Live Your Life For Half The Price

Also by Mary Hunt

Debt-Proof Living

Debt-Proof Your Marriage

Debt-Proof Your Kids

Debt-Proof Your Holidays

The Financially Confident Woman

Tiptionary

Cheapskate Gourmet

Everyday Cheapskate's Greatest Tips

The Complete Cheapskate

Money Makeover

Live Your Life
For Half The Price

*Without Sacrificing
the Life You Love*

Mary Hunt

DPL Press   Los Angeles

Live Your Life For Half The Price, Debt-Proof Living, Live the Plan!, Cheapskate Monthly, Rapid Debt-Repayment Plan, Rapid Debt-Repayment Plan Calculator, Tiptionary, and Everyday Cheapskate are registered trademarks of Mary Hunt.

PRINTED IN THE UNITED STATES OF AMERICA

This book is designed to provide accurate and authoritative information on the subject of personal money management. It is sold with the understanding that neither the author nor the publisher is engaged in rendering legal, accounting, or other professional services by publishing this book. As each individual situation is unique, questions relevant to personal finances and specific to the individual should be addressed to an appropriate professional to ensure that the situation has been evaluated carefully and appropriately. The author and publisher specifically disclaim any liability, loss, or risk that is incurred as a consequence, directly or indirectly, of the use and application of any of the contents of this work.

Cover Design: Jeremy Hunt, *www.SDMFX.com*

Author Photos: Beth Herzhaft Photography, *www.Herzco.com*

For information regarding special discounts for bulk purchases, please contact:

DPL Press, Inc., P.O. Box 2135, Los Angeles, CA 90723; Special Sales: 800-550-3502. Visit us at *www.DPLPress.com*

First edition published 2005

Library of Congress Cataloging-in-Publication Data
Information Available by Request from Publisher

ISBN 10   0-9760791-0-0
ISBN 13 978-0-9760791-0-1

1   2   3   4   5   6   7   8   9   10   11   12   13   14   15

This book is dedicated to you.

In your lifetime you will manage millions of dollars.

You are getting your fortune in installments—one paycheck at a time.

The money you don't spend will ultimately give you

the freedom to live the life you love.

Table of Contents

Acknowledgments

I owe a huge debt of gratitude to many people whose assistance, support, and friendship, at work and in life, have given me the reasons and the motivation to fill the pages of this book.

Thanks to Harold, my partner in life and business, for managing everything in our lives so well and giving me the freedom I need to do my work. Without you none of this would make sense; with you it's all perfectly clear.

Thanks to Jeremy and Joshua for your involvement in this project. I like knowing you're proud of your mom.

Thanks to Cathy Hollenbeck for your unwavering commitment to our mission, for helping me get my message of financial help and hope to the masses, for holding the business together, for the untold "light bulb" moments, for the countless hours of slogging through muddy manuscripts, but most of all for daring to dream with us for what lies ahead. I simply could not do this without you.

Thanks to Kim Penrose, my faithful assistant, for your gentle strength, timely reminders, and uncanny sense of timing. You always know just seconds ahead what I need and where to find it. Thanks for keeping me on track so "Everyday Cheapskate" column lands in hundreds of newspapers every day, *Debt-Proof Living* (formerly *Cheapskate Monthly*) newsletter makes it to press every month; and for seeing this project through.

Thanks to Christy Rocha for managing so well our thousands of newsletter subscribers and bookstore customers. How you manage to keep that ship upright and moving forward with such seeming ease never ceases to amaze me.

Thanks to our Friday night friends—Mark, Rosalie, Paul, and Jan—who never give up on me finally finishing a project. Just knowing that Friday is coming has pulled me through some long days of lonely writing.

And finally I thank God for blessings beyond my comprehension through his son, Jesus Christ, who willingly paid the *full price* for my salvation. My life is in your hands.

Mary Hunt, California

An Interview

Over the past fifteen years I've had many interviews, and I'm grateful for each and every one. One interview in particular stands out in my mind, however, because of an unfortunate case of "host laryngitis." It was the first time I'd ever been asked to interview Myself. Seriously.

I can't say it was unpleasant. In fact, I rather enjoyed Myself. I responded candidly to each of My questions; I knew all the answers and didn't stump Myself even once.

Now I find Myself in a similar situation. There you are and here I am. I know you have questions, but alas your voice is silent. So as I did that day for a radio audience, I've decided to do here for you: I will interview Myself.

Me: *Why did you write this book? There are plenty of books out there on personal finances already.*

Myself: I know this looks like a personal finance book, and it is in a way, but not really. This book zeroes in on just one segment of the art of managing your money—

Me: *You're going to make me ask?*

Myself: I wasn't finished. (now, don't start interrupting)...the part about limiting your spending so that it does not exceed 80 percent of your income.

Me: *Oh, so this is a budget book!*

Myself: No, not really.

Me: *A bargain guide?*

Myself: No, not that either. This is a book about how to live below your means—how to spend less than you earn. Living below your means is a decision, an attitude—it's a way of life.

Me: *Forgive me, but I don't understand the difference between living below your means and finding great bargains.*

Myself: If you are committed to maintaining a healthy margin between what you earn and what you spend you're going to be a deal hunter. But the bargain isn't the issue—the bargain simply is the means to the end. The *real* issue is achieving a lifestyle where you buy what you need and want what you have—a consistent way of life where you live below your means.

Me: *Who did you write this book for?*

Myself: Since 1992 I've devoted my life to helping people make the shift from spender to saver—showing them how to stop spending all they have, how to get out of debt and how to live below their means. Millions have taken me up on my offer and proven that my simple debt-proof living plan works!

I can't tell you how many people have gotten out of debt and gone on to do amazing things with their lives and their money. I really can't. But I know—and this breaks my heart—that for every success there are ten thousand more who don't get it or if they do, procrastinate. They make good money, they're not horribly in debt but they just spend all of their money—all the time. These are the people who need this book.

Me: *Who would not benefit from this book?*

Myself: Well, I'd like to think that I'm such an entertaining writer anyone would find this a real page-turner (I once knew a girl, Paige Turner). But those who never spend beyond their means; who give, save and are building wealth will probably not find much inspiration. They are already doing what I'm talking about here. While I'd be honored if they flipped a few pages, I did not write this for those who are seasoned LBYMers (live below your means) looking for ways to go lower and lower. And lower.

Me: *So what can we expect in the pages that follow?*

Myself: You may have noticed this is a single volume, not a ninety-six-volume matched set. That's why you are not going to find every possible consumer product and service together with details on how and where to buy it for 50 percent off. As I said before this is not *Mary Hunt's Guide to Bargains*. I hope to empower my readers to action by teaching them the principles of living below their means and showing them how to reduce the cost of some of their major expenses.

Me: *Thanks for being My guest today. Where can our readers find you if they have questions?*

Myself: It was my pleasure! These days I spend most of my time hanging out at my website: *DebtProofLiving.com*, where it's open house 24/7.

Introduction

Affluence is *not* measured by your annual income. Affluence is determined by how many of your resources you manage not to spend—the amount of income you keep.

Live Your Life for Half the Price is about how to spend less than you earn, how to make better choices with what you have so you can keep more of what you make. Who should read it? Anyone ready to achieve extraordinary results on an ordinary income.

The idea that you should live below your means is obvious, isn't it? It's not like this is the first time you've ever heard of the concept. You know that cutting spending is hard work. But living paycheck to paycheck is much harder work. So if you knew how to stop spending so much, it's safe to say you'd be doing that by now.

Living on less than you earn takes effort. Like swimming upstream or walking up the down escalator, you have to work at going against the flow. It takes a conscious effort to spend less on everything from food to ATM fees, insurance to clothes, and the fun things in life, too.

Sadly, by the looks of climbing credit-card debt and personal bankruptcy filings in the U.S., too few people are willing to put forth the effort. It seems easier to just spend all you have and then depend on credit to cover the gap between what you need and how much you make. At the time it seems fine to have it all now and pay later. Yet we eventually learn the long-term effects of that spending error.

If you are not where you'd like to be with your money, don't assume that's because you make less money than you desire. Increased income does not guarantee a better life.

Think about it: Ten years ago your annual income was less than it is now. Perhaps it was a lot less. You believed then if you only made more money you'd be out of debt and on your way to building wealth and securing your future.

Then you got a raise or changed careers. Your annual income improved, but then you added new expenses and accepted new debt. Before long you got to thinking that if you only made more money you'd be out of debt, and on your way to building wealth and securing your future.

Then you got a raise or changed careers. You made more money. You took on more expenses, added more debt. I know I am repeating myself and that is my point. You're caught in a vicious cycle that insists more money is the only way to improve one's financial situation.

More money alone is not likely to change your life. You've proven that. But making the decision to stop spending all of it so you can keep more of it—that's the solution.

It took me decades to wise up. But finally I found the key to the life I love. I hope it doesn't take you that long. How much more time can you afford to waste? No matter your current income, you can do better with what you have without giving up the life you love. Just the fact that you are reading these words right now means you have an important resource within your grasp.

As you read this book, make it a personal challenge to see how much of your money you can manage to keep. Make it a game. Try different strategies. Some things will work better for you than others. I ask only that you be open to many options.

I know that with the right information, motivation, and encouragement you can shift your energy from treading financial water to achieving financial freedom. What makes me so sure? For fifteen years I've been helping people get out of debt. Their success can be directly connected to their personal decisions to live on less—to stop spending everything they make. None of these stories were overnight miracles. It takes time and hard work to right the wrongs of past mistakes and to change behaviors, habits, and attitudes. But it is so doable. The stories are amazing.

I am handing you the opportunity to change the course of your life. I am giving you a chance to take charge of your finances, to do better with what you have so you can start making the kind of progress with your money about which you've only dreamed.

And now you have a decision to make. I hope you will grab this opportunity to finally stop living beyond your means—regardless of your income level or current financial situation. You're about to discover you can do more with what you have—more than you dream possible. If you're ready to take on the challenge, so am I.

Let's get started!

Chapter One

The Life
You Love

I was asked to interview sixty millionaires from Oklahoma. What I learned
from them was simple, yet the message had a lasting impact on me: You cannot
enjoy life if you are addicted to consumption and the use of credit.

~ Thomas J. Stanley, Ph.D. in *The Millionaire Next Door*

Shortly after graduating from college I married the love of my life.
We had no debt but we had new sheets and towels. Life was wonderful. In fact, my life had never been this good. I was finally done with
school, I loved my job, and my new husband adored me.

Had you knocked on the front door of our tiny home (three hundred
square feet, no kidding) and asked me to rate the quality of my life, I
would have given it the highest possible marks and without hesitation.

The Card

I got my first credit card for convenience, pure and simple. Harold, my
conservative banker husband, did not share my enthusiasm but finally

agreed. I didn't see this as a way to build our credit history or spend money we didn't have; I thought it would be more convenient to use this Texaco card and pay the bill once a month rather than scramble for money every few days to put gas in my car. I would save time too.

The minute my new card came in the mail I took it for a test-drive. For fun, I pulled up to a full-service pump (back when they had those) just as proud as I could be. I felt like royalty because within seconds several attendants addressed my every automotive need.

My quality of life took a bounce. For a moment I felt a sense of privilege I'd never known. It felt good. And with this magic card I didn't have to worry about a thing, because my husband would take care of the bill.

You don't think the Queen of England actually pays her bills, do you? Of course not, and why should I? Privilege. Entitlement. Quality of life. As long ago as this was, I remember the incident as if it happened this morning, right down to what I was wearing. I guess you might say this was one of my life's "defining moments."

Blinded by flawed thinking that suggests if one is good, two must be better, I added several more credit cards to my collection. My quality of life began to improve in other areas, little by little. I couldn't believe all the quality I'd been missing.

Having the freedom to buy stuff whenever I wanted was a big deal to me. I'd grown up with very little. Now, for the first time in my life, I could act on my compulsive urges. No waiting; just make a snap decision and move on.

We got a new car. We had a baby. Make that two. The best toys. More Legos. Star Wars action figures, video games, cool clothes, hobbies, vacations, more new cars. More new clothes, new swimming pool. Ah, quality of life, standard of living.

Our family vacations and big Christmases added even more to my quality of life. We enrolled the kids in private schools. They participated in sports and other enrichment programs. We even bought a recreational vehicle to improve the quality of our lives. It worked for a while.

We crossed a significant threshold the month we were unable to pay the credit card bills in full. Enter consumer debt.

Debt Turns Ugly

Let me tell you about high-interest, unsecured, revolving credit-card debt. It's like cancer. It begins as a single cell, and you don't even feel it. Opting to pay the minimum payment rather than the full balance was effortless, painless…no noticeable negative effect at all.

It was easier to pay $40 than $400. Breathing space, relieved pressure. It was like a gift—as if we were getting away with something.

At that point I would have told you—and meant it with all my heart—that consumer debt improved our lives. It allowed us to do more things and get more stuff. It was like getting a big raise even though our income had not increased.

But like a single cancer cell that begins to multiply, so did our debt. It grew and multiplied until it nearly killed us. We missed payments, incurred late fees, and had to borrow more and more to handle our ever-growing minimum payments.

The very thing that had "improved" our quality of life began to eat away at it instead.

By the time we celebrated twelve years of marriage, we were in our third home, our two bundles of baby boy joy were six and seven, and we were driving two fancy new cars. We changed careers and also tried self-employment.

If I could stop here you might assume that our quality of life had improved even more remarkably. But lest you jump to that conclusion, let me also tell you that we had amassed more than $100,000 in unsecured (mostly credit-card) debt. Things were way out of hand.

We were horribly in debt and our business had failed; we were unemployed, months behind on our bills, and facing foreclosure on our home. We had no savings, no retirement accounts to cash in, and no rich uncles in the family tree. Let me assure you, there was little quality in our lives.

True Quality

I longed for the simple life in our cozy 300 hundred-square-foot home when we got regular paychecks, paid our bills on time, paid cash for our day-to-day living, and—on top of that—had money in the bank. We were so happy. Our quality of life was authentic. That was the life I loved.

I loathed the trap that now held us so tightly. I discovered too late that having it all now and paying for it later was a hollow promise—a torturous trap. The availability of credit that promised the freedom to have and do anything I wanted now held us in bondage.

I didn't set out to ruin our lives. I didn't sit down one day and dream up a foolproof plan to plunge me and my family into the kind of financial distress from which few recover. I thought I was making our lives better. I was driven by this thing we call "quality of life."

The Pit of Despair

I wish I could say I woke up and came to my senses on my own. The truth is, I hit rock-bottom so hard it shook me to the core of my being. Never before or since have I experienced such pain, defeat, and despair.

I had to reach my lowest point, where I could do nothing but let go of my stubborn demands to be in charge of my life. On that day, I humbled myself before God and admitted that I could not fix this. I was out of options. I poured my heart out to God, asking for forgiveness and help. So terribly afraid of losing my husband, my boys, and my home, I promised that day that I would do anything to repair the damage I'd done and repay the debt I'd amassed.

Our journey back is a story for another place and time, but what I need to tell you is that we did make it—we paid the entire debt without filing for bankruptcy or asking for a single concession from our creditors. Our home did not go through foreclosure, our marriage survives to this day, and our boys are now financially responsible adults.

While it took thirteen years to completely repay our debt, the quality of our lives began to improve from the first day of the journey back. But it was a different kind of quality—authentic and rock solid.

I learned so much on that journey back to solvency. No doubt, things can improve the quality of our lives—but only to the extent that we own them and they do not own us. Material things satisfy physical needs. But it takes more than meeting physical needs to find satisfaction and experience true quality of life. We need contentment, joy, and peace of mind too.

Here's what I want you to know and understand: reducing our spending was the catalyst that started the dramatic and permanent change in our lives. And that change was not limited to our finances. It was all-pervasive. Learning the power of living below our means gave us the life we love. It affected our relationship, our spiritual lives, our home life, our children's lives, and now—your life.

May I Ask You a Question?

I have asked many people this question: What contributes to the quality of your life and brings you satisfaction? Typically I get a blank stare. If I wait long enough, I get a fairly predictable response in the form of a list.

Take a look at the following list of the responses I have received most often.

- *All my bills paid*
- *Peace of mind*
- *Love*
- *A fast computer*
- *Good health*
- *My garden*
- *A great meal*
- *Walking in the country*
- *Good friends*
- *A week in Yosemite*
- *A week away anywhere*
- *A good book*
- *Great clothes*
- *Knowing my purpose*

- *Money in the bank*
- *Contentment*
- *A paid-for home*
- *A fine leather handbag*
- *A beautiful quilt*
- *Spending time with kids (grandkids, spouse)*
- *Cell phone*
- *Pets*
- *A massage*
- *Warm fire, cold night*
- *Makeup*
- *Helping others in need*
- *Freedom to do what I want*

Not surprisingly, in all the times I have asked people what brings quality to their lives, no one has responded, "A closet full of clothes I never wear" or "A garage that is so packed with stuff there's no room for a car." No one has mentioned the forty-eight remaining payments on the pair of Jet Skis.

As you read through that list, did you see anything you would place on your list? Would your list fall in line with the one above or would yours be completely different? What would you add or subtract? There are no right or wrong answers. But I can assure you that making such a list for yourself will be enlightening.

What contributes to the quality of your life? Now take a minute and narrow that to the top ten things that define your quality of life.

Would a boatload of money help?

If you're holding out for the life you love to magically appear once a boatload of money gets dumped into your life, don't count on it.

You may believe in your heart that winning the lotto or getting an unexpected inheritance one day will make your life perfect. Perhaps you're convinced that getting in on the ground floor of the latest and greatest multilevel marketing opportunity will make you rich overnight. That won't happen.

If you can figure a way to get that kind of money, good for you. But if you think money alone—and plenty of it—will give you the life you love, forget it. Money alone, no matter how much of it flows through your life, will not automatically materialize into the life you love.

Either you are living the life you love or you aren't. If you are, you may be fearful that reducing your spending or not relying on credit to get by will force you to live a life you hate. That's a real fear, one with which I can identify. After all, if you've never consciously worked at living below your means, the fear of becoming a penny-pinching miser may give you the creeps.

Or if you aren't happy with your life, you may be dreaming about what it would be like to really love your life. You know it's out there, you can imagine what it will be like, but it is forever out of reach. No matter how hard you try or how fast you go, you cannot quite grab onto it. You believe that what stands between you and the life you love is more money. That is probably not the case at all.

Whether you fear losing the life you love or only dream of living it, here's the bottom line: You need to learn how to live on 80 percent of your income. You have to cap your spending at 80 percent of the money you bring home, no matter what. Make it a habit as fundamental as stopping for red lights. Realize once and for all that if you can't pay for it today from the money you have, then you can't afford it.

The Stuff Factor

Stuff alone does not make our lives better. Sure, a good computer, a comfortable home, and a reliable car add quality to our lives. But without peace of mind, someone to love, and a good sense of why on earth you are here in the first place, all of that is just stuff. And more of it is just more stuff.

When you picked up this book, I promised you that you can live your life for half the price without sacrificing the life you love. I mean that and I believe it with all my heart.

Satisfaction Saturation

I'll never forget the time I asked one of my young piano students what he wanted for Christmas. It was a generic question, a pleasantry. I wasn't looking for make, model, and serial number, but that's what I got. He whipped out a sixty-page list. I gulped, checked to see if this child was serious (he was), and quickly proceeded with his music lesson.

I don't know how many toys, electronics, and gadgets he had on that sixty-page Christmas list, but at five things per page that would be three hundred entries! I'll admit to participating in a few overly indulged Christmases in my foolish past, but even I cannot imagine what that child's dream Christmas would look like.

Somehow I think that most of us have a bit of that kid in us. We want it all. And every bank and credit card company out there is affirming the notion and willing to make it happen.

In time, however, we reach the maximum level of satisfaction. And the more we attempt to increase that level, the more difficult it becomes to retain a sense of fulfillment. More becomes less as our feelings of satisfaction diminish.

By the looks of some of our closets and garages, we've been doing a pretty good job of trying to get it all. But how much of it satisfies?

What portion of what we have is actually contributing to the quality of our lives?

The secret of living the life you love is the ability to identify the point of maximum fulfillment, the point of "enough." More than enough will not increase your happiness; in fact, it begins eating away at your sense of satisfaction.

Get in touch with your internal satisfaction "meter." Doing this will be very revealing. Rate your possessions. How much satisfaction do they give you? If you consider everything in your life, rating its level of satisfaction, you will learn a lot about yourself and your current situation.

Review, Not Regret

Imagine how different your current financial picture might be had you not spent so much of your past income on stuff and activities that did not improve the quality of your life. Or worse—actually diminished your happiness. It makes you wish you'd never purchased anything that wasn't needed or wanted, doesn't it? While I am not suggesting that you should live with regret, a thoughtful review of how you've managed your money up to now can head off repeating the same mistakes in the future.

As you begin to review your life and possessions through the filter of how they contribute to or subtract from the quality of your life, you will make some startling discoveries. You've been hanging on to things that don't make a positive contribution to your life. They do not serve you, yet they take up space in your world. They keep you from the peace you could be experiencing. Or worse, they steal your joy.

Living below your means does not mean giving up life's pleasures and what really matters to you. On the contrary, spending less than you earn is the way to have and do those things that will maximize the quality of your life.

Chapter Two

Found
Money

*The bottom line is that we think we work to pay the bills—but we spend
more than we make on more than we need, which sends us back to work to get
the money to spend to get more stuff to ....*

~ Joe Dominguez, author *Your Money or Your Life*

Money in the bank. Bills paid. No debts. Paid-for home. A healthy
retirement plan. All contribute to feelings of peace and security.
No doubt, money plays a major role in determining the quality of our
lives. Still, we have seen that once our basic needs are met, more money
will not necessarily bring more happiness. Instead, what we do with our
money makes the difference in how we live our lives.

Finding Money

So here you are, determined to improve the quality of your life by living below your means. The situation seems perfectly clear—you need

to find more money. You have two choices: increase your income or reduce your spending.

Option 1: Increase Income

Making more money does seem like the most logical way to fix a financial problem. There are only a limited number of ways to do that:

Beef up your paycheck. You can ask for a raise; you can land a new job that pays a lot more than your current job. Or you could even get a second (or third) job to supplement your current income.

Land a windfall. I mention this in case winning the lottery or getting a big inheritance is on your list of realistic options for changing your financial picture. Theoretically both are options, but I don't suggest you count on either as a realistic way to increase your income. Your chances of being struck by lightning are much better than winning the lottery. As for that inheritance, you be the judge.

Sell assets. Finding a cash buyer for your grandmother's sterling silver, the boat, all of the clothes and household items you never use, a piece of real estate or any other asset you own is another option for increasing your income.

All of these are ways to increase your income and improve your financial picture. But let's get real. If you could do any of these things, you would have done them already and we wouldn't be having this conversation.

The Other Side of a Pay Increase

While increasing your income is a way to change your financial picture, the change may not be good for you. Believe it or not, increasing your income could worsen your financial position.

Increased expenses. Let's say you ask for that raise and (surprise!) get a nice annual increase of $5,000. First, you'll never see the entire $5,000 due to payroll and federal income taxes. What you do take home will come in small increments. In addition (I hate to be the bearer of bad news), you have to consider that a raise could push you into a higher tax bracket. Once your impressive raise is subjected to taxes and other withholding, you'll be lucky to see an extra $60 in your weekly paycheck. Ditto if you work overtime.

Let me point out one more fact: Even if you can start working overtime or arrange for that raise to be effective today, it will take several weeks for you see any of it. However, any increases in related expenses—additional childcare, gasoline, and other expenses incurred because of additional time away from home—will kick in immediately.

I am certainly not impugning pay increases. I just want you to be aware of all aspects and the true benefit and cost of a pay increase.

Enhanced lifestyle. Something odd happens when you get a big boost in income. If you aren't careful, it can encourage increased feelings of entitlement. Suddenly you deserve a new outfit, better birthday parties, a better cell phone, a faster computer, a great vacation, a newer car, a larger house.

Let's say you decide that $5,000 looks like a down payment on a vehicle upgrade. You could sure use a minivan. So you buy one—a great new van with $469 monthly payments. Of course you do this before you see that $5,000 boils down to $60 a week. You've just worsened your financial situation with new debt and a monthly payment that exceeds your net increase.

You may discover after you've added up your entitlements that your $60 a week increase doesn't go far. In fact, your increased income has put you further behind.

Old habits. Let's say that you can find a way to increase your income sufficiently to actually improve your financial situation. Not bad. But here's the problem. Just exactly what caused those money problems in the first place? Overspending? Too much credit-card debt?

Your newly enhanced income may do little more than stick a financial Band-Aid on a pile of bad habits. If you fail to address them, nothing will change. In fact, statistics suggest that more money only makes your financial problems worse, not better.

Option 2: Reduce Spending

Your other option for improving your financial picture is to systematically, methodically, and intelligently reduce your spending. If you are currently spending $1, you need to find a way to reduce that to 80 cents.

Unless you live below the poverty line—in which case you have a different set of challenges—I am confident that with persistence you can reduce your outgo. You can. This effort will have all the positive effects of increasing your income without the challenges mentioned above.

It's instantaneous. Reducing your expenses brings instant gratification. Here's an example: You normally spend $140 a week at the supermarket. This week you spend only $100 but come home with the same kinds of food you normally purchase. This means you have $40 tax-free in your wallet for some other use. No waiting and no begging; no loans, no debt, no payback. It's your money, already taxed.

Every expense you have—not only your grocery tab—is a candidate for some type of systematic reduction.

Less stress. Assessing the way you spend your money forces you to focus on what really matters. You begin to notice unneeded "baggage," you're more willing to acknowledge what brings you joy, what needs to go, and how to create the life you love. Chaos slips away, leaving calm and simplicity in its place. Reducing your expenses will have a far-reaching effect on more than just the balance in your bank account.

More contentment. Examining what is meaningful and then having the courage to confront the rest will bring a sense of contentment to you and your family. Instead of being so concerned about getting everything you want, you'll find contentment in wanting what you have. Overindulging in stuff complicates life and causes much stress.

The Best Option

I'm sure it will come as no surprise to you that I'm partial to reducing spending over increasing income as the way to improve your financial situation. You knew that all along. The title of this book gave it away.

The majority of adults in the U.S. live beyond their means, if credit-card statistics are the gauge. More than 60 percent of active credit cards carry a balance from one month to the next. That tells me that the cardholder is unable to pay that balance in full in a single month. The debt is greater than the ability to pay.

If you're in this group, you're in trouble, digging yourself into a horrible pit of debt. You're spending your future. Run, do not walk, to the closest copy of my book *Debt-Proof Living*. I'll be there waiting, ready to help you get out of debt.

The 80-Percent Solution

The key to achieving financial freedom is to live below your means. Specifically, to limit your overall spending to 80 percent of your net income. Spend only 80 cents for each $1 you see in your paycheck. Impossible? No. It takes skill, effort, and determination. It takes desire and commitment to live below your means—to be fully committed to living the best life you can on 80 percent of your income without sacrificing the life you love.

You may wonder about the other 20 percent of your paycheck. What happens to that? It's all part of a plan that creates the financial balance necessary for living below your means. For each dollar that flows into your life, you give away 10 cents and put 10 cents into your emergency or Contingency Fund, as I refer to it. Giving and saving are the magic bullets that will quiet your insatiable desires, put to rest your fears, and give you incentive to live the life you love on 80 percent of your take-home pay.

So, you may be wondering, how does this "80 percent solution" square with "half-price" living. Studies indicate that the typical American family is now spending upwards of $1.25 for every $1 of income and saves little if any. Let's say that describes you. Here I come suggesting that not only should you stop spending more than you earn, you need to reduce your living expenses even further to 80 percent so you can start saving money consistently, and also become a generous giver. I know. That is an overwhelming expectation, particularly if you are currently struggling while living beyond your means. Now you can see that living your life for half the price is necessary if you ever hope to practice the 80 percent solution.

Average over Time

Don't worry about losing your dignity. In fact, no one needs to know about your new resolve to find ways to drastically cut your expenses. You don't have to print, "I'm cheap!" on your forehead. A better option is to engrave this motto on your mind: *Wherever I am, whatever I do, I can find a way to do it for less.*

It is unrealistic to think that in order to reduce spending you will never pay full price again or that everything is available somewhere for just half price. But if your goal is to pay only half price and you are willing to work at it, you can drastically reduce your expenses without sacrificing the aspects of your life that mean the most. It will average out over time. This is a mind-set, an attitude.

Your Money Temperament

To loosely assess your money temperament, consider the following premise, then choose the response closest to what you would do:

Your rich uncle gets wind of your desperate need for transportation. In a surprise move he sends you $15,000 with instructions to buy a car. What do you do?

A. Make a $15,000 down payment on your dream car.

B. Pay cash for a $15,000 car.

C. Exercise extreme patience, flexibility, consumer savvy and negotiating skills to find a dandy used, late-model, low-mileage, well-maintained car for $7,500 and then stash $7,500 into a savings account.

Putting aside your humble author's obvious bias, let's analyze these options.

Twice the price. If you responded *A,* you are prone to live your life for twice the price. You don't mind paying interest and monthly payments because that's the way to get what you want. You're just doing the best you can to maximize your income so you can drive the car you desire.

You depend on consumer credit to bridge the gap between your income and your expenses. It's easy and convenient. Because you pay double-digit interest rates on your revolving debt, you end up paying twice, or more, for the goods and services you charge. However, you don't think about paying double. You live for today, assuming that tomorrow will take care of itself.

Full price. If your response was *B,* you are okay with full price. When you have money, you don't hesitate to spend it. You're a cash buyer, not a wheeler-dealer, and you prefer to just pay the asking price. No hassles, no problems. You have a cash mentality. You pay as you go. If you like it you buy it. If you don't, you wait.

You don't pay attention to price that much. As a result, your income matches your lifestyle. You don't live beyond your means and never carry credit-card debt. Still, it takes every penny to pay the bills. You live from one paycheck to the next. It seems as if you can never get ahead.

Half Price. If your choice was *C,* your mind-set is to live your life for half the price. You enjoy the challenge of living below your means; you try to never pay the full price. You get a thrill whenever you beat the system. You earn more than you spend and save the difference.

You know your prices, you're patient, and you know how to pay less than the going price for just about everything. In fact, you pride yourself on living your life for half the price. You live an understated lifestyle and find great satisfaction in being prepared for the unexpected. You live below your means, and that creates contentment, joy, and a financially stress-free life.

Back to reality. Of course no one pays "twice the price" for everything, nor can anyone be assured of never paying more than half. My point is, with every spending opportunity comes a choice: choose to go into debt, determine to not spend more than you have, or work hard to pay half the price.

Toil and Trouble

A couple hundred years ago Adam Smith, economist and philosopher, wrote, "The real price of everything, what everything really costs to the man who wants to acquire it, is the toil and trouble of acquiring it."

I'm not trying to fool you into thinking it's a simple thing to live below your means. I'll admit that it is easier to just buy what you want and then switch to credit when you run out of money. That's as easy as walking downhill. Or rolling off a log.

There is a component of toil and trouble in half-price living, and at times it is more toilsome than other choices. In some ways living below your means is like having a part-time job with this job description: plan, research, wait, negotiate, strategize, compare, and consider.

What better part-time job could you hope for than one where you set your hours, agenda, and pace and you're the boss. The more toil and trouble you choose to contribute, the closer you'll come to living your life for half the price. And don't forget: the "wages" are tax-free because every dollar you manage not to spend is a dollar on which you have already been taxed.

Toil-and-Trouble Factor on Wheels

Remember the $15,000-for-a-car question? Let's revisit the three options, taking into consideration the toil-and-trouble factor.

Buying the new car in option *A* took all of one hour. It was simple and convenient, and given the fierce competition among new car dealers, probably quite pain-free. The salesman was more than willing to handle every detail and made the transaction so simple. You didn't even have to think about the full price of the deal. Just knowing you could handle the monthly payment gave you a sense of satisfaction. No toil, no trouble.

Paying cash in option *B* required diligence to locate the car. Because this is not a new vehicle, add in the time and expense of a trip to the mechanic for a checkup and inspection. However, paying a lot less in the long run for a good car was offset by the effort or "toil and trouble" this buyer was willing to contribute to the deal.

Finding a cream puff of a car for just $7,500 in option *C* was even harder work. It took weeks of patience, test-driving, calling, and networking. Finally all of the toil and trouble paid off when this amazing low-mileage, single-owner, pampered car turned up. A great deal for sure, but look at the "paycheck" this buyer received in exchange for his toil and trouble: $7,500 in the bank and a decent car to drive as well.

If This Were Sports

In their book *The Millionaire Next Door* authors Thomas Stanley and William Danko relate this matter of increased income versus reduced spending to sports. Earning more money, landing a big windfall, or in any other way of increasing one's income is like playing offense. Reducing expenses, on the other hand, is playing defense. And doing it well is *great* defense.

When it comes to personal finance, choosing to always play offense is exhausting. Playing a great defense is a common thread that Stanley and Danko discovered as they analyzed the day-to-day habits and lifestyles of self-made millionaires.

Half-Price Mind-Set

While "half price" does refer to the cost of things, half-price living is also an attitude, a new way of thinking, a learned behavior. It is a mind-set that sees a bigger picture and exercises personal discipline and respect for the money one is entrusted to manage.

I hope that what follows will make you excited about what can happen in your life when you begin to live below your means. And if you've already begun the journey, I want to inspire you to do even better.

Chapter Three

Handy Tools, Secret Weapons

*If you don't make the shift from spender to saver at some point
in your lifetime, you are dooming yourself to poverty
or having to work forever.*

~ Ted Benna, Father of the 40l(k)

It takes determination not to spend beyond your means. And it takes even greater strength to stop spending before you come to the end of your income. Stopping while there is still a healthy margin between what you earn and what you spend requires self-imposed limitations. You have to choose to place a cap on your spending and then stick to it. Sounds so simple, doesn't it? It's not.

Living beyond your means is the easy way. Almost anyone who can sign a credit slip can do it. Why would anyone choose the more difficult option of living on less? For the payoff, my friend. It is simply fabulous. Living below your means is your best hope to turn your ordinary income into something extraordinary.

In this chapter I'll describe the tools and weapons you need to successfully and consistently spend less money than you have available. The more determined you are to equip yourself and be willing to use these tools and weapons, the more successful you will be in living your life for half the price.

Handy Tools

These tools are tangible items—things you need in your possession to allow you to accomplish specific tasks. Any craftsman knows the right tools for the right job make all the difference in a project's outcome. Some of the tools, as you will learn, you can actually hold in your hands. Others you can view on paper or your computer monitor. Their commonality is that you must acquire them if you do not have them already.

Secret Weapons

No tangible items here. For our purposes weapons are attitudes, values, activities, and behaviors required to stand strong against your opponent. Think of these weapons as your armament—the bulletproof attire you need so you come out a winner.

The big, bad advertising world does everything it can to control your behavior as a consumer—to get all of the money you have now plus a big promissory note for what you will earn in the future. Going into debt, spending beyond your means, being consumed by stuff—all these results prove that you lose and they win.

For our purposes, consumer advertising encompasses everything from preapproved credit-card invitations you receive in the mail to store sales, television commercials, online offers, flashy ads for hot new cars, and the entire gamut in between. The ad industry is bent on manipulating your behavior by creating desire and promising fulfillment.

This formidable foe requires weapons to protect yourself and secure your freedom to spend your money in ways that are consistent with your values, not the values that advertisers would impose on you. Weapons, for our purposes here, are intangibles—attitudes, skills, and abilities.

By the way, if you happen to be employed in the advertising industry, do not quit your job! I am a huge fan of capitalism and the free-enterprise system. I love the freedom we enjoy that allows merchants to advertise in an effort to compel people to buy their goods and services. I also believe that consumers need to be at least as smart as the merchants who court them. So, consider yourself fortunate to have access to the inside scoop. You have a decided edge in building a counterattack.

Tools

Cash

Cold, hard cash is as powerful a tool as you can hope to find for the task of spending less of your hard-earned money. Living with cash means you carry currency. You use cash to pay for all your day-to-day expenses—gasoline, food, dry cleaning—expenditures that are not tax-deductible and for which you do not need long-term proof of purchase.

Adopting a cash lifestyle requires determination, because for most people it is so new, so foreign. We are so used to dealing with money's stand-ins—credit cards, debit cards, ATM payment cards, and checkbooks. If you are not used to living with cash, at first it feels scary, or at least wrong. Blame it on the consumer-credit industry.

Decades of clever credit-card marketing campaigns have finally made believers of a nation of consumers. Finally we believe that carrying cash is not safe, certainly not convenient, and that we'd be foolish to even try to live that way. They've made it sound as if this is for our own good, personal safety, and convenience. We learned all of this from the very industry that stands to make a fortune if they can convince us to stop paying with cash!

What about safety? Of course you need to practice caution with cash. You shouldn't be carrying thousands of dollars in cash. You need a reasonable way to keep cash at home (a small home safe is a good investment). But keep this in mind: far fewer people are mugged for their cash than have their identities stolen through credit- and debit-card thievery.

The danger of plastic. The credit-card industry knows that people spend more when they pay with a credit card than they would if they paid with cash. They know because that is how they designed credit cards to work. They promise improved profits to merchants who accept credit cards.

A Visa USA marketing brochure assures merchants, "A recent Visa study of 100,000 QSR (quick service restaurant) transactions showed that customers using payment cards spent an average of 30 percent more than those who paid with cash. Other industry studies suggest that the average increase may be even higher."

MasterCard International makes this promise: "Consumers spend more when they're not constrained by cash on hand. You may see increased purchases of higher-margin products as well as specialty items. And customers may visit your store more often."

A study by Dun & Bradstreet showed that the credit-card user spends 12 to 18 percent more when using credit instead of cash.

Spend cash, spend less. It is a simple principle: it hurts to spend cash, so you spend less to avoid the pain. The credit-card industry makes clever use of this principle. They offer a money substitute to relieve the pain. And without the pain, it is much easier to spend and spend and spend.

There really is something magical about credit cards. *They make money disappear!* Here's an example:

Let's say you need groceries. You plan to spend $50. If you walk into the store with $50 cash in your pocket and no backups (credit cards, debit cards, or a checkbook) you cannot spend $51. You have a self-imposed spending cap. You simply cannot go over. Instantly you become a different kind of shopper: You are more careful. You compare prices, look for sales. You are not tempted to pick up items impulsively because they look good, because you are focused on what things cost. What a concept!

Okay, now hit rewind.

You need groceries. You plan to spend $50. You arrive with a credit card, debit card, ATM card, checkbook, and $2.43. You can't believe all the great sales; the produce is spectacular; the bakery smells divine. Forty-five minutes later you roll through the checkout with a final tally of $124.37. Whoops. Went over just a little, but it doesn't matter. You have all kinds of backup to pay for the loot.

A real pain. Cash is a powerful weapon in your mission to live below your means because committing to cash is not easy or convenient. You have to plan ahead and pay attention to how much cash you have with you before you go into the store. It is, in fact, a royal pain. That is what's good about it. Living with cash requires you to think, be aware, and remain engaged. It also requires that you exercise personal discipline.

The lack of convenience and ease is what makes this tool so effective. If you purposely make it difficult to spend your money, you will spend less of it.

Cash has limitations. Of course it is not altogether possible to live with cash only, but you can come surprisingly close. Do not get rid of your checkbook or your credit card. You cannot mail cash; you should not use cash to pay your bills.

You need to pay for online and mail-order purchases with a credit card (not a debit card as we will discuss later) so as to be protected in the event your order does not show up, is of poor quality, or is damaged. You need your ATM card to access your cash. Each piece of plastic has a place and proper function in your life. But for all of your day-to-day spending opportunities, forcing yourself to be constrained by the cash you have on hand will make a huge impact on how much of your money you get to keep.

Envelopes

Plain, lowly letter envelopes are a handy tool. Now that you are committed to living with cash, you need a simple way to manage it. It's hard to find a better system. Label your envelopes according to your spending requirements (food, gas, dry cleaning, lunches, and so on) and then divide the cash between them.

As you spend, take the money from the appropriate envelope. You'll know it's time to stop spending when the envelope is empty. Could life be any simpler?

Mvelopes. Someone was bound to create "electronic" envelopes. A clever and reputable system for managing your money online can be found at *http://DebtProofLiving.mvelopes.com.* While there is a fee for this service (it works out to as little as $7.40 a month when you sign up for two years), it is certainly worth your consideration. (Note: I have negotiated a lower rate for friends and family of my company Debt-Proof Living and you can count yourself as one of that group. If you access using the URL above, you will get a discounted rate whether you sign up for three months, one year or two. The company offers an excellent demonstration and a 30-day free trial. Simply use the above URL to find both. I suggest that you take advantage of the trial period just to make sure Mvelopes is right for you.) Mvelopes is not software but rather an online money management service. It is as safe as it is simple to use.

Computer

You need this tool. The days are gone when computer literacy was an option. Whether you own a computer or have access to one (almost every public library these days has computers available for limited use to the public), you need basic computer literacy skills to go along with the hardware. These skills include accessing the Internet, email, and word processing.

With the advent of the Internet, the world has become a much different place. You will be far more successful living your life for half the price because of the research capability and online resources you have at the click of a mouse.

Financial Software

Knowing where you are with your money will keep you from slipping out of reality. One of the best uses you can make of your computer is to keep track of your money electronically. Add a good financial software program to your computer and learn to use it. This will revolutionize your financial life. It is like hiring a smart assistant.

Programs like Microsoft Money (*Microsoft.com/money*), Intuit's Quicken (*Quicken.com*), and the online money management system, Mvelopes (as mentioned above) are useful yet friendly. A simple accounting program, even simple spreadsheets you create with a program like Excel, will help you manage and keep track of your money. It doesn't have to be complicated or expensive. What works for you is exactly what you should use.

If you have any hang-ups with things mathematical, you need this kind of personal assistance. You will love knowing your checking account is always balanced. You can pay your bills online (some banks will charge a fee for this, although some do not; Mvelopes service includes online bill paying) and even track your spending by category to monitor your progress. Financial software also can assist you with setting up a long-term financial plan and preparing for your tax returns.

As trite as it may sound, it is true that if you take care of your money it will take care of you. When left unattended, money has the odd ability to vaporize—to vanish without a trace if not cared for and looked after. Nothing is quite so expensive as denial.

Proper Plastic

You are about to learn that I am opinionated—if not biased—in this area of plastic. As opposed as I am to credit-card debt, my position on credit cards may surprise you.

Credit card. You need one good, all-purpose credit card. You need only one, two at the most. Let me explain. Credit cards are not inherently bad. On the contrary, used in the right way, a credit card is an important tool. Credit-card debt is the problem to avoid!

Think back to when credit cards were first introduced (of course, we cannot remember such a time, but we've heard others speak of those days, right?). They were called "charge" cards. You had to pay the entire balance at the end of the month. No interest accrued; it was a consumer convenience.

Today American Express is considered by most as a "charge card" because the balance must be paid in full each month (although now even AmEx has jumped onto the consumer interest bandwagon with cards that allow for minimum payments and big rates of interest with a line of credit cards). But you as a savvy consumer can use any credit card as a charge card by simply making certain you pay it off before any interest accrues and never charging more than you can reasonably pay in a given month.

A good all-purpose credit card has these primary features: no annual fee, at least a twenty-five-day grace period, and accepted in many places. Ideally it also has a low rate of interest, although this is not a primary requirement because you will not carry a balance.

A credit card is a tool. You use it solely for your benefit, which means you get all the benefits without paying for them—no annual fee, no interest. To be accepted in most places it should be a MasterCard or Visa. When making your selection from those you may already have, always opt for the card you've had the longest.

Your credit limit on your one good, all-purpose credit card is only as important as its ratio to any balance you may carry on it (your goal is to get this to $0 balance and keep it there). In these days of computer generated credit scores (you can get your score at *MyFico.com,* for a fee), the ratio of debt to available credit is very important, as is the length of time you've had your credit card. Carrying balances close to your limit will pull your score down just as maintaining a large space between what you owe and your credit limit will improve your score.

Debit card. I include this here so you will not leave this chapter confused. You do not need a debit card. Because a debit card does not carry the consumer protection afforded by federal law the way a personal credit card does, it has greater potential danger.

If a thief gets hold of your MasterCard- or Visa-branded debit-card number, that thug has all he needs to clean out your bank account and every account attached to it. While your bank might have some kind of protection against fraudulent use on your debit card, it is not required by law to do so. And bank provisions can be changed at any time. Even if they have some kind of plan in place to protect you, this could leave you in the position of having to prove you weren't the one who went on a major spending binge (remember, online you can use a debit card without producing a PIN or signature).

ATM card. In these times when banks charge a fee to speak with a teller (can you even believe that?), you need an ATM card to have fee-free access to your cash or to make deposits. Many banks have eliminated the lowly ATM card in favor of a MasterCard- or Visa-branded ATM/debit card combo. I'm sure that by now you can figure out their reasoning. While you need ATM access, you don't need a debit card. Finding a bank that offers a simple ATM card may be worth your while.

Credit Score

Your credit score (also known as a FICO score) is a three-digit number that determines the interest rate you will pay on your credit cards, car loan, and home mortgage. It also determines whether you can get a cell phone or rent a home or apartment. A low credit score translates into paying higher interest rates on cards, loans, and insurance premiums; it can even affect your ability to get a job. You live in a world where your credit score is considered a direct reflection of your character.

Your credit score is based on your spending and bill-paying habits and your overall debt load. As such, two of the most important factors are the age of your credit card (how long you've had it) and the ratio of the debt balance (if any) to your available credit. Your current balance should be no more than 30 percent of the available credit to get the optimum credit score. See resources for more on how to get your credit score.

Tracking

Before I describe this tool (or is it a weapon?—you be the judge) let me tell you why it is so important: You need to know where all your money goes. If you are part of a couple, this applies to you collectively.

For most of us (I have a feeling there are far more natural-born spenders than those born with that rare "savers gene," who are not likely reading this book), money comes into our lives and is gone so fast we don't have a clue what really happened to it. The simple act of carefully tracking spending will give you the power of truth in your life versus what you imagine.

Tracking simply means counting—writing down how you spend your money. If two of you spend the household income, ideally both of you should keep this kind of daily record.

While you can use a PDA or other electronic device, all you really need for this tool is a small notebook or a stack of business cards that are blank on one side. Keep it simple and you'll improve your chances of sticking with it.

Start each morning with a fresh page or card. Put the day's date at the top, then write down each purchase made that day (gasoline, coffee, rent, new Jag...whatever) followed by the amount. Do this for every transaction, even the small ones, even the secret ones and embarrassing ones. If you spend it, record it.

At the end of the day put that day's record into a drawer or other safe place. The next morning start with a new page or card. Repeat every day for the entire month.

At the end of your first month of tracking, you will be a lot smarter than when you started. You will have a new vision.

And now you have a job to do: Pull out your month's worth of daily spending records. Categorize all of your spending. Don't make this more difficult than it is. You should be able to see ten to fifteen common areas of spending (groceries, fast food, clothing, utilities, housing, transportation, and so on). Don't assume this single month will give you an exact picture of your normal monthly spending. Many expenses do not repeat every month. Still, this is an excellent way to get a feel for how you are spending your money.

Don't be surprised, but do be encouraged, when you see that without doing much more than simply writing down how you spend your money you are becoming a more careful spender. This alone starts you on the path to living your life for a lot less.

Simply seeing where the money goes has an awakening effect on most people, encouraging them to keep more of what they earn. But the real value of this initial exercise is that it allows you to make changes for the coming month. Areas of spending that are really out of control can be tamed by deciding ahead of time how much to spend in that category and then capping it. When you reach the limit in an area, no more spending!

Creating a written spending plan will be as useful, if not more, than tracking your spending. But nothing will do you more good than exercising the personal discipline to both track and plan.

Weapons

Your Attitude

The most powerful weapon you have against spending all that you have is your ability to control your thoughts and responses to every circumstance in your life.

Think about it: Your attitude is the only thing over which you have complete control. It is more important than education or experience; more important than how much money you have, how much you owe, what you would like to do, or where you want to go.

You cannot tailor the circumstances of your life, but you can tailor your attitudes in response to those situations. The way you choose to respond to your circumstances—from the mundane to the major—can change the course of your life.

Here are some ideas for putting your attitude to work for you:

1. *Get angry!* If you have consumer debt, you know it's the pits. Debt eliminates your options, keeps you awake at night, and can make you lie to your creditors—even to your spouse. I know; I've been there. Terribly—worse than horribly—in debt!

So what are you going to do about it? Whine, complain, continue feeling sorry for yourself? I have a better idea. Get mad! Decide once and for all that you will not sell your soul to the likes of MasterCard and Visa—not one more day, not one more purchase. Get righteously indignant at the very idea of transferring your future wealth to creditors. Repeat after me: *I've had it, and I'm not going to live on credit anymore!*

If you do not have debt, you can still be angry about how it has affected your life. You pay more for things because of consumer debt. Millions of people file for bankruptcy every year, and that affects how much you have to pay to live your life.

2. *Campaign.* Think of your attitude as your personal ad agency, pub-

lic relations firm, and marketing organization all rolled into one. Flood your mind with so many compelling messages of hope and encouragement that no space remains for doubt and discouragement.

3. *Be content.* Choosing to be content doesn't mean you toss out your goals and dreams. Contentment is not complacency but rather a decision to want what you have. Contentment is the way to deal with self-pity and other destructive behaviors. Contentment is the equivalent of an emotional massage. It feels that good.

4. *Be grateful.* The simple act of choosing to be grateful for what you have rather than focusing on what you don't have is powerful beyond words. Sounds cheesy perhaps, but once you experience the power of a grateful heart, you will understand what a powerful antidote thankfulness is for the negative attitudes of greed, anger, and fear. Gratitude is a choice that builds a layer of insulation around your life, protecting you from focusing on what you don't have.

5. *Visualize.* Create a "mental camera" and keep it with you at all times. When faced with a situation or decision, step out of the picture and look at it through your mind's camera. Focus. Zoom out slowly to see this circumstance in the light of tomorrow, or the coming week. This will give you a new perspective—more realistic than a close-up view that only considers the moment.

Pull away even further so you view an entire month, then a year. (Don't go too far or you'll be no more than a speck of dust on the frame of time, which defeats the purpose of this little attitudinal exercise.) What impact will the decision you make now have on the big picture?

Choosing to control your attitude by viewing things in a new way will help you to make better decisions.

6. *Isolate.* If you are easily dissatisfied or prone to impulsive behaviors, identify your weak spots so you can avoid them. Turn off the television. Skip past the magazine ads. Isolate yourself from mindless

shopping. Avoid places you are most likely to slip back into your old ways of spending beyond your means.

7. *Self-talk.* Get into the habit of having heart-to-heart talks with yourself. This is so effective in stopping mindless spending. Ask yourself some questions before making a purchase of any significance. Then expect honest answers from yourself:

- *Do I need it?*

- *Do I want to dust (dry clean, insure, store, fuel, or otherwise maintain) it?*

- *Don't I already have something that will do just as well?*

- *Could I borrow it from a friend or family member?*

- *Is this is a good value?*

- *Do I have the cash to pay for it?*

- *How many hours will I have to work to pay for it?*

- *Could I possibly delay the purchase for a few weeks? Months?*

- *Am I willing to wait twenty-four hours before acting?*

The single greatest money-saving strategy I've learned over the years: when I run across something I think I have to own, I just wait a little while.

Know Your Prices

As simplistic as it might sound, knowing what things cost is one of the most useful weapons against all the forces that conspire to separate you from your money. To not know how much things cost is to be in denial.

Denial is a terrible thing: It tells us that the full price doesn't matter as long as we can handle the monthly payment; or that as long as there's room on your credit card, the price doesn't matter. Denial whispers that as long as swiping the debit card completes the purchase so the kids get what they have their hearts set on, then the price doesn't matters.

Denial says it's cool to not pay attention to price tags—that somehow this indicates a carefree, fabulous way of life where money is "no object." But all of that is just hogwash. Price *does* matter, and people who actually have money know what stuff costs. They memorize prices. They are not tricked by sales or "specials."

On the other hand, people who live beyond their means prefer not to know what they are spending. It's just easier that way. So know your prices and focus on what things really cost. This practice keeps you engaged and aware. Knowledge is an important tool, so start paying attention.

The Power of "No"

At times your most valuable weapon of all is the willingness to simply exercise good old-fashioned personal restraint—the power to say no!

I have a theory that those of us born with the overspending gene don't overspend on $5,000 designer bags or $1,100 jars of wrinkle cream. Instead, the bargains get us. And the really great bargains really get us.

Just because you can get something for half price doesn't mean you should buy it. It takes a powerful weapon—the power of no—to step away from the bargain, even if buying it would not require you to go into debt.

Discovering ways to radically reduce the cost of your lifestyle could prompt you to buy twice as much just because you can. That would not only defeat the purpose but it would be foolish.

Various forces and temptations will attempt to sabotage your efforts not to spend all of your money. Clever marketing and enticing advertising campaigns will appear to be offering authentic ways to help you save more. The willingness to just say no is powerful beyond words.

Make It Automatic

When it comes to managing your money, just about any automatic resource you can arrange will become a powerful weapon against spending beyond your means. The secret lies in our ability as humans to forget. This can either work for us or against us.

If you forget to pay your credit-card bill, prepare for trouble. If you forget to record several ATM withdrawals, and your wife is at the same time writing checks against the balance in the checkbook register, prepare for an unpleasant surprise and the possibility of a chain of bounced checks.

But on the other hand, if you forget about the $50 you've authorized as a deduction from your weekly paycheck to be deposited to your 401(k), forgetfulness is a good thing. Soon you don't miss the money because you are not used to receiving it. You forget about it.

Arrange to have your house payment or insurance premium automatically deducted from your checking account each month. This benefits you in ways other than insuring on-time payments: many mortgage lenders give a preferred interest rate for automatic payment, and some insurers waive fees in exchange for auto pay.

I am a big fan of all things automatic: lawn sprinkler timers, transmissions, washing machines, savings deposits, bill paying, and just about anything else I can arrange. What I don't see, I don't miss.

If you're like me (somehow I think we may be alike), you can easily let things slip. I have a tendency to forget. And in these times when paying late on any bill can cause the equivalent of a natural disaster with your credit score, "automatic" creates a safety net. Having things set up to happen automatically has saved my hide on more than one occasion. The power of automatic payments and deposits can do the same for you.

Cautionary note. Forgetfulness and "automatic" are helpful when it comes to making deposits and paying bills, but this doesn't let you off the hook when it comes to keeping a watchful eye over your bank account, your credit-card account, your invoices, and other statements.

Secondary Market

Gently used, previously owned, second hand, consignment—all refer to the secondary marketplace of consumer goods. In this country of affluence and abundance the secondary market is huge! Bigger than I ever dreamed before the advent of the Internet.

Secondary does not always mean the commodity has been used or worn. All it means for our purposes is that it was purchased originally and is now being sold for a second time and at a tremendous price reduction.

While I am hesitant to make any promises I cannot keep, I am nearly certain that I could locate just about anything in the secondary market and buy it for a fraction of the new price. It is amazing what is available in this country if you are patient and willing to work hard to find it.

Find your comfort zone. If you decide to participate in the secondary market, you need to find your comfort zone. Some people are more sensitive to the subject of buying "used" than others. However, the secondary market refers to much more than shopping in thrift stores and frequenting garage sales.

Consignment stores are popping up all over the country—offering everything from baby clothes to designer furniture. With the added competition comes higher standards. Many thrift stores have become more upscale in an effort to stay current and relevant to their more discriminating customers. These days it is not uncommon to find brand-new items in the secondary market, especially with the explosion of online auction sites.

Now let me warn you. The secondary marketplace offers as many opportunities to overspend as any shopping mall or online shopping opportunity. Just because you find something in excellent condition at an unbelievable price does not mean you need it or should buy it.

Online auctions. While there are plenty of Internet online auction sites (*Onsale.com, Ubid.com, Overstock.com, Bidz.com, BidVille.com*, Yahoo! Auctions, and even non-auction classified-ad sites like Craig's List, to name a few), *eBay.com* remains the most popular place to buy, sell, and research. Imagine every antique store in the country together with the contents of every individual's garage and attic all assembled under one roof—that's a small picture of eBay.

Almost everything shows up in the secondary market eventually, and when it does, you'll see it on eBay. Whether you want to know what your grandmother's antique Gorham figurine is worth or where to find the companion piece, eBay is an amazing resource for discovering the current value of anything in the secondary market. It is also dangerous. You can go broke loading up on other people's junk.

If you do not need something specific, do not log on to eBay. This is a dangerous place for a compulsive shopper who has no specific need or the personal discipline to get in and get out.

Meet the seller. If you find the item you are looking for, don't make a bid until you first meet the seller. Send this person a friendly email message. Confirm the cost of shipping and handling. While your inquiry is sincere, learning the answer is not your primary purpose in making the contact. You want to find out with whom you are dealing. Is this an individual or a big commercial clearinghouse for junk? Be brief and kind. If you do not receive a cordial response within twenty-four hours, you may be dealing with a large merchandiser, not an individual. That could be a red flag, so proceed with caution. Do not continue if you have any doubts or misgivings.

Check the seller. Read the seller's feedback to learn about others' experience with this seller. Negative feedback? Move on. If everything looks positive, look at the seller's number of completed auctions. One seller I tried to communicate with had more than 58,000 completed auctions with only 94 percent positive. Six percent may not seem like an unreasonable rate until you realize that means 3,480 unsatisfied buyers. I never received a reply. I learned later that this company buys carloads of returned, damaged, and worn items from major retailers. Too risky for me.

Calculate the shipping. This is part of the purchase price. Always look at the cost of shipping before you do anything else. Many sellers pad the shipping beyond reason. Do not be swayed by a seller who offers, for example, new lamps for 99 cents with no reserve (a reserve price is the minimum price a seller is willing to accept for the item). What's the trick? The shipping/handling fee is $50, something a bidder might miss in the frenzy to get a lamp for a buck. You must include the cost of shipping when considering the full price of the item.

Check the primary market. Before you make a commitment to buy, make a quick search with a shopping "bot" that will scour the Internet to see if you are about to pay too much. It happens frequently: items are priced higher on an auction site than can be purchased new elsewhere. There are several shopping bots, such as Froogle (*Froogle.Google.com*) or *Shopping.com*. If what you are looking for is available elsewhere on the Internet, it will pop up here together with the price. You don't want to pay more for an item on eBay than you could buy it new elsewhere. That happens frequently, so buyers beware.

Set your limit. If everything checks out and you decide to make a bid, determine the most you are willing to pay for this item, including shipping and handling, and stick with it. If the bidding goes beyond your limit, walk away. It is easy to keep bidding because you are determined to win. That can be dangerous.

If you are interested in selling things on eBay, go to *eBay.com* and click on "Sell." This will take you to a seller's tutorial and the eBay Learning Center. Advanced learners may wish to enroll in eBay University (*eBay.com/university*).

Courage to Negotiate

You may believe negotiating means asking for a discount or haggling with a seller. You're right, but it is more than that. Negotiating is the way you get what you want. Everything is negotiable, whether a major purchase, a larger discount, a better price, getting your teenage son to put the seat down, or receiving a refund on a product or service that did not meet your expectations.

In fact, you are already a negotiator. You negotiate with your kids, spouse, bosses, coworkers, employees, creditors, vendors, friends, clerks, and salespeople. You negotiate with telemarketers and repair people, teachers, and neighbors. You negotiate using your words, your tone, your body language, even your silence. The secondary marketplace is a good place to put your negotiation skills to work for you.

Something for everyone. The goal is not that everyone comes out an equal winner but that everyone walks away satisfied. Negotiating a deal that gives something of value to each party is the mark of a wise negotiator.

Go overboard. The point here is to ask for more than you are willing to settle for. To illustrate, let's say you want to make an offer on a house, an offer considerably less than the asking price. You write the offer, but in a surprise move stipulate that the price includes the laundry-room appliances, pool table, dining-room suite, and piano that you saw on your initial tour.

The seller responds that the price of the house is acceptable, "But that certainly does not include the personal property!" You win because you get your price (you didn't really want the twenty-five-year-old stuff, anyway), and the seller wins because he stood firm against what he considered an unreasonable request.

Knowledge wins. The person with the most knowledge wins. Never forget that knowledge is power. The more you know, the better your chances of getting what you want. The true skill comes in keeping what you know to yourself, revealing only a bit at a time and only when doing so is to your advantage. Remember that negotiating is a game, and the most skilled player usually wins.

The least motivated party is in control. If the other party finds out how desperate you are to make the deal, you've just lost power. Anytime you can send nonverbal cues that you are not desperate—that you are willing to cancel if you do not get what you want—you retain control. This drives a desperate opponent crazy!

No matter how anxious you may be on the inside, never let it show. The simple act of calmly and slowly closing (never slamming) a notebook, briefcase, purse, calendar, newspaper—whatever is handy—is an effective negotiator's most powerful tool. Without saying a word, you send a message that fills your opponent with worry that you are going to walk away.

You need to learn these basic negotiating skills to become an effective negotiator:

1. *Prepare.* Do the research. Carefully formulate exactly what you want.

2. *Set limits.* Know in your mind exactly how far you are willing to go, and stick with it. This allows you to focus on your alternatives and keeps you from appearing desperate.

3. *Create emotional distance.* Stick to the facts. Put your emotions away. Never utter the words "feel" or "feelings" in a negotiation.

4. *Listen effectively.* Remember what your mother always told you about the reason you have two ears and one mouth. No one knows better than I how easy it is to focus so intently on what you want to say next that you fail to really hear what your opponent is saying.

5. *Communicate clearly.* Choose your words carefully, express them succinctly, and then be quiet. Silence is a good thing.

In fact, the first party to break the silence is likely to lose the negotiation.

6. *Always remain a fragrance.* No matter how things go or turn out, remain kind and respectful so that your presence is fragrant. You never want to become an odor.

There, you have it—the tools and weapons you need to begin moving forward with living below your means. But just like the tools in a workshop or weapons in an arsenal, they are only as good as your willingness to pick them up and use them.

Refer to this chapter often as you pick up one tool after another, and rely on these weapons as the need arises. They will give you the power to better manage your money so you can keep more of it!

Chapter Four

Food Shopping: The Jarring Truth

How come the odds of going to the store for a loaf of bread and coming out with ONLY a loaf of bread are three billion to one?

~ Erma Bombeck

Food prices in the U.S. have climbed so dramatically in recent months, a stroll through the aisles of a typical supermarket is enough to kill your appetite. If that was the only place we spent our food dollars that would be one thing. But most families these days spend as much eating out as they do for food to prepare at home.

The huge food expense for most households—food in all of its forms—adds up to the second-highest monthly expense, second only to housing. Because it is such a huge financial area eating up so much of your income, we will break this down into several chapters. This chapter is devoted entirely to the challenge of cutting the cost of groceries to half price.

If price were the only criterion for reducing the cost of groceries, the possibilities would be endless, starting of course with a garden and some well-chosen highly productive farm animals.

Another option for slashing the cost of groceries would be to spend days on end going from store to store, town to town picking up each and every store's special-of-the-week. I sure don't have the time or gasoline for that, and I'm guessing that you don't either. What we need is an easy, efficient plan for grocery shopping that meets this simple set of criteria:

1. Takes no more than two hours a week.

2. Does not require that I shop at multiple stores each week.

3. Does not require that I buy store brands.

4. Includes a wide variety of name-brand, high-quality, nutritious foods that cover the USDA's current food pyramid and are family friendly.

5. Does not require that I buy in bulk quantities that are difficult to handle and cause a storage problem in my home.

6. Cost effective. I decide how much I am going to spend each week, and that amount may change depending on my circumstances.

Tall order? Yes, but fortunately you can accomplish all of this realistically while slashing the cost of your groceries to half the price or more. However, this requires that you trade in your old way of thinking and open your mind to a new way of food shopping.

But first, let's dissect this activity known as grocery shopping...

Two Methods of Grocery Shopping

There must be dozens of ways to shop for groceries, and I'm certain I've tried them all. But when it comes right down to it, every possible method falls into one of two categories—needs shopping or reserve shopping.

Needs shopping. You buy what you need now at the best price possible and enough to last until you go shopping again.

Reserve shopping. You buy what's on sale even if you don't need it now so that you don't have to overpay for it when you do need it. Reserve shopping is the process of building a small in-house grocery store. When it's time to make dinner you visit your own store.

Needs shopping is, in my opinion, a flawed system. Even the most diligent needs shopper—who shops with cash, builds the week's menus around what's on sale, and is careful to avoid all impulsive purchases—will eventually need something that is not on sale. That's what the stores count on. When you pay full price for some of the items in your cart, the store's plan works. They win. Mission accomplished.

Consider this needs-shopping dilemma: You need mayonnaise. The best price today is $2.99 a quart for the store brand. You need it; you buy it. It's not a horrible deal but it's not great.

Four weeks ago at the high-priced supermarket across town where they do crazy things like double coupons to attract shoppers, the quart size of Hellman's mayonnaise (aka Best Foods, the Cadillac of mayonnaise among those who rate their condiments), was on sale: 2/$5. That same week there was a $.75 manufacturer's coupon for Hellman's mayonnaise in the Sunday paper.

Here's the way that deal would have played out had you been aware of the sale and clipped that all-important coupon: $2.50 for one quart, less $1.50 for the coupon ($.75 x 2 = $1.50). Final price for the Hellman's: $1. That beats your store-brand deal by 66 percent.

As a needs shopper this is your dilemma: You didn't need mayonnaise a month ago. You need it now. The coupon has long expired and the sale is over. So you pay $2.99 for the off-brand mayonnaise because that's the best deal at the time you need it. To make matters worse, you discover that your friend, a reserve shopper, bought three quarts of Hellman's for $1 each and won't have to restock until it goes on sale again.

Reserve shopping is the best way I know to consistently pay less than half price for name-brand groceries. This method requires a minimal investment of time and energy. It's a reliable system—you can count on it to work for you week after week. You will enjoy a wide variety of foods in all of the food groups, including meat, produce, dairy, and household cleaning products and personal care items. Rather than coming up with menus before you go shopping, you look to the store's sales cycles to determine your food purchases. You create menus after the fact once you go shopping in your pantry's grocery stockpile.

Reserve shopping is an ideal grocery method for singles, families with kids, big families, little families, seniors with no kids—for all situations. You are not locked into narrow selections but have lots of freedom to choose the foods you want to buy. The amount of food is limited by the amount of money you wish to spend. You simply spend up to that limit and stop.

Eventually you will have a month's worth of basic groceries on hand. This insulates you against wild price fluctuations at the grocery store. You won't find yourself running to the store for one or two things, forced to pay the highly inflated full price.

When challenges come your way—you lose your job or get sick; there's a blizzard; you're hit with unexpected car repairs—whatever the setback, with food in the pantry, hard times are less hard.

Create a Price Book

Knowing the everyday and various sales prices on items you buy regularly is important no matter which method of grocery shopping you embrace. You need a practical way to track this important information. Creating a price book unique to your shopping habits and your particular store(s) is an effective way to do this.

If you frequent several stores (for example the grocery store in your town that has the lowest overall price, the supermarket that doubles coupons, a bakery outlet store, and a produce stand) list in your price book the prices of the items you buy regularly in each of these stores. It's possible you live in a more rural area where you have no choice— it's the one food market in town or nothing. Still you need a reliable way to track prices.

Let's say the high-priced supermarket has whole-grain bread regularly priced at $3.29 on sale, buy-one-get-one free. You also have a $1 manufacturer's coupon for that item that the store will double. According to my math, with that deal you can buy two loaves of high-quality bread for 65 cents each. The best price you've ever seen in your bakery outlet store is 99 cents, and that was a long time ago. Without this valuable information in your price book you might walk right past an excellent bargain.

Now I have no doubt that you can create a perfect price book on your own, but just in case you need ideas and inspiration, here are resources for your consideration:

- Organized Home (*OrganizedHome.com*) offers free printable pages to create a price book.

- It's Your Money (*MoneySpot.org*) offers a free downloadable price book using Excel, which allows you to track the prices of commonly purchased items. This particular tool calculates price-per-weight-unit, price-per-quantity-unit, and price-per-use if applicable.

- Dollar Stretcher (*Stretcher.com*) offers a price book with pocket pages and a calculator for $14.95 plus shipping and handling.

- Grocery Book (*GroceryBook.com*) offers a price book as part of a package with the book by the same name ($19) that you can either print or download to your computer.

- Cheap Cooking (*CheapCooking.com/pricebook.htm*) has a terrific Excel spreadsheet you can copy to create your price book.

- Practical Saver (*PracticalSaver.com*) offers *Real World Grocery Savings*, a $9.95 e-book download that offers a good plan for tracking sales, organizing coupons and creating a Price Book.

I Have a Confession...

I used to be a fanatic needs shopper. And I didn't keep that to myself. In my early books and also my *Debt-Proof Living* newsletter (formerly *Cheapskate Monthly*), I advised my readers to shop with cash and to buy only what they needed.

While I'm confessing let me also say that I was a coupon snob. I could not be bothered with clipping and filing coupons. I tried it once and it gave me a rash. I am not an organized person. Coupons get lost in the bottom of my purse. They give me a headache. I had a long list of good reasons why clipping coupons was a waste of time and money.

In 2001, as a kind of research project for *Cheapskate Monthly* (known today as *Debt-Proof Living* newsletter) readers, I set out to prove my position. I couldn't do it. As a result of that experiment I converted to reserve shopping, and remain an avid fan to this day.

One last confession: I do not keep a price book and I do not track grocery prices. Some people are naturally gifted in that area of data collection and mathematics. I am not one of them.

Objections and Misgivings

Before telling you exactly how reserve shopping works (my method of choice) and what you need to transition to being a reserve shopper, I want to address the objections and misgivings you may have about this way of buying food.

I Will Spend More Money Reserve Shopping

On the surface, this does make sense, but it is not the case. You first need to determine your grocery spending limit. If that is $100 a week, be firm and do not exceed that amount even if that means leaving bargains at the store. Your stockpile will grow slowly at first, and that's perfectly acceptable.

I Will Need a Lot of Extra Storage Space

You'll be surprised how many places you have already where you can store your reserve. Nonperishable items can be stashed just about anywhere—under a bed, under the staircase, in the garage or basement. A single cupboard or closet devoted to your food reserve is all you need. I predict in no time you'll be sizing up a broom closet for shelves or clearing space in a cupboard currently filled with stuff you never use.

I Need a Chest Freezer

Again, not true. The freezer space in your refrigerator is sufficient to handle your frozen reserves. Just make sure to empty, clean, and reorganize your freezer at least monthly. And keep in mind that only a portion of your grocery stockpile will be frozen.

It Takes a Lot of Time

Once you get the hang of it you will spend no more time reserve shopping than you do now as a needs shopper. It could be less because you will visit only one store weekly. Just think of all the time you will save when you cut out those last-minute runs to the store for one or two things.

How to Reserve Shop

This is a perfectly legal and ethical way to pay less than half price for groceries—and to do that consistently, week after week after week. I only mention this because once you understand how it works and why it works, it seems too good to be true. And you know what they say about that. It usually is. But not this time.

This shopping method utilizes these tools: the supermarket's weekly sales and two coupon circulars from the biggest Sunday newspaper in your area. These coupons are published by Valassis (*Valassis.com*) and Smart Source (*SmartSource.com*) and inserted into all major newspapers in the U.S. That's all the coupons you need. More may send your brain into serious overload.

Each week, go through the stores' ads using your method of choice (more on this follows) and make a list of the sale items priced low enough to be worthy of your business. Next find the coupons that match those items. You're ready to head to the supermarket.

To be successful at this kind of shopping, a person needs to be organized, somewhat gifted with numbers, and a whiz when it comes to tracking a store's sales cycles. Sadly, I possess none of those qualities. Still I am proud to say, in spite of my lack of mathematical and organizational skills I have built and maintained an amazing stockpile of groceries for many years now.

May I show you my stockpile?

I have so many groceries in my stockpile that I provide lunch for my entire office staff at least three times a week. I took two months off from grocery shopping recently because the stockpile had grown too large and I needed to pare down. (What could you do with two months of grocery money if you didn't have to use it to buy food?) Over the years we've also given away loads of food to help people going through difficult times.

You want to know my secret, don't you?

I have help. You can have help too. Here's the way I look at this: Why do the tedious work of keeping track of prices and sales cycles— work that makes me crazy—when others are more than willing to do that for me?

I want to introduce you to two separate websites owned by two smart ladies who do this work and then let me have a copy of their shopping lists. While both of these websites offer a similar service, they are quite different. Moreover, one site requires a membership fee; the other is free and open to the public.

Thanks to this help, I don't have to do the dirty work. And I routinely walk out of the supermarket with savings of at least 50 percent. My all-time high was a whopping 74 percent savings.

The Grocery Game

Every Saturday I go to *TheGroceryGame.com* to get "The List." This is more than a listing of all of the items that are on sale at my supermarket this week (that is a list that would be so long, it would take too much paper to print). The list I'm after is the one that goes through the sale items and identifies those that are an authentic sale—not "fake" sales trying to trick me.

Let me explain the difference between a real sale and a fake one, using General Mills Cheerios as an example. A 15-ounce box has a regular price of $4.29. If you track that one item over the course of a year you'll have a graph that looks like a wild roller-coaster ride.

One week the price drops to $3.99, then down to $2.49, then back to $4.29 for a few weeks. Then one week it plunges to $2. That's when it shows up on The List because that's an authentic "rock-bottom" price. I have a 50-cent coupon for Cheerios that when doubled makes my net price $1. One dollar! I just wait patiently until The List tells me it's time to buy. The only reason I have the luxury of waiting is that I've done the same thing in the past, so we have plenty of cereal at home in our food storage area.

The Grocery Game tracks and offers The List for nearly every supermarket chain across the country. Members invest thirty minutes to one hour each week preparing for their shopping trip and come out with an average of 67 percent savings. A subscription is $10 for eight weeks. A four-week trial membership is available ($1 for four weeks) and highly recommended. Go to *TheGroceryGame.com* for more information and to sign up for a trial membership.

Coupon Mom

This website is every grocery shopper's fondest dream come true: *CouponMom.com*. It is completely free and requires no registration or log-in. You could go there right now if you weren't busy reading this.

When you do go to this site look for your state and click on a grocery store chain. You'll see a list of the current week's "Best Deals," including the coupon you need to match with it to get an even better deal. Prepare to be amazed. But it doesn't stop there.

While Stephanie Nelson, *The Coupon Mom* and founder of the Cut Out Hunger program is anxious to help you cut your grocery bills in half, she has another agenda. Her mission is to feed the hungry. She sees so many unbelievable bargains each week (many items you can pick up for just 25 cents if you have the right coupon) and encourages those of us who use the information on her site to donate at least one item from our weekly grocery trek to a food pantry or other charity in our local communities. She will even help us find donation locations.

Can you imagine what could happen if every person in the U.S. who grocery shops any given week were to donate only one item to help feed the hungry? We could wipe out hunger in this country and create such amazing reserves that charitable organizations would beg us to stop. Narrow that to just the people in your neighborhood, church, or school group. In very little time you would be helping individuals and families through difficult times and back on track.

Do It Yourself

If neither of these resources applies to your situation—or you simply prefer to track your grocery store's data on your own—here are the steps:

1. *Select a supermarket.* For optimum stockpiling you want to shop at

the pricey big-name chain supermarket in your area that accepts and hopefully doubles manufacturer's coupons. Supermarket chain stores like Kroger, Publix, Thrift Way, Frys, Smith's Safeway, Vons, Pavilions, Ralph's, King Soopers, Winn-Dixie, Shoprite, and Albertsons are great candidates. Depending on the location, these stores often double (some triple) your coupon's value. (If there are no stores that double coupons in your area, that's okay. This method will still work for you.)

High-priced supermarkets are the best place to reserve shop because while the regular prices are much higher than prices at other stores, their sale prices come in consistently lower. And when matched to a coupon, the net price of the items you buy for your at-home stock-pile will consistently beat the cheapest no-frills store in town.

Remember, the supermarkets do all they can to appear to be the cheapest source for groceries in hope that you will pay full price for many of the items in your grocery cart. It doesn't take many full-price purchases in a high-priced store to wipe out a lot of hard work.

2. *Know your prices.* This is critical. To achieve dramatic savings you have to be a price wizard, knowing both the regular prices and the various sales prices of the items you buy. Supermarkets are clever. They know shoppers are impressed by sales. But many sales are teasers. You'll need to track for a while to discover the sales cycles and patterns. Your detailed price book or database will let you know when the sale price is at its lowest. That's the time to stock up.

3. *Collect coupons.* Every Sunday rescue those two coupon circulars from the biggest newspaper in your area (published by Valassis and Smart Source and inserted into all major newspapers in the U.S.). That's all the coupons you need.

4. *Match sales prices with coupons.* This is where the radical savings bring prices down to look like "loss leaders." Once an item is on sale at its lowest price, match it with a coupon and make your buy. And buy as many as you can at that price according to the number of coupons you

have for it, the store's policy on multiple coupons, and your financial condition. Then watch your stockpile take off.

5. *Stick to your spending limit.* Stockpiling can run amok for the compulsive shopper who is driven to buy good deals. You must set a spending limit and be willing to leave bargains in the store once you have reached that limit. Spending twice as much because you are stockpiling makes you an overspender. No matter what, that's not good.

Organizing Coupons

Whether you depend on one or both of the grocery list services mentioned above—or you create your own list—the one job likely to drive you nuts is organizing your coupons.

Done well, reserve shopping requires that you manage hundreds of coupons—and keep them until they expire but not one day longer. Okay, it's not that critical, but you want to purge as often as possible. When you need a particular coupon, you don't want to spend hours trying to remember where you filed it.

The Virtual Coupon Organizer. A free online tool that is perfect for those of us who dislike clipping and filing coupons, this interactive database at *VirtualCouponOrganizer.com* lists all the coupons that have come with the Sunday paper that have not yet expired. Think of it as an electronic coupon caddy. You can search a coupon by brand name, food category, or the date it was released. If you are diligent to keep the coupon circulars from your Sunday paper, this organizer becomes an electronic index of what you have in your coupon drawer.

Using this electronic organizer, you may never have to file stacks of individual coupons again. Instead keep the entire coupon booklets from each week's newspaper. Because the interactive coupon caddy knows exactly where a coupon is in your stack, all you do is let the organizer tell you where it is in your stack of booklets, go to that page, and clip the coupons as you need them.

This works in another way as well. Let's say you need cereal and cannot wait until next week's grocery shopping trip (you will run out of items from time to time). Go to your virtual coupon caddy, look up "cereal," and up will pop a list of all the cereal coupons you have in your stack of coupon booklets. So even if the item is not at a deeply discounted sale price, you will have the benefit of a coupon to get the price down.

Create a coupon index. Kara Rosendaal (*PracticalSaver.com*) offers a user-friendly system using your computer and either Word or Excel to create and maintain a table of contents for your coupon file. In her forty-nine-page book *Real World Grocery Savings*, a $9.95 ebook (you can read a sample chapter online), she describes this method in detail.

Make the Transition

If you are a needs-based shopper wanting to transition to the reserve method, there is an easy way to do so. It will take about twelve weeks to make the switch and end up with a respectable stockpile.

First, identify the supermarket where you will do your reserve shopping. If you have a supermarket in your area that doubles coupons, that should be your store of choice.

Begin to make some stockpiling purchases each week, making sure you buy only items that are at rock-bottom prices and for which you have a coupon. Consider using one of the grocery list services described above as a resource to help you determine which items are the best deals and which coupons to use.

Continue to make your needs purchases at a no-frills, cheap store. Each week your needs will diminish and you will begin to shop from your stockpile. After twelve weeks you will have a well-rounded stockpile. You're on your way.

Supermarket Alternatives

Under most circumstances, you will do well reserve shopping in a single supermarket. However, you can certainly build and maintain your stockpile from just about any place that sells food. Since each situation is unique, and every area of the country offers different options, you have to assess all of your options and then determine what is best for you. There is no one-size-fits-all.

No Frills Grocery

Stores like Food 4 Less, Hy Vee, Pak 'n' Save, and Scratch 'n' Dent are examples of discount food markets known for their lower everyday prices. Countless other super-discounted, no-frills grocery outlets and stores are available all over the country in small cities as well as large. Get out there and look. Make it your business to learn everything you can about the no-frills in your community. Learn the ropes; ask the right questions. Some of these stores will have everything you need, all at lower prices. Others will concentrate on just non-perishables.

Discount Warehouse Clubs

If you do all of your food shopping at Costco, Sam's Club, or BJ's you will spend a lot of money. It is difficult, if not impossible, to consistently slash your food costs at these "big box" stores. You will, however, come home with greater quantities of high-quality foods, meats, and name-brand items. If you have the personal discipline to be selective and you possess industrial-strength restraint, you can make excellent buys.

You can always count on these items to be cheaper at one of these clubs than at the typical supermarket, even when on sale there: milk, cheese, eggs, butter, frozen chicken breasts, and laundry detergent.

ALDI

This important worldwide discount grocery chain operates over seven hundred stores in twenty-six states, primarily from Kansas to the East Coast (see *Aldi.com* for store locator). ALDI carries only private-label foods and boasts to pricing everything 50 percent less than their competitors.

Most customers find they can do 90 percent of their weekly shopping at ALDI. When you shop at ALDI you don't worry about coupons, sales, or other marketing ploys. A true no-frills operation, expect to put a quarter into the slot to "rent" a shopping cart (you'll get it back when you leave) and also to pay a small fee for grocery bags. Of course you can bring your own bags. ALDI encourages recycling.

Wal-Mart

All Wal-Mart stores have food departments. A Super Center combines a typical Wal-Mart store with a full-service supermarket. Not yet available in every area, those who are familiar with these stores report that the savings are impressive. Wal-Mart accepts manufacturer's coupons, but does not double them.

The unique feature of Wal-Mart is the price match. The reason behind this policy is to preclude you from having to drive to many stores to pick up the lowest-priced sale items. Provided you have the competition's weekly ads with you at the checkout to verify the competing price, Wal-Mart's policy is that you will get that lower price.

As a wise shopper be sure to check on the way this policy is handled in your local store to preclude a time-consuming snag at the checkout.

Green Markets

While we normally think of produce, green markets also offer other items like bakery goods, meat, and so forth. This is an opportunity to buy directly from the grower, maker, butcher, or baker. The appeal? No middleman.

You should find prices at a green market lower than the supermarket, and these prices are generally negotiable. Simply ask, "Is this your best price?" Shopping at a green market may be a way to reduce your food costs, but be careful. It's easy to overshop and overspend because the bargains at a green market can be so enticing.

Bakery Outlet

Most cities have an outlet store where the overstock from a commercial bakery can be sold quickly at bargain-basement prices. While you might think such a place would be well-known and in a location you cannot miss, this is not always the case. You need to ask around or look in your phone book.

While the prices at such an outlet are already amazingly low (remember they need to get rid of this stuff quickly to make room for tomorrow's overruns), to get even better deals, shop on the day when everything is marked down even further. This makes it possible to buy bread and other bakery items for just pennies on the dollar.

Wherever there's a Wonder Bread bakery for example, you'll find an outlet for the overstock. Find an Entenmann's Orowheat Bakery Outlet or simply search your phone book for "bakery outlets." Local independent bakeries may not have a separate outlet store, but often reduce the prices at the end of the day.

Organic and Natural Foods

If you are committed to a diet of organic foods, you know that decision can be expensive. Still, if you are as committed to reducing the cost as you are to keeping true to an organic way of life, you can accomplish that for a reduced price.

The most expensive way to purchase organic foods is at a high-priced store like Whole Foods. If you must shop at such a store, apply the principles of reserve shopping: buy only what's on sale in the expensive organic store, then do your needs shopping elsewhere.

Grow Your Own

The only way you can be 100 percent sure of what goes into your produce is to grow it yourself. If you require organic foods and you are not supporting a garden, you are allowing a lot of money to leak out of your life. It does not take a great deal of space to grow basic vegetables and herbs. You can do it in containers on a balcony or you can grow fresh herbs year-round in a windowsill.

Farmer's Market

Produce is typically cheaper and fresher at a green or "farmer's market." If you don't see a sign saying the produce is organic, ask. Many farmers are making the transition to organic farming. The key to making good deals at these kinds of markets is to ask lots of questions. Ask the produce manager about seconds (produce that isn't perfect) that may be available at a discount. A simple "Are you discounting any sub-prime produce today?" is an easy way to find out what kind of bargains are waiting for you in the back of the store.

Community Gardens

If you do not have space at your home for a garden, you may be able to join a community garden where you rent a plot of ground. If eating organic produce is important to you, making the time and effort in this way will save you a ton of money. Ask if there is a community garden in your area or perhaps help to start one. Often there are people with land lying dormant who are happy to let a group farm it free of charge. In a community garden everyone contributes and divides the harvest.

Community-Supported Agriculture (CSA)

Consumers and farmers work together to produce organic produce. While the farmer is tending the crops, consumers share the costs of supporting the farm and share the risk of variable harvests (and also share the overabundance of a particularly fruitful year). Membership in the CSA is based on shares of the harvest. Members are called shareholders and underwrite the harvest for the entire season in advance.

A share in a CSA costs about $300 to $400 for a twenty-four- to twenty-six-week growing season. Many programs accept monthly payments. Most CSAs allow singles or small families to buy a half share. Each project handles this relationship in their own fashion. To find a CSA in your area go to the website *NAL.usda.gov/afsic/csa* and click on "National State-by-State Database of CSA Farms."

Join a Grocery Co-Op

Such an organization will be much cheaper than a supermarket like Whole Foods. But don't expect this to be fancy. In fact, your co-op may be housed in a warehouse or garage. Foods are usually sold in bulk and co-op members are often asked to volunteer time to run the co-op.

Buying food is the best and easiest place for you to begin living your life for half the price. Yes, this will require some amount of toil and trouble, but the payoff will be more than worth your effort. Just make sure you set a spending limit before you clip a single coupon or print a weekly shopping list.

And one more thing. Clear a space for your stockpile. If I've convinced you to become a reserve shopper, you're going to need it!

Chapter Five

News Flash! There's a Kitchen in Your House

Dinner in half an hour? Even if you're working all day, why buy Chinese take-out food, or frozen dinners, or eat at a fast food joint when you can make a fresh, informal home-cooked meal even in a minuscule kitchen— and you will know exactly what you are eating.

~ Julia Child, chef and TV host

Having a well-stocked pantry, freezer, and refrigerator is fabulous. But alas, acquiring the food is only half the job. It takes commitment to turn that food into quick, easy, and delicious meals so you can stay out of the drive-thru.

Your success in buying groceries for half the price will be for naught unless you follow through by turning that food into home-cooked meals instead of eating out. This is critical because failure to exercise the discipline required to eat your meals from your stockpile of groceries will result in paying twice: Once for the groceries and then again to eat out because you're too tired, don't know how, or simply cannot be bothered spending time in that area of your home known as a kitchen.

I want to motivate and inspire you to fix family-friendly fare in less time than it takes to have pizza delivered. Or the time it takes to find your keys, drive to a take-out restaurant, wait in line, drive forward to the menu board, decide what you want, count your money, place your order, pay at the first window, wait for your order at the second window, drive home hoping nothing spills, carry all of it into the house, and finally look in the bag to discover half your order is missing. Don't you hate when that happens?

If there's only one thing you take from this chapter, let it be this: you do not have to be a seasoned home chef to create tasty meals and in thirty minutes or less. You don't even have to be a good cook. If you can open packages, use a measuring cup, lift the lid from a slow cooker, slide a chicken into the oven, and boil a pan of water, I believe you have what it takes to get started.

No matter where you fall in the demographic spectrum—a single guy in a big city apartment with a kitchen the size of a postage stamp on the one end, to the mom of a big, busy family with a kitchen to match on the other—or any of the many possibilities between—I have confidence that you can turn out quick and easy meals for a lot less than you currently spend on food.

I'm assuming that you've begun grocery shopping in keeping with the principles and instructions in the previous chapter. As such, I know what will be making up your stockpile. The same things come on sale like clockwork. But before we go over what you can expect to find in your stockpile, let's talk about that place known to many of us as the "State of Overwhelmed." That is where you could easily find yourself if you take stockpiling seriously. But please, do not despair, do not leave me now! I promise to not leave you overwhelmed.

Because I can't leave you now and come back in a few months once you've gone through the gradual process of building a reserve of food, I need to approach this as if you have your reserve established. And while you won't find recipes in this chapter, I couldn't help myself. I had to make sure you would have access to a handy supply of my can't-live-without recipes and instructions for how to turn a food reserve into fabulous meals that will keep you and the family eating at home. You will find these in Appendix A at the back of the book.

So take a deep breath...and let's move on with an overview of the foods you'll see a lot of in the coming months.

Chicken

You need a good chicken repertoire because once you begin to diligently buy mainly what's on sale, you'll be eating a lot of chicken—whether you are needs shopping or reserve shopping. You'll have whole chickens as well as boneless chicken breasts, cut-up fryers, wings, thighs, and drumsticks. All of it is good for your health and your spending plan.

Rice

Not only is rice cheap, it is a healthy and delicious side dish for almost any meat entree. You need to know the tricks to making perfect rice quickly and efficiently. Decide now to add brown rice to your diet and your repertoire. It is healthier and extraordinarily delicious when prepared properly. Just keep in mind that white rice cooks more rapidly than brown and is always an excellent side dish.

Beef

Once you get into the swing of things, you will find yourself buying lots of London broil or other cheaper cuts of beef because often they will be on sale at bargain prices. You need a variety of ways to prepare this so that it comes out tender and flavorful. That's a challenge because cheaper cuts of meat can easily turn out tough and bland.

Pasta

When eaten in moderation, pasta is an important part of a well-rounded nutritious diet. And believe me when I say you will have lots of pasta in your grocery cart once you begin buying what's on sale. When pasta is on sale and you have a coupon to match, it is an almost-free pantry item. You need many options for using pasta in your homemade meals.

Legumes

Otherwise known as beans, legumes should find a place in your regular meal lineup. I suggest that one meal each week should have legumes as the entree. Pinto beans, limas, black-eyed peas, lentils, and navy beans are always cheap. And while legumes may never make the list of sensational sale items the way cold cereal and salad dressings do, they are always a bargain—even when you pay the full retail asking price. And those times when they are on sale, load up.

Ground Beef

You'll find ground beef on sale often. Sometimes it will be the leanest variety, but quite often not. Regardless, you should buy ground beef when the price is right. Then you need to know how to quickly and efficiently get that ground beef cooked and virtually fat-free. It's easy as you will learn when you cruise through appendix A. Cooked ground beef is a basic staple item you should freeze to be available at a minute's notice.

Freezer-Ready

This is what I call anything like ground beef, rice, sliced turkey, chicken stock, beef broth, lasagna, and homemade cookies, all of which I've prepared partway then frozen in portion sizes for future use. If you could peek into my freezer right now you'd see about twenty zip-type bags, each containing about one pound of browned ground beef and bags of cooked rice in individual-portion sizes; two pans of homemade lasagna; dozens of one-cup frozen portions of homemade chicken stock; ditto on the beef broth. It is so quick and easy for me to put together a meal in no time flat from this odd collection of meal ingredients.

Cake Mixes

They go on sale often. Priced at their lowest, you will get cake mixes for 75 cents each or less. Knowing what to do with a cake mix other than following the package instructions will bring great variety to your meals, because you'll have quick and easy desserts on the menu.

You can make cookies from cake mix or use a cake mix as a quick-and easy-base for a more elaborate dessert that tastes and looks like you made it from scratch (my favorite way to cook, sometimes called "semi-homemade").

Produce

This question may have crossed your mind: *Is it possible to eat a healthy diet on a tight budget?* The answer is yes. Still, many believe that a cheap diet is one loaded with carbohydrates, lacking in the required amounts of fruits and vegetables that we know are necessary in a healthy diet.

The Department of Agriculture put this question to rest in July 2004 with publication of the study *How Much Do Americans Pay for Fruits and Vegetables?* Americans can meet fruit-and-vegetable food pyramid recommendations for as little as 64 cents a day. The same report found 127 different ways to eat a serving of fruits and vegetables for less than the price of a 3-ounce candy bar. The full report, an easy read and quite enlightening, is available free online at *http://Ers.usda.gov/publications/aib790/aib790.pdf.*

If you depend on a grocery list service like The Grocery Game or The Coupon Mom (see chap. 4), expect to see a variety of fruits and vegetables on those lists each week, year-round. The healthy-diet conscious shopper will zero in on these items on The List and stock up as dictated by the ages and gender of family members. If you don't depend on such a list, you can rely on the fact that most grocery stores have a variety of fruits and vegetables on sale each week.

The fresh produce department is not the only place to find fruits and vegetables. You will find items that meet the standards in the canned, frozen, and dried fruits aisles of the supermarket too. This will vary according to the season, so let the sales be your guide. What's in season is usually the cheapest. The big three in the fresh produce department will be apples, oranges, and grapes—they are on sale most often, but not all the time. This means you will need to change your thinking away from shopping for the familiar standbys to trying new things when the price is right.

Have you ever wondered what constitutes "a serving" in the context of the daily recommendations from the U.S. Department of Agriculture? It is likely less than you might think. A small apple, for example, is considered one serving. But a large apple counts as two servings.

The National Cancer Institute, cosponsor of the "5-a-Day for Better Health" program (*5day.com*) defines a serving as:

- 4 ounces of applesauce (any variety or brand)

- One medium-size fruit (or 4 ounces by weight)

- 1/2 cup raw, cooked, frozen or canned fruits (in 100 percent juice)

- 1/2 cup raw, cooked, frozen or canned vegetables

- 3/4 cup (6 oz.) 100 percent fruit or vegetable juice

- 1/2 cup cooked, canned or frozen legumes (beans and peas)

- 1 cup raw, leafy vegetables

- 1/8 cup raisins

- 1/4 cup other dried fruit

Getting five or more servings of fruits and vegetables into your diet every day is easier than you think. It's also much more likely now that you have taken control of your grocery shopping and committed to eating most of your meals from that food.

A glass of 100 percent juice and a handful of berries on your cereal equals two servings for breakfast. An apple or banana is a great one-serving mid-morning snack. A small, mixed-green salad adds another serving with lunch. Try a fruit smoothie as an afternoon pick-me-up for one to two more servings.

Mushrooms in your stir-fry? Tomato sauce on your spaghetti? A snack of dried fruits and nuts? There are so many ways to add more servings of fruits and vegetables to your daily diet.

Specials of the House

You need a repertoire of simple dishes, six to eight entrees or meals you can make with speed and confidence that you and your family enjoy. You may already have such a list. If not here are some ideas to help you get started (you will find specific recipes and directions for some of these and others in appendix A). Just make sure you keep it simple or you'll not likely stick with it.

Spaghetti is always a family-pleasing entree, so learn to make that. You'll need a couple of good, reliable entrees that use ground beef, such as chili or meat sauce (for spaghetti or a host of other uses). You need to know how to make a great stir-fry from ingredients you have on hand (even leftovers) and a great casserole (you're going to love the ideas in the appendix A for "designer cuisine"). Homemade pizza has every hope of becoming your number-one favorite quick-and-easy home-cooked meal.

Once you hit on the meals you enjoy, claim them as your specialties of the house. Fix them on a regular basis. Yes, over and over again. Aren't you and your family eating the same fast food over and over? The same principles apply with the great food you fix at home for half the price and in half the time.

Your family will beg you not to eat out again once they realize what a great cook you are—and fast too. Well, perhaps "beg" is a bit strong, but you get my point.

Return of the Slow Cooker

The slow cooker (known to many by the brand name Crock-Pot, however there are other brands) is back, having made a comeback from the 1970s, and in a big way.

If you have a slow cooker (a recent study says 77.8 percent of us do), now would be a great time to drag it out of storage and give it another chance.

I know what you're thinking: the reason that slow cooker landed where it did is because it produced overcooked and bland meals that could, at best, be considered semi-edible. I hear you. The problem is we probably didn't know (much less follow) the basic fundamental culinary techniques of slow cooking.

But that was then, now is now, and a slow cooker may well become your culinary lifesaver.

One of the best things about slow cooking is that it requires some level of planning ahead. It does cook very slowly, after all. Loading the cooker in the morning guarantees a more stress-free afternoon and evening because you've already done the minimum amount of work required. And as a bonus you'll have a delicious meal waiting when everyone returns home that day. You will bless the day you took my advice to call this wonderful appliance back into service.

Why Slow Cook?

Convenience. A slow cooker can be left unattended all day. You can put in ingredients in the morning and forget about it until dinnertime without the worry of burning your house down. It's as safe as a night light.

Economy. The best slow-cooked ingredients are often the least expensive (tough cuts of beef, the dark part of the chicken, root vegetables). Knowing dinner is all ready to go precludes unscheduled fast-food runs and relieves guilt. The folks at Sunbeam say it costs only a penny to operate a slow cooker for six to eight hours. How awesome is that?

Basic Guidelines

Best size and style. Popular sizes are 3 1/2-, 4-, and 5-quart models. Most have removable liners. The 3 1/2-quart models are fine for most dishes and needs, but the 5-quart models allow you to insert other dishes, springform pans, or pudding molds, giving you a wider range of options.

Rival's latest Crock-Pot models, Smart-Pots, have fancy timers; some are programmable and allow you to set the time and temperature to cook in thirty-minute increments for up to twenty. As interesting as all that might sound, you don't need anything that fancy to get started with slow cooking.

Manufacturers usually recommend filling the pot half to three-quarters full, so if you're cooking for two, this might be an important consideration. You can get a good slow cooker for less than $50. Watch for sales at stores like Target or Wal-Mart. Go to *Froogle.google.com* and type in "slow cooker" to see the vast array of choices.

Know your cooker. A traditional slow cooker where the heat surrounds the cooking insert is better than a slow cooker where the heat comes from underneath. The most common models have a removable pot insert. The two heat settings are low (200 degrees) and high (300 degrees). The slow cooker, or "multicooker" usually cooks from the bottom and might have a thermostat allowing a wide range of temperatures.

Slow cooker recipes. Until you become slow-cooker proficient, stick closely to a recipe that has been specifically developed for slow cooking. Go to the Food and Beverage area of *About.com* where you will find thousands of recipes for slow cooking and everything you ever wanted to know about the technique. Bookmark that site because you will use it frequently.

Rival's Crock-Pot website (*CrockPot.com*) has a nice collection of slow cooking recipes. Another favorite source of recipes for slow cooking is Crockery Kitchen (*CrockPot.cdkitchen.com*). There are many cookbooks in print for slow cooking. But rather than buying, borrow them from the library.

Master the Stir-Fry

If you want to learn to do something impressive in the kitchen, this is it. Who doesn't love a good stir-fry? The reason I love it: no recipe; only technique. If your family is anti-leftovers, do not tell them this part: it's the perfect way to clean out the refrigerator. You need some of this and a little of that.

The reason most home stir-fry comes out a soggy mess is that our home stovetops don't get as hot as restaurant woks. The secret is to cook everything very quickly on very high heat, but in small batches. Then remove those small batches from the skillet or wok until the end when you put all the cooked batches back into the same pot and toss with a great sauce.

I have such confidence in you, I'm going to make this bold statement: you can make stir-fry start to finish in less than thirty minutes. The secret is to get all of your ingredients ready and within easy reach before you start, and to get your skillet as hot as possible.

You will find my favorite instructions (and recipes for the sauce too) in Appendix A, together with some of my favorite shortcuts and kitchen helps. Enjoy!

You Deserve Some Help

Internet

The Internet has untold sites filled with recipes (I've already given you several that specialize in recipes for slow cooking), so many, in fact, you could find yourself paralyzed and unable to cook a meal for all of the information.

So in an act of mercy, I offer my single most favorite recipe website: *Allrecipes.com*. At this site you can search by the ingredients you have on hand, by recipe title, or by recipe collection, such as their "Quick and Easy" collection.

The most helpful feature on this site, in my opinion, is the reviews by others who have tested these recipes. I feel as if I've been to cooking school after reading comments and suggestions. It gives me confidence to try new things, improve my recipes, or make the same strategic changes to recipes as reviewers describe.

Cookbooks

I hesitate even to bring this up. The typical kitchen has at least seventeen cookbooks already, most of them doubling as colorful dust collectors. However, I find several cookbooks invaluable. Before buying them, however, see if you can find them at the library. Take them home for a couple of weeks and see how they work for you.

Desperation Dinners! by Beverly Mills and Alicia Ross (Workman, 1997; *DesperationDinners.com*). Written by two working moms with four kids between them, this friendly cookbook fulfills its promise to supply families with more than 250 recipes that can be made from start to finish in twenty minutes.

The Rush-Hour Cook's Weekly Wonders by Brook Noel (Champion Press, 2003). Part of a series of Rush Hour Cook publications, this book presents nineteen weekly dinner menus complete with grocery lists for today's busy families.

Quick & Healthy Low-fat, Carb-Conscious Cooking by Brenda Ponichtera, R.D. (ScaleDown Publishing, Inc., 2005). Help for people who say they don't have time to cook healthy meals.

Saving Dinner by Leanne Ely (Ballantine Books, 2003). Menus, recipes, and shopping lists to bring your family back to the table.

e-Mealz

You know you should stick to buying what's on sale each week. But for many that presents a bigger problem than it's meant to solve! What are you supposed to do with all of this seemingly unrelated sale bounty? Sure it was cheap, but it's no bargain if you don't use it.

An online service, *e-Mealz* offers a solution that may be right for you. Each week a team of clever moms create dinner menus from the food items that will be on sale in your supermarket this week.

Once each week members receive an e-mail with a menu plan for six dinners, the recipes and instructions to make the meals, and a grocery shopping list to go with it. The shopping list is in aisle order for the store layout and includes the sale prices (expect to spend about $75 at the grocery store for the sale items required to feed a family of four to six).

If you are just too busy and frazzled to wade through the store's weekly sales ads, buy what's on sale, and then find recipes for the coming week that uses those ingredients—*e-Mealz* is anxious to come to your rescue.

Currently *e-Mealz* offers specific plans for four supermarket chains: Winn Dixie (Thrift Way), Publix, Wal-Mart Super Center, and some Kroger stores. Additionally they offer an "any store" low-carb plan. A $5 monthly fee allows you to print your menus and shopping list from the site. Visit *e-Mealz.com* for more information.

Menu Mailer

Have you ever wished you could hire a nutritionist to do the hard work of planning healthy meals, then have her simply hand you the recipes with a grocery list for the ingredients you'll need to prepare them? You can stop dreaming. Leanne Ely, nutritionist and author of *Saving Dinner* provides a service known as Menu Mailer (find it at *Savingdinner.com*) to give busy families the help they need.

Fabulous menus, delicious recipes, and shopping lists for everything necessary to prepare healthy, nutritious meals, are delivered weekly to your email address. You decide if you want a regular menu, low-carb, Kosher, frugal, or vegetarian, and whether you want this for two people or six. You even select your menus for the hemisphere in which you live so your recipes will match your seasons. (She's thought of everything.)

The menus are wonderful and healthy, the recipes are easy, and the fact that the grocery list is already made up is a dream. You're on your own to purchase the ingredients in your store of choice. Menu planning has never been so easy, because all the work is done for you. For just pennies a day ($29.95 for twelve months or $9.95 for a three-month trial), you will never panic about what's for dinner again. Go to *SavingDinner.com* to learn more and to sign up for your trial membership.

Chapter Six

Eating Out: The Mother of All Budget-Busters

I've been so busy, I don't even have time to cook for my kids.
I don't want to say we eat out a lot, but I've noticed lately when
I call them for dinner they run to the car.

~ Julie Kidd, comedian

For most people, eating out is such a normal and acceptable part of daily living, it is like breathing. They go in and out, hardly aware of what they are doing. Unfortunately, for many it's like breathing polluted air for all the damage it is doing to their finances. As minor as eating out may seem, it is likely one of the biggest drains on your disposable income. It just might be an area of spending ripe for serious reduction without sacrificing the life you love.

Here's the problem in a nutshell: ready-to-eat food and drinks are so available it's a no-brainer—literally. You don't even have to think about it. It takes more brain power and effort to get dinner on the table than to stop for take-out on the way home from work. Packing a lunch at home takes more time and effort than grabbing something on the run.

My definition of "eating out" is paying for food prepared by others instead of eating your meals from the groceries you buy. That makes eating out a very broad category because it refers to donut shops, lunches purchased at work and school, coffee breaks, trips to the vending machine, fast food, diners, and cafes. It includes picking up take-out, ordering pizza delivered, multiple-course meals in fancy restaurants, and everything between.

To get a handle on this runaway expense, it is best that we divide eating out into two categories: meal replacements and entertainment.

Because You Have to . . . or for Enjoyment?

Meal replacements are necessary at those times when for one reason or the other you are not at home and cannot get to your food at home. It's meal time and you gotta' eat!

Eating out for the pure joy of it may contribute to the quality of your life. If so, that should be seen as a form of entertainment. But for now it is essential to see eating out as two separate activities—one to be avoided whenever possible, and the other treated as one of the good things in life, so plan accordingly.

Nothing will sabotage your efforts to slash your grocery bill and drain your finances faster than unnecessary meal replacements. You can corral it by making a commitment to eat as many of your meals as humanly possible at home from the groceries you purchase.

Meal Replacements

You can't predict the unpredictable, but when it comes to replacing meals you can come close. Simply becoming aware of how much you and your family members eat out and how much it costs you should help tame this runaway expense. And then when it cannot be avoided, make sure you eat out as inexpensively as possible. After all, wouldn't you rather spend your eating-out dollars on a planned meal you count as entertainment than let so much money leak out of your life through a meaningless "gulp and go" replacement meal?

Unless you live in a remote area or are extremely disciplined, it is likely you won't banish all meal replacements from your life. After you've identified which eating-out activities count as entertainment, what's left should be considered meal replacements. Your goal is this: when you can't ban, plan! You want to eliminate as many meal replacements as possible and then plan ahead for those you cannot avoid.

Here's an example of how to logically plan for simple meal replacements. Let's say you have a $3.50-a-day latte routine. You hardly consider this entertainment—but you don't want to give up your coffee either. What you may not be aware of is the significant drain this places on your income. You need to make an allowance for this by planning ahead. Here are your choices:

1. Once each month put $75.83 cash into an envelope to allow for this daily excursion into Latte Land. Didn't know it would be that much? It gets even better: At a rate of five lattes-a-week you will spend $910 in a year's time. Or ...

2. Switch from a latte to a large coffee of the day (typically half the cost at most coffee bars), step to the side, and pour in your own creamer from the supplies provided at no additional cost. Remarkably it tastes about the same. This reduces your morning coffee expense to about $38.50 a month, freeing up $455 in a year's time. Or ...

3. Invest in a coffee maker with a timer. Once a month purchase good quality coffee beans along with your groceries. The cost of coffee and milk (to replicate the lattes) will run about $20, or half of option 2. Annual recoup? Another $225. Or ...

4. Invest a little toil and trouble in the effort to roast your own coffee beans (one of my personal favorite hobbies, something I will

explain in Appendix B). Now you will spend about $10 a month, have better-tasting coffee than you will find at any coffee bar in town, pick up a new hobby, and reclaim an additional $225 of your hard-earned money each year. Tip: Spend $5 every couple of months to purchase sturdy disposable cups with lids at a restaurant supply or discount warehouse club and you're ready to go.

This is intended to demonstrate how the simple task of analyzing and planning your meal replacements can reduce the cost or eliminate the replacement altogether.

Lunch-at-Work

Here's another common meal-replacement situation. You eat lunch out every day because you work and that's just what you prefer to do. Okay. What's the tab? About $7 a day? Fine. Just make sure you are planning ahead with $35 cash in an envelope each week earmarked for work lunches. And it's $3 more for coffee breaks each day? Better add another $15 to the envelope—that's $50 a week.

By my calculations, if you work fifty weeks a year, that's $2,500 of after-tax dollars that go toward replacing one meal each day for one person in the family, and some kind of snack or beverage at break time. I'm not saying this is wrong or even that you shouldn't do it. I am only holding up a mirror and a light for you to see for yourself the high cost of meal replacements.

What options do you have? As elementary as it may seem, preparing a meal at home and bringing it with you is an option. It takes time and a modicum of planning. You have to decide if the financial result is worth the toil and trouble.

Instead of going cold turkey (pun intended) all five days, start by bringing your lunch two or three days a week. Calculating the savings is likely to encourage you to put forth the effort, or at the very least to give it a try. Multiplying this effort times the number of people in the household who pay for lunch meal replacements could add up to some serious money over a year's time.

The Challenges of a Busy Lifestyle

I don't know all of the challenges you face that prompt meal replacements. But let's say that Tuesday is your kids' soccer practice day. By the time you drive carpool, there is no time to go home for dinner before getting the kids to the field.

Logistically you have to eat out. That's fine. Just plan now to put $20 into an envelope each week for that excursion into Fast-Food Land. And while we're talking about kids and school, there are school lunches, ice cream treats, sodas, pizza, fries, an occasional snack from the corner store...what do you think? Another $40 a week? Okay, set it aside. In cash. In a trusty envelope.

It All Adds Up

Start adding up all the known meal replacements you will face over a week's time (or a month if you are brave). That's a lot of dough! You can't ignore it and hope it will go away. Either you plan ahead and have the cash to pay, or you depend on plastic to pay for meal replacements.

Unfortunately, now most fast-food places allow you to swipe any kind of plastic you happen to have handy. It is a dreadful thought to think some people add the cost of burgers and fries to an already out-of-control credit-card balance. It might have happened to you.

What if you could move away from meal replacements altogether by planning ahead, packing lunches, making coffee at home, arranging things so you bring food with you from home on soccer practice night and so forth? Now you are eating from the food you purchased at the grocery store. You are preparing meals from your stockpile.

Much of the money you spend on meal replacements could be channeled elsewhere. You do not have unlimited sources of money, and it is a shame to think of how much of what you have simply leaks out of your life in meaningless meal replacements. At the very least those funds could be moved over to your entertainment fund so you could actually take joy in eating out rather than allowing that money to vanish into thin air with nothing to show for it. Perhaps that's the money you need to build an emergency fund or to pay off your debts.

McLeakage

I received a letter from a reader who explained that she and her mother live together and enjoy eating at McDonald's. As a regular routine they stop in for a simple breakfast and coffee, nothing elaborate. In their minds this was quite a benign activity. That is until they took me up on my challenge to track their spending for a month. With an amazing degree of shock they told me that in one month together they spent more than $385 at McDonald's. That's two elderly ladies having their muffins and coffee (plus a little something more apparently given this works out to an average of $12.83 a day) in the morning.

Can you imagine how much the typical family spends on fast food in a month? How about your family? Don't imagine any more. Do the work to find out.

While your goal is to eliminate meal replacements, getting to that point may take some time. But you can start now. Wean yourself from your drive-thru habit. When you have food at home and plan ahead for preparing that food, you won't have the continual need to eat out, which will be your saving grace. You won't have a nagging sense that you have nothing to eat at home and no time to run to the market.

From now on when you eat a replacement meal because you have no choice (dubious), see that money as coming out of your grocery allotment for the week or month.

It won't take long to begin thinking differently about that pathetic-looking salad or skimpy burger. You'll find yourself saying, "I can make this at home for so much less and it will taste a lot better too." And when that meal replacement tab comes to $20, $25, or more…you will see it as more than an expensive effort for so little payoff. You'll see it in terms of how many groceries that same amount of money could have purchased.

If you are successful in eliminating meal replacements altogether, good for you. If not, it's important you replace meals as economically as possible.

There Are Ways to Do That

Plan ahead. Let's say it's Tuesday again, the day your kids have soccer practice. Despite your best efforts to get dinner on the table in plenty of time to make practice or to bring food with you from home, something came up. You must feed the kids on the run to make it to practice on time. To pop into the first place you see for a round of burgers, fries, and drinks could prove very expensive. A better option: hit the taco joint down the street because it's Taco Tuesday! You can get a bag of ten tacos for $3—a bargain in any book.

While you hope to replace meals rarely, it's good to have a survival plan. Find out where the Taco Tuesdays are in your town. Look through the paper and mailers for coupons. Fast-food chains often have these midweek family specials, typically on Tuesday, the day that supermarkets and restaurants see the fewest customers. Know what they are so you can make a good decision when the need arises.

Discounts. Many restaurants offer a reduced-price menu for seniors and children. If you or someone in your party qualifies, be sure to inquire if this doesn't show up on the regular menu. Typically these discounted menus offer smaller portions at significantly reduced prices.

Order down. It never hurts in a regular restaurant to ask if older children or even adults can order from the kids menu. Quick-serve restaurants are not likely to have age restrictions, which makes a kids meal an excellent alternative for any age.

Share. Splitting a meal these days is socially acceptable and economically savvy. While some restaurants charge a minimal charge for splitting, most are accommodating. Even if you have to pay a dollar or two to split, it's still better than paying for two meals you cannot eat completely.

If you're embarrassed about sharing, don't be. Many restaurants are so accommodating they'll split the meal in the kitchen and bring it on two plates. Just don't shortchange your waitperson when it comes time to tip. He (or she) served two people even if you split the meal. You can also take half a meal home these days, because servings are so large; then you have lunch for tomorrow.

Specials. Many restaurants have daily specials that are not on the menu. Often specials are priced below their menu price. Be sure to ask about any specials if the server does not volunteer. Don't want the entire dinner or lunch? Ask for just the entree a la carte.

Early birds. Many restaurants, in an effort to build business during their quiet hours, offer half-off meals or some other enticingly priced deal, but only if you're there before the regular dinner crowd, typically from 4:00 to 5:30 PM. Look in your local newspaper and your mailbox for advertisements and information.

Skip the sodas. Skip the pricey drinks and dubious "free refills" altogether and you'll save at least $1 per person. One of my readers rewards herself whenever she opts for water by stuffing two bucks into her savings account.

One mom wrote saying she pays her kids $1 to order water. Not only does that save money, it gives the children an incentive to break the soda habit. Everyone's happy.

Appetizers. Before you opt for a full meal, check the appetizer menu. You'll find generous portions minus the add-ons like salad or soup. And the price is right. Just request that your selection be served as an entree and you'll fit right in.

Coupons. Call the high school to find out who is selling local restaurant discount books or discount cards. Or go to *Entertainment.com* to find one a book of coupons specific to your area. But exercise extreme caution. By the time you adhere to all the conditions some restaurants impose, and tip the waiter as if you had paid full price for even the discounted meal, you could end up paying more than you would have had you not used a coupon from the Entertainment Book.

Play tourist. It's not unusual for restaurants to have special offers directed at tourists. Local residents can avail themselves of these offers too, if they can find out about them. Stop by the lobby of a local hotel and peruse the local attraction brochures. You'll find all kinds of offers for local restaurants. Your local tourism board and chamber of commerce will have this kind of information as well.

Lunch menu. Many restaurants have a lunch menu that is slightly different from the one for dinner, the difference being the portion size and price. Ask to order from the lunch menu.

Strategize. Many fast-food chains are competing with each other and trying to drive business with their "99-Cents Menus." Some also offer upgrades to their already substantial value meals, resulting in increased portion sizes. You can use both ends of the spectrum to your advantage. Get creative, do some figuring ahead of time so you know with certainty which combination of items in several quick-service chains make for the cheapest meal replacements for you or your family. Think of it as a survival plan—something that is not part of your daily routine but that you know where to find in a hurry if you find yourself in a pickle.

Here's how one family of four eats at McDonald's for $8. Their secret? No Happy Meals. For the kids (ages three and five) they order one two-cheeseburger value meal (about $3.50). Dad gets a value meal ($3.50), Mom gets a 99-cent sandwich and shares the fries from the other meals. They still have food left over. It's all about strategy and having a plan before you go.

Websites. All of the quick-serve chain restaurants have websites with details about their menus. You won't find prices and specials, however, but cost is not the only factor. Nutrition needs to be of utmost importance. Visiting a few of these websites (McDonald's, Burger King, Jack in the Box, and so on) and clicking on their nutritional lists will be enlightening. It's possible to consume an entire week's worth of fat as dictated by any reasonable eating plan in a single meal.

It is also possible to learn which menu items are low in fat or carbs and so on. Most of these chains profile their value meals. Some restaurants to consider are *JackInTheBox.com*, *BK.com*, *ChickFila.com*, *McDonalds.com*, *KFC.com*, and *ElPolloLoco.com*.

Semi-Fast Food

Semi-fast food is combining quick-service food with home cooking. Here's an example:

Pizza. The take-out pizza store in my neighborhood sells ready-to-roll pizza dough. I can buy a large ball of dough that makes a sixteen-inch pizza for $2.50. That's slightly more than it costs to make dough from scratch. But when time is of the essence, this is a fast, cheap, high-quality alternative.

Using my own sauce and toppings, I can have really great pizza on the table in no time at all. I do rely on this option quite often, particularly when we have last-minute guests. It is impressive to turn out such a high-quality delicious pizza so quickly. It is my little secret.

Not all pizza stores sell their dough (the national chains in my area look at me as if I have three eyes when I inquire), but independents are typically more than happy for the business—any business. In fact, one store near me even lists this on their menu board.

Find a pizza take-out nearby that sells raw dough so you'll know what to do when you're in a bind. Hint: You can freeze the dough and use it to make breadsticks and calzones too.

Chicken. Just because you don't have an entree for dinner doesn't mean you have to replace the entire meal. You can supplement a big bucket of chicken at home with your own salad and bread. Or maybe you have the chicken but no sides. Large cole slaw and corn plus fresh biscuits from the drive-thru will turn that into a complete meal for far less money than buying the entire meal.

Rice. As easy as it is to make at home, it pains me to suggest buying rice at a quick-service or other restaurant. But this is a great solution that can reduce an otherwise expensive meal replacement.

All Asian restaurants, even the quick-service variety, offer plain white rice as a menu option—usually dirt cheap. I can pick up a large container of white rice for $2 or $3 in my neighborhood. It's hot, fluffy, and perfectly cooked. At home I can serve it plain or enhance it by adding scrambled eggs, soy sauce, left-over chicken, peas, carrots, and so on.

Soup du jour. The fanciest fish restaurant in my community has a pricey menu. I mean take-your-breath-away expensive to the point that getting the check all but ruins an otherwise fabulous meal. However, their to-die-for New England clam chowder is renown and available for take-out at a reasonable price. I can only imagine they are trying to discourage the annoying customers who come in on a cold winter night, take up space at a lovely linen-covered table, and linger over big steaming bowls of hearty chowder, turning down the complete meals and dessert.

That's fine with me because picking up a quart of steaming hot chowder and sourdough rolls (also their specialty) is a terrific way to avoid a huge restaurant tab when needing a meal replacement. Lots of restaurants serve homemade soups that are available for take-out. Check around and then put that on your list of options when you need to fill out or replace a meal inexpensively.

The big salad. Pizza restaurants are notorious for offering big salads on their take-out menus. It might be called a large antipasto salad. Typically it's a big bed of lettuce and other greens plus a variety of pizza toppings, such as onions, olives, peppers, tomatoes, pepperoni, and cheese. Fantastico! Toss it at home with your favorite dressing and you have a large, satisfying, family-sized salad at a side-dish price. In fact, you could make the salad the dinner entree by adding your own ingredients at home, such as hard-cooked eggs, garbanzo beans (chick peas), left-over chicken, beef, and so on.

Start Now

Now is the time to start planning how to replace a regular meal more economically. You're smart, so I am confident you will come up with ideas and strategies I've not considered. But don't get too excited. You want meal replacements to be as rare an event as possible. Otherwise all of the money you are not spending on groceries will get sucked into the big black hole of fast food while the food you buy at the grocery store goes to waste.

Eating Out as Entertainment

Entertainment dollars can be eaten up in a hurry with restaurant meals. But there are ways to stretch your eating-out budget so that you can enjoy—not eliminate—this important entertainment factor. Like all areas of living your life for half the price, you need specific strategies together with a plan and the discipline to stick with it.

Self-Serve

You can drop 15 to 20 percent (the cost of a tip) from your eating out tab just by serving yourselves in a restaurant that offers this type of service. Pizza parlors, buffets, and many steak houses to name a few, offer this type of dining experience. It may seem minor, but that extra $5 or $10 that you don't leave as a tip will add up over time.

Coupon Certificates

If you know where to look, you can purchase restaurant gift certificates for a fraction of the face value. Of course there are conditions, but it's worth your consideration. *Restaurant.com* acts as a community matchmaker introducing great restaurants to local people. Not all offers are the same, so it makes sense to peruse the restaurants' offerings in your area. From this site you buy gift certificates for these restaurants at a great discount. For example a $25 food certificate can cost $10. There are conditions you should read before purchasing, however these conditions are more than reasonable and certainly not difficult to comply with. You can purchase multiple certificates.

The website that helps grocery shoppers, *CouponMom.com*, also has some terrific coupon codes and discounts for restaurant dining.

Kids Eat Free

Many restaurants assign Tuesday as the day that kids eat free when parents purchase a meal. This marketing tactic if acted upon well, can save you a lot of dough.

Chapter Seven

No More Back-of-the-Closet Mistakes

Women usually love what they buy, yet hate two-thirds of what is in their closets.

~ Mignon McLaughlin, *The Neurotic's Notebook*

If what they say is true, we wear 20 percent of the clothes we own while 80 percent are banished to the dark side of our closets. Even if these quotable experts are way off and it's more like 50/50, that still means we waste a lot of money trying to get it right.

Imagine for a moment that by some stroke of luck you had all the cash you've spent in your wardrobe-buying lifetime on clothes that you didn't wear. That's the kind of money you'll be able to keep in the future, once you learn how to stop making those back-of-the-closet mistakes.

Here's the problem. We shop for clothes with no particular plan in mind. If it fits it's a definite candidate; if it is also on sale it's a done deal. And eight purchases out of ten are not right, so they end up in the back of the closet or stuffed into a cupboard or drawer. That's an expensive approach to wardrobe building.

What, Where, and When

Slashing the cost of a wardrobe is less about bargains and more about knowing what to buy, where to buy, and when to stop buying. The way to cut your clothing costs by half the price is to reduce your wardrobe to the equivalent of the 20 percent of individual pieces and outfits you wear now and stop wasting money on back-of-the-closet mistakes.

With this mind-set not only will you buy clothes in an entirely new way than you have in the past, you will recognize when your wardrobe is complete. And you will be willing to stop buying clothes even though unbelievable bargains remain to be had. The ability to stop shopping is critical to your success in dressing well for half the price.

The best wardrobes are built around classic designs and are developed over time, pieces at a time. And they last. This minimalist approach to building a wardrobe makes so much sense—fashion sense and economic sense. When you have well-chosen classic and timeless items in your closet that you like and that fit well and look good on you, you can create thirty or forty different outfits. Even if all twelve or fifteen items are high-quality designer labels, there's no doubt you will spend far less with this approach than buying hundreds of items from sale racks, none of which complement each other or fit very well either.

You Need a Uniform

Your "uniform" is your look, your signature style. Everyone needs to create a personal uniform that addresses his or her taste or personal style, color palette, and body type. When determining your uniform, incorporate all of these things.

Think about your favorite outfit. Without knowing more than it is your favorite, I can nearly guarantee that it is one of your most flattering colors, it fits you well, and reflects your taste and style. It's you! Color, style, and fit working together make it work for you.

It's just a guess, but I'll bet the 80 percent of your wardrobe that you don't wear is all over the map. It's likely those items don't fit right and are the wrong colors and styles for you. Individually some things might look great on the hanger; still, they are just not you.

Why did you buy those clothes? Let me guess. They were on sale. That dress was really cute. It didn't quite fit, but you figured that would be your incentive to lose ten pounds.

You justified that the color would be passable if you wore the right blush and lipstick. Do you wonder why that dress languishes in the back of your closet—tags still attached, next to so many other completely wrong choices? Those items are not you and never will be you. Even at rock-bottom prices, you're looking at very expensive closet stuffers.

Your uniform is a filter through which every clothing purchase will pass, whether it's a sweater you knit by hand, a designer blazer from the thrift store, or jeans from the department store. Your uniform is your personal fashion safety net that will keep you from being seduced by clothes that are simply not right for you, even if they are fantastic bargains.

Know Your Colors

Each of us has natural coloring that is part of our DNA. It shows up in the color of our hair, eyes, and skin. The premise behind color analysis is that certain colors enhance one's looks, and a person will look healthier, radiant, and more alive; whereas other colors will make the person look washed out or sallow. The predominant tone or color just under your skin is what determines if you have blue/red (cool) undertones or yellow/orange (warm) undertones. The colors you wear close to your face should complement these natural tones.

Some department stores offer color analysis service for a fee. You can go to *StyleMakeovers.com* for a simple, free online analysis. Or check your library for the book *Color Me Beautiful* by Carole Jackson. (Ballantine Books, 1987). This book, now a classic, has been around for many years and is still relevant.

With a big mirror, good lighting, and a friend to offer a second opinion, you should be able to confidently determine your color palette. Your confidence will grow once you can tell that something is the right color for you and also when something that may fit well is simply not right because it is the wrong color.

Discover Your Personality

If you find yourself always gravitating to the same types and styles of clothes—tailored, feminine, dramatic, sporty—you are simply expressing your clothing personality. Most of us have an inborn tendency to favor a particular style and type of apparel. Whether frilly feminine, sporty natural, simply classic, or head-turning dramatic—that is you. Your clothing personality will give you clues to establish your uniform. Trust your taste.

Living your life for half the price does not mean you deny your style and taste. On the contrary, embracing a specific uniform will assist you greatly in doing that because you will stop buying things that are not you.

The Shape of You

You do not need a model's figure or physique to look great in your clothes. No matter your height, weight, and proportions, if you know what you should wear for your body type, you'll stop wasting your money on clothes that look great on the hanger but are all wrong in the mirror.

Your silhouette—the essential frame you are born with—should always be the number-one consideration when making a clothing decision. If it's the wrong shape it will never fit you no matter what size you try on. Your measurements will change as you go through the seasons of life, but your frame is the one part of your clothing equation that will never change. You need to identify your body type, make friends with it just the way it is, and then learn how to dress it to your best advantage.

Once you know for sure your body type, determined by the shape of your torso, it will be easier to discover the right pant style for you, the best necklines, which skirt length you should wear, what to avoid, and the exact style and cut of jean that will make you feel and look great. It's like slipping a key into a door that has been locked to open a new world of clothing understanding and half-price living.

Basic Body Shapes

Several theories and explanation of body types can be found in countless books, even Internet websites. The simplest and my personal favorite is found in *The Pocket Stylist* by Kendall Farr (Gotham, 2004). Clothing is always designed for silhouette first, measurements second, and that is true of all clothing from low end to high, cheap to expensive.

An item of clothing that is not cut to your silhouette will never fit your shape—no matter what size it is, no matter how cute it is, no matter that it's your perfect color, and most of all, no matter how many times it has been marked down.

A simple way to describe your shape uses letters and a number: If you are an A, you are smaller at the top than the bottom; V just the opposite; H is straight up and down while 8 is curvaceous. Some analysts call these body types apple-shaped, pear-shaped, triangle-shaped, and so on.

Take me, for example. At the risk of destroying any mental images you have of your humble author, I'll use myself as an example. I am an

A-type female. That's my body type. My shoulders slope slightly and I carry my weight below my waist. There, I said it.

My height dictates my need for clothes that are cut and designed for petites (under 5 feet, 4 inches is considered petite), because the length of sleeves, jackets, skirts, and pants are shorter than regular sizing.

Let's talk about pants. I know that I should never wear cropped pants because they visually shorten the legs. I need to make my legs appear longer, not cut off mid calf. Part of my uniform is a pant that is straight all the way to the bottom or flares out a bit. It should be long so that it sits right at the top of my shoes when wearing heels. It's a visual thing. And because I know this, I am not even tempted a tiny bit to buy cropped capri pants—even if they fit, even if they are the right color, and even if they are on sale. That is a fashion risk I'm not willing to take. And on a positive note, that's an entire fashion trend I won't be wasting money on!

I have specific guidelines in my uniform for the necklines best for me (boat neck, ballet neck, square neck, V-necks, and a plethora of other shapes that draw the eye upward). I don't wear bulky textures or large prints. In fact, my uniform pretty much rules out prints altogether. I could go on but I think you get the point.

Knowing what to buy makes buying the right clothes a lot easier. Knowing my colors, body type, and personal taste is the best insurance against expensive mistakes—clothes that look great on the hanger but I'll never wear because they are so wrong for me.

Wardrobe Plan

As you can tell by now, I'm into plans. There's just one thing I need to tell you about a wardrobe plan: you need one. This is a plan you design specifically for your lifestyle and uniform. Your wardrobe plan will save you money, frustration, and time.

Building your wardrobe should not be a never-ending endeavor. In fact, it is possible you are already well on your way with the clothes you have already. You'll never know without a plan. And there comes a time when your wardrobe is complete and you move into maintenance mode. But without a plan you will not know when that day arrives. Without a plan you'll just keep spending money, very likely needlessly.

There is no one-size-fits-all wardrobe plan. It depends on your lifestyle. A single career woman in Manhattan who participates in sports on the weekends will have a completely different plan than a stay-at-home mom in Missoula who is involved in community activities. But both need a written plan if they are determined to live below their means.

Basically a wardrobe plan establishes basic colors and clothing items. Even the most extensive plan is still quite simple compared to the quantity of clothes most people have. Any professional stylist will tell you that the key to making this work is for all the pieces in your wardrobe to coordinate in both style and color. Once you have the basic pieces, you can create many looks, many outfits within the framework of the clothes you have.

Below are simple samples of wardrobe plans for career adults (you'll find kids' wardrobe plans later in this chapter). I could fill pages making up plans for all kinds of situations, but I know that is not necessary. Once you see how simple this is, I have every confidence you will be able to create a wardrobe plan that fits perfectly for each person in your family.

Career Woman

  3-pc suit—skirt, jacket, and pants (navy or black)

  3 skirts (taupe, gray, black)

  2 dresses (one should be a basic black dress)

  5 blouses (at least one button-front shirt)

  2 blazer-type jackets

  3 pairs slacks

3 coats (rain, between seasons, and winter for your area)

2 sweatshirts

5 T-shirts

2 jeans

2 jackets (one sporty, one parka-type)

2 pairs pumps

2 pairs low shoes

1 pair sneakers

Career Man

2-pc suit (navy or black)

5 shirts

5 ties

2 sports jackets

3 pairs slacks

2 coats (trench for rain and winter coat)

2 sweatshirts

5 T-shirts

2 jeans

2 jackets (one sporty, one parka-type)

2 pairs shoes (dress, casual)

1 pair sneakers

Closet Sweep

While many items in your wardrobe are not right for you and should be purged, you may be surprised to discover how many items you have already to plug into your wardrobe plan. However, before you can do this effectively you may need to separate the useful from the "get-rid-ofs." Not easy. Believe me.

I find it difficult to let loose of anything with a perceived value. I guess as long as I store it there's a chance that one day I may actually wear it. And I tend to hang on to things that hold promise because they look so great on the hanger. We both know that it's time to give them up. I have a painless way to do this.

Grab Everything and Get It Outta' Here!

Move everything out of your closet and your drawers too, if you can manage. Put them into a spare room closet or armoire if at all possible. Do a clean sweep on your closet, leaving it empty. If you cannot manage that, push everything to one side to make a visual separation.

For clothes and outfits to earn a spot in your clean closet and empty drawers: (1) each item must be listed on your wardrobe plan, and (2) you must actually wear it.

In a short time you should have figured out what you wear regularly and what you don't. You can safely purge the losers. Unless it's a seasonal issue (your winter coat is fabulous, you just don't wear it in the summer), take the clothes that are not right for you to a donation location or consignment shop, price them for a garage sale or to sell them on eBay, or arrange a clothing swap with your friends and relatives.

Whatever method you choose, be strong. You can do this, and oh, what a sense of accomplishment you will have once you have accomplished a successful purge.

Plan into Action

You have a uniform based on your colors, clothing personality, and body type (it can be a loose idea for now), and you have a wardrobe plan. You know with certainty what, if anything, you need to flesh out your plan. Now you are in the position to buy what you need and want what you have. You have options—more options now than ever before.

Because you have a need for a pair of khaki slacks in a particular style, you can shop sales, consignment shops, thrift stores, eBay, Target, or Nordstrom's half-yearly sale. If you are replacing a pair of pants that fit well and that you've enjoyed for a long time, make a note of the brand and style number. Now you can shop strategically. When you find them at the right price, you will have no question whether it is a good purchase.

Your confidence will soar as your clothing costs plummet. Why? Because you will avoid buying five pairs of the wrong pants on your way to finally getting the right pair.

Tape Measure

Before you buy another piece of clothing, you need eight critical measurements and a cloth tape measure to carry with you at all times. With this information, you can take all the hassle out of fitting rooms by taking a few strategic measurements of those pants or that top while they are hanging on the rack.

Why try it on if there is no chance it will fit? Or look at it this way: each item you take with you into the fitting room will have a high likelihood of being right for you because before you even try it on you have determined that you need it and can afford it, and that it is the right color, shape, and size to fit you.

Here are the eight standard measurements you need for yourself, your spouse, your children, and anyone else for whom you purchase clothes:

1. Shoulder to shoulder: from the edge of one shoulder to the edge of the other shoulder

2. Bust: under your arms, around the fullest part of your chest

3. Natural waist: at your navel

4. Low waist: approximately one inch down below your natural waist

5. High hip: four to five inches below your natural waist

6. Low hip: eight to nine inches below your natural waist

7. Thigh: at its widest point

8. Rise: measure from natural waist down to crotch, holding the tape a little loose, through the legs up to waistband in the back; repeat for low waist

Okay, you've got your measurements and your cloth tape in your bag or pocket. You need a pair of jeans. You check the rack and see a pair of jeans in your size (a dubious distinction, as every manufacturer sizes items differently, especially jeans). You know from your measurements that your hips are forty-four inches. You whip out your tape measure and measure side to side across the widest place. You multiply by two and come up with forty-one inches. You can put that pair back on the rack and move on. You don't need to waste your time in the fitting room. Those pants will not fit.

You can continue measuring pants on the rack, saving yourself time and frustration, until you come to a pair that measure out correctly for you. You check the rise and it's at least in the right ballpark. Now you have a pair of jeans with a high likelihood of fitting. You try on that pair.

Find a Tailor

Now that you understand how important it is that your clothes fit well, you also will understand that ready-to-wear for adults isn't always. Having a good tailor to lift a hem, take in a seam, and shorten a sleeve is vital. With this option, so many more opportunities will open to you. A good tailor can take a garment down two sizes, which will come as good news if you find a jacket or skirt that is perfect in every way for your wardrobe plan, but is two sizes too big.

The cost for altering tailored clothing can vary significantly from city to suburbs, so it's best to check with several to get a lay of the land. Compare the costs at two or three alterations shops for: replacing a zipper, changing the hem in a dress, and shortening a pair of slacks with cuffs.

If you do not know of a good tailor in your area, check with your local dry cleaners. Many now have on-site alterations and tailoring service. A good tailor has a changing room available because he or see must check for fit and mark for alterations while you are wearing the garment. No changing room? Keep looking.

If you have a sewing machine and are inclined to learn a skill, sign up for a class in basic alterations and tailoring. You'll bless the day you made the decision to learn how to do make your own basic alterations.

Where to Buy

The best thing about having a uniform and knowing your strategic measurements is that a whole new world of opportunity for acquiring clothes is now open to you.

Let's say your wardrobe plan calls for a brown wool herringbone jacket with a black velvet collar. You have a specific need. It doesn't matter where you get this jacket as long as it is the right style, color, and size (or can easily be made the right size to fit you exactly).

Consignment, vintage, discount, warehouse club, outlet, thrift, high-end retail (yes, they do have sales!), even eBay—all of these places are possibilities for you.

Consignment Is Chic

You'll find the cream of the crop in clothing if you look for these stores in tony areas. Also known as resale, reclothery, and repeats, this secondary market offering gently worn clothes, for women primarily, but also for men and children, is gaining acceptance and popularity.

Consignment stores run the gamut from no frills to opulent. What they share are great prices on high-quality, excellent clothes. Items in consignment shops are typically priced at least 60 percent off the original new retail price. You can expect a higher level of quality and care with clothes on consignment than in thrift stores. Sellers are required to deliver the items freshly cleaned and still in dry-cleaner bags. Some stores accept only clothes from a standard list of designers, while others may have a more broad list but require garments to be in pristine condition.

A really great consignment shop has a fast turnover of product. Your best clue for how quickly a shop turns its inventory is to keep your eye on the window displays. If they change every week, you know it's an active store.

Outlets Are Tricky

It used to be that an outlet store was at the back of a factory where slightly irregular items, samples, and overstocks of first-run products were sold for a fraction of the new retail price. Talk about bargains!

But that has all changed. Nowadays some major retailers have more outlet stores than regular retail stores, and that is a clue about where the inventory originates. Some retailers manufacture low-end discount lines just for their outlets. So outlets definitely can be a mixed bag.

An example of an authentic outlet store is Dansko, the shoe manufacturer. Remarkably, it is an online manufacturer's outlet store. Curiously, this manufacturer does not sell its shoes to the public. If you go to the Dansko website (*Dansko.com*) you will be referred to either an online dealer or retailers in your area. However, at the top of the

Dansko homepage are those beautiful words "Shop Outlet Store," where you can buy "seconds" direct from the manufacturer for 30 percent to 50 percent off regular retail prices. These are not first-quality shoes—they have visible flaws—however, the company is up front and shows up-close examples of these flaws.

Then there are the outlets that are little more than a repository for last season's leftovers, and also manufacturer's goofs that are too good for the landfill but not good enough for the real store. Perhaps the items were mislabeled at the factory, or cut off-grain, or more likely mis-sized. While that might not matter while it is hanging on the rack, that garment will never hang just right, feel just right, or look right even if it measures up correctly. All that to say, you have to be cautious. Never buy something from an outlet store that you have not tried on. If you are diligent, you can find some real treasures in outlet stores. Even then, if it does not have a place in your wardrobe plan, step away from the outlet.

Retail on Sale

Waiting for the big sales at mainstream retailers can stretch your clothing dollars to cover first-quality, in-season clothing. Inquire with the sales force as to when a particular line or item might be marked down. In fact, don't be surprised if they offer to put the item aside pending the sale or call you when the sale is announced. Most retailers have extensive websites where you can peruse the season's offerings and devise a strategy. You can do a great deal of research without leaving home.

Thrift Stores

These days, thrift stores, also known as second-hand or used-clothing stores, vary as much as retail. Some are so fancy you'd think you were in a unique boutique of some type. Others are...well, down and dirty. What they share in common is that their entire inventory has been donated for a charitable cause, as opposed to consignment stores, whose offerings are generally more gently worn and a portion of the sale returns to the original owner.

One thrift-store shopper sadly tells me that thrift-store bargains are not what they used to be, as these stores now have more inventory from which to choose. They can be more discriminating in what they are willing to accept in donations. The prices reflect this.

While thrift stores are still a viable venue for acquiring clothes that fit into your wardrobe plan, you need to be wise in your assessments. And of course, once you have an alterations service or tailor at the ready, exact fit is not as critical as quality—provided it is a style, color, and quality that can be tailored for a perfect fit. Just make sure you have your eight critical measurements and a measuring tape handy.

Deep Discounters

Stores like T.J. Maxx, Marshalls, Stein Mart, and Ross move merchandise like it's going out of style! There are some good deals to be found provided you happen to be there at the right time and are willing to dig. The real steals are often found in the back on these stores' clearance racks.

Brace yourself, though. You will find rips and missing buttons and all kinds of challenges. But if you approach this with your tailor in mind, your measurements in tow, and your tape measure ready, you just might find a gem. These stores carry designer labels and high-end merchandise that for one reason or another couldn't make it on Fifth Avenue.

A good rule of thumb is that a professional tailor can take a garment down two sizes without losing the classic lines and proportion. More than that becomes a real challenge and expense. But if that $350 Ralph Lauren wool blazer in the exact color and style you have been searching for has two buttons missing and a ripped lining, and is a size twelve when you wear a ten, don't be so quick to walk on by. At $19.99 it may be the buried treasure you hoped to find.

Discount Department Stores

Kmart, Target, Wal-Mart, and Kohl's (to name just a few) offer a haven of bargains, particularly for children's clothes. Remember to always match quality with need.

A growing child does not need quality clothing designed to wear well for many years. For kids, shop for low-end clothes that will hold up as long as needed. These stores' sales can make the bargains even sweeter. Find out the store's schedule for marking things down. One reader wrote to say her Target marks down every Tuesday evening. She times her trips accordingly.

Online Auctions

While there are many online auction sites, *eBay.com* is the most well-known, and clothing is one of its largest categories. You really can find just about every type, brand, designer, color, and style of garment imaginable on eBay. But you have to be careful.

You don't know where that garment came from. It might be brand-new hanging in someone else's closet. It could be brand-new, first-quality offered by a small distributor of that particular brand of clothes. Or it could be part of a truckload of store returns from Bloomingdales. Could be stained, hopelessly stretched out of shape, faded, or reeking of cigarette smoke. You just don't know. But you can find out. Provided you are willing to follow very cautious guidelines (see page 46) you may discover you can build your entire wardrobe from eBay. The secret is to know your prices and your products.

Take the two brands of clothes that I buy on eBay. I know these designers and manufacturers inside and out. I go to a local department store to touch and try on. I know the specific colors by name, how the sizes run, and the difference between, for example, what one designer calls a "tunic" and a "top." When a piece from this line shows up on eBay, I know exactly what it is and how it fits. A quick communication with the seller gives me a good idea of the origin of the garment and what I can expect to receive.

A friend of mine enjoys the Tommy Bahama line of men's clothes. When I recommended he bid for the items he needs on eBay, he was more than a little skeptical. But he did as I suggested and visited a department store to get familiar with the different styles of pants and so forth. Sure enough, when items he wanted hit the eBay auction, he was able to close the auction at far less than half of the new price, including the shipping.

Clothes for Kids

Using the basic principles of color, style, and clothing personality, create wardrobe plans for every member of your family, even your kids—especially for growing kids. It simply does not make economic sense to pay full retail for clothes that will be worn for such a short time.

Recent studies warn parents that kids who've been given too much too soon grow up to be adults who have difficulty coping with life's disappointments. They have a distorted sense of entitlement that gets in the way of success both in the workplace and in relationships.

Psychologists say parents who overindulge their kids may be setting them up to be more vulnerable to future anxiety and depression. Overindulging children in clothes, toys, and possessions affects them as adults with higher incidents of depression and divorce. Just because you can afford to fill your child's closet with designer duds doesn't mean you should. Sometimes it's harder to say no than yes.

To keep yourself on track and from going overboard on impulse buys (oh, it's so cute), make a simple wardrobe plan for each child. Then be willing to stick to it. Here are examples:

Boy's Wardrobe Plan

4 washable pants (two jeans, two pants)

3-5 shirts for pants

4-5 T-shirts

2 sweatshirts

1 light jacket

1 heavy coat

1 pair sneakers

1 pair shoes

Girl's Wardrobe Plan

4 washable pants (two jeans, two pants)

3-5 tops for pants

3 T-shirts

2 skirts

1-2 dresses

2 sweatshirts

1 light jacket

1 heavy coat

1 pair sneakers

2 pairs shoes

Children don't need many clothes. The more they have, the more your laundry will pile up and the more outfits will find their way to the back of the closet, never to be seen again. Too many choices translate to clutter, guilt, and waste.

Basic colors. A child's wardrobe functions on the same principles of color as an adult's. But instead of seeing all colors in that child's natural palette as candidates for his or her clothes, stick to a few basic colors. You'll be able to mix and match with ease, make more outfits, and coordinate with other clothes already in your child's closet.

Hand-me-downs. My best advice is to accept gratefully any trades, swaps, or outright gifts of clothes from relatives, friends, or others. And when you're done with those clothes, pass them along to others as appropriate.

Strategic gifting. If grandparents and others give your children gifts for Christmas and birthdays, suggest the items that will plug in the gaps in that child's wardrobe plan. Most people appreciate specifics of size, color, and style.

Consignment and resale. Stores just for kids, from newborn through preteen, are opening up in communities everywhere. And why not? Kids grow so fast, often their clothes are barely worn. Consignment is a great way to turn gently worn items into cash.

One such example is the national chain of consignment stores Once upon a Child (see *OUAC.com* for a store locator). You'll be amazed how many new-with-tags designer labels you'll find at these stores—baby furniture and equipment too—all at prices close to half of retail.

KidVantage Club. While Sears is a good source for affordable kids' clothes, what sets the chain apart from the competition is their KidVantage Club. No matter how old or how roughly treated, if kids' clothes purchased at Sears ever wear out, the KidVantage Club guarantee will replace any item, as long as it is in the same size and they can replace it with the same brand at a similar price.

With this advantage you can be sure all your hand-me-downs purchased from Sears will be brand-new for the next child. Sears's policy is not only amazing, it is for real. The wear guarantee is straightforward and good at any Sears location chainwide. My experience is that provided the wear is visible, there are no questions asked. It's a good idea to keep your receipts in the event you need to provide proof-of-purchase if the brand is other than a Sears label. Note: Kids brand clothing and shoes purchased on *Sears.com* are not eligible for KidVantage Club benefits.

Now and later. When you come across a particularly excellent sale for something that works perfectly for your child, consider buying that item in several sizes for now and for next year too.

Deals on eBay. eBay is especially rich with high-quality, designer-brand, excellent-condition clothes for kids. Once you peruse the bargains available you may find it impossible to pay full retail elsewhere.

Other online sites also offer excellent bargains direct to the public from time to time. An excellent example is the well-known OshKosh brand at *OshKoshBGosh.com*. Look for the markdowns; just make sure you consider the shipping costs too.

Chapter Eight

Attack of
the Killer Fees

*Money is not just pieces of paper or electronic blips
with prices attached. It is far more: Our fondest hopes,
our most fervent dreams, our worst nightmares, all balled up
into an explosively emotional package.*

~ Jason Zweig, Columnist, *Money Magazine*

Listen. Hear that loud whooshing sound? It's money being sucked out of millions of individual bank accounts, credit-card accounts, and mortgage-repayment plans in fees—big, bad, budget-busting fees—most of them completely hidden from the consumers who are paying them.

So take a guess. How much of your household income disappears out of your bank account each year just in service fees so that you can have access to your money? A conservative estimate is that the typical family in the U.S. pays between $600 and $1,000 a year in service fees alone. This figure doesn't include interest or punitive (late, overlimit, and so on) fees—only the fees you pay for access to your money.

You can stop the attack of the killer fees on your money. You don't have to contribute to banks' and credit-card companies' huge profit centers (more than 30 percent of the $100 billion in profits the banks made in 2003 came from fees) to have checking and savings accounts, a credit card, debit card, and ATM access too.

By following a few simple strategies, you can easily keep that $600 to $1,000 from being sucked out of your accounts every year. It is possible to enjoy all the safety and convenience of banking, credit-card, debit-card, and ATM services without paying a cent in fees. But before I can show you how to do that, we need to sort through the myriad of fees being imposed on you—most of them buried in the fine print.

Fees on financial services fall into two categories: service fees and punitive fees. Service fees are the fees banks, credit unions, and credit grantors charge for their services. Penalty or punitive fees are "punishment" fees charged to customers who break the rules.

Bank Accounts

Service fees

You signed up for a free checking account. So what are all those fees piled up at the bottom of your account statement very month? Maybe it's time to take a closer look.

Service fees (sometimes called maintenance fees) on bank checking accounts can include a flat monthly fee, per-check fees, fees for speaking to an account representative ($3 per conversation at one of the nation's largest banks), fees for checking your account balance by phone, fees for using out-of-network automated teller machines (ATMs), fees for receiving copies of your paid checks, and fees for using telephone banking.

Have you analyzed your bank statement recently? That's where you will find these kinds of mystery fees. Question everything! You should not have to pay a cent to have access to your own money.

Penalty Fees

These are the fees banks slap on their customers who break the rules. While you will never find a bank or credit union that allows you to break the rules without consequence, and rightly so, you should place your business where the consequences for infractions of the rules are the most reasonable.

Minimum balance. Many checking accounts have minimum balance requirements. In exchange for your promise to keep plenty of money in your account at all times, you receive interest on the balance. If you allow the balance to fall below that predetermined amount, a penalty fee is assessed or the interest is withheld, or both.

Overdraft. Fees for bouncing a check can be horrendous. And with more banks availing themselves of the provisions of the recently enacted law "Check 21," your paper check can now clear as fast as a debit-card transaction. Depending on what type of arrangement you have with your bank, a single bounced check could cost you a small fortune. First, there's the overdraft fee. You'll get this no matter what. And if the check is paid from your overdraft protection account or with the bank's funds, the fees plus interest will begin to pile up quickly.

ATM fees. Some financial institutions do not charge a fee to use an ATM machine provided you use that bank's machine. However, this is not universal. Some banks charge a fee to use even their bank's machine, and an additional fee if you use an outside ATM.

Free Bank Accounts

Nearly every bank and credit union offers some kind of personal "free" checking account. They have to, because that's what the competition is doing. But what looks like a free account at first glance may not be so free when you look more carefully.

A totally free checking account should charge you no service fees at all. In fact, you should not even have to pay for your checks. And you should get interest on your checking account balance too.

Credit union. This is a good option for finding a free checking account. Unlike a bank, which is a for-profit corporation, a credit union is a not-for-profit corporation with the purpose of making money for its members and accountholders. The profits of a credit union are used to reduce the cost of services, including interest rates on loans, and are also returned to the members in the form of dividends. To find a credit union you can join, go to *CreditUnion.coop* and click on "Locate a Credit Union."

Be sure to ask all the right questions: Is there a minimum balance requirement? Is there a charge for personalized checks? (If so, order directly from a check printer like *ChecksInTheMail.com*). What are the overdraft penalty fees? What are fees to use ATM machines and what are the restrictions?

Local independent bank. Your best option for a truly free checking account in a local bank is with one that is independent. Unless you travel a lot and need access to a branch of your bank in every major city, there is no benefit to banking with a big national bank.

USAA Federal Savings Bank. This is it—the only place I know where you can get a 100-percent-free checking account including free checks, free postage-paid envelopes, pay no charge whatsoever to access your money and get paid interest, too.

This bank is a cross between a bank and credit union because it is owned by its 4.3 million members—many of them connected to the U.S. military in some way. However, the banking services are available to the public.

USAA Bank offers a free checking account with no conditions, minimums, or requirements; free personalized checks; free deposit slips; and free postage-paid and pre-addressed envelopes to make deposits.

And not only for your initial order—at this writing reorders are free too.

Located in San Antonio, Texas, USAA Federal Savings Bank does not have branch offices. But USAA can be your branch bank no matter where you live. Online banking is available 24/7. You mail deposits in postage-paid envelopes or have automatic deposits if you prefer (it's not required). You can use an ATM machine anywhere, and USAA will reimburse you $1.50 per ATM use up to ten per month. This amount will show on your statement as a credit to offset charges you may receive for using any ATM machine. Note: If you use the ATM more than ten times a month, you need to evaluate your ATM usage and adjust accordingly.

USAA pays interest on checking accounts, a rate higher than some banks' basic savings account, but only on balances of more than $1,000. That's not a minimum balance of any kind or an average balance. Your account is scanned every day and if the balance is $1,000 or more, they pay you interest for that day.

You can add online bill-paying privileges to your free checking account. There is a small monthly fee of $4.95 for this service. But if you have automatic deposit of your paycheck, even online bill paying is completely free.

USAA Federal Savings Bank offers overdraft protection that is tied to either your savings account or credit-card account. If you use your overdraft protection by drawing on your credit or savings accounts, there is no fee. The service to transfer those funds is free. If you do not have overdraft protection, checks are returned "NSF" and a $25 fee assessed. That's the most reasonable penalty structure you will find at any bank or credit union.

Joining USAA is tricky, so stay with me. When you access the website (*USAA.com*) you will be confused. I guarantee it. Everything you read on the site will lead you to believe that unless you are presently an active member of the U.S. military—or have a connection through a family member—you are not eligible to join USAA. But this is not true. You are eligible. Let me explain.

USAA has a huge family of financial services; banking is just one of those services. However (and trust me on this) the banking services are available to anyone over age eighteen with a Social Security number. All you need is a membership number. You must make a one-time toll-free phone call to 800-531-2265 to get a membership number so that you can open a new checking or savings account. Automated service is always available, customer service representatives are available Monday through Friday, 7:30 A.M.- 10 P.M., CT; Saturday, 8 A.M.- 6 P.M., CT: Sunday 1 P.M. - 6 P.M., CT. Once you have your membership number you can either ask for an application to be mailed to you or you can go to *USAA.com* and click on "Register Now."

Once you have established a password and log-in account, you can open a checking account online. You will have the option to receive an ATM card or a debit card to go with your account.

Once a member, you are also eligible to open a savings account that will earn a better rate of interest than on money left in your checking account. You can make transfers between your USAA bank accounts online or by phone.

You will receive your debit card or ATM card and deposit envelopes in the mail, as well as a supply of personalized checks.

ING Direct Savings Bank. This is not like any other bank and is possibly the best place to have your savings account. You cannot walk into the ING Bank. Instead you do business with ING online, by phone, or through the mail.

Without the overhead and high operational costs of other banks, ING can pass those savings onto customers. And they do. As proof, the Orange Savings Account lets you save with no fees, no minimums, and the best interest rates on savings in the nation. And no required minimum balances ever. By way of comparison, at this writing the savings rate at ING Direct is a full percentage point higher than even with USAA.

You must have a checking account with another institution (like USAA Federal Savings Bank or your bank or credit union). Then ING links your personal checking account to your ING savings account. You can easily transfer funds to or from your ING account without any fees or charges. You can conduct transactions online at *IngDirect.com* by using the interactive phone system or by calling an ING Direct associate. There are no fees, no service charges, no penalties, and no hidden costs.

I can understand that you may not want to bank online or through the mail because you like the option of walking into your bank and seeing real, live people. But it shouldn't cost you a fortune in fees to bank this way. Now that you know there are banks that do not charge any fees to checking account customers, use them as a benchmark against which to evaluate your bank. And don't be afraid to ask questions. Find out the entire fee structure—service and penalty fees as well.

Credit-Card Accounts

Service fees

Many credit-card issuers charge an annual fee ranging from $35 to $300 or more. More companies than ever before are also tacking on a monthly maintenance fee of $6 to $9. These are not punishment fees, but they sure look like it. They are fees charged simply for the privilege of spending with plastic.

Penalty fees

Interest. The penalty fee with the greatest impact on a credit-card account is, of course, the interest on the unpaid balance—the penalty for living beyond your means. It can be steep, and the interest rate on credit-card accounts always is variable—even if the issuer says you have a fixed rate.

Fixed-rate interest on a credit card account is very misleading. On a credit card or "open-ended credit account," fixed means the interest rate is not tied to an index. It can, however, be increased with only fifteen days notice to the cardholder. That's the law.

The fine print on the initial credit-card application or the sheet that came with the credit card itself reveals the interest rate structure, complicated as it may be. First, there is the interest on balance transfers, then the interest on new purchases. The interest on cash advances is always different and usually the highest rate allowed in that state. Many cards also have a "default rate" built in, which is the interest rate that will kick in if the cardholder defaults on any of the provisions of the credit-card agreement. A default can occur with something as minor as being five minutes late with a payment.

Late payment. Making a credit card payment late can be deadly. It's like knocking down the first domino. It starts with a severe late fee of at least $29 added to your account. Your first thought might be, "Well, just don't do that!" But it's not that simple to make an on-time payment. It takes more than an ordinary effort.

First, you must discover what constitutes "late." Your statement will show a due date, but what you do not know is the time of day on that date before which your payment must be received to be considered paid on time. It may be one minute past midnight. That means if your due date is September 18, and the due time on that due date is 12:01 A.M., your payment is late if it arrives in the morning mail on September 18. You must have had it there in time to post on the 17th to get in under the wire.

Credit-card companies have been criticized severely for not disclosing this time aspect, and also for not sending out statements in a timely manner to allow a customer sufficient time to mail a statement. It appears to many that this is a clear example of a credit-card company intentionally manipulating customers into a late position for the purpose of collecting lucrative fees. Makes you mad, doesn't it?

Overlimit. Most credit-card accounts have a credit limit. And unlike years ago when you could not charge beyond your limit, banks and credit-card companies are quite happy for a customer to break through that barrier. They happily charge you interest on the growing balance and then sock you with an overlimit penalty fee of $29 to $35 every month until the balance is reduced sufficiently to be under your limit. Ka-ching.

Don't Let This Happen to You

A late fee added to a credit-card account can push an almost-maxed-out account balance overlimit, which then triggers an automatic over-limit penalty fee. Together they can add $70 to an account balance.

The following month the minimum monthly payment is not sufficient to bring that balance below the credit limit, so that triggers another overlimit penalty of $35. Without using the card at all, the balance grows all on its own and at a rate faster than the minimum payments can bring it down. But wait! It gets worse.

Remember, a late fee started all of this, and being late even one time gives the company a window of opportunity to increase the interest rate on the account to its "default" rate, which for many card issuers is now the highest rate allowed in that account holders' state—28 percent or more. This snowball effect can be an unrelenting punishment for the cardholder. The problem is that the card company encourages and enables this by allowing a customer to charge past his or her credit limit. And if that's not enough, late payments wreak havoc on one's credit score.

Free Credit Card

You need one good, all-purpose credit card. Just one. That card should have no annual fee, a grace period of at least twenty-five days, and should be accepted in many places (VISA or MasterCard are accepted most widely). If you use it, faithfully pay the balance in full long before the due date. Now you have a totally fee-free credit card.

Where can you find a card like that (if you do not have one already)? Log on to *CardTrak.com* and click on "Search." Under "Consumer Services" click on "Find a Card." Next click on "No Annual Fee." You will have a fairly lengthy choice of cards for your consideration.

As a member of USAA Federal Savings Bank (honest, I'm not their spokesperson), you can apply for their USAA MasterCard. It fits all of the fee-free specifications, plus has a relatively low interest rate and penalty fee structure. Once you are a member of USAA's banking services (see above for how to join), you can apply for this at *USAA.com*.

Debit Cards

Service Fees

More banks are now charging a fee for debit-card use. It can range from 25 cents to $1 per use when you select "debit" at the time of purchase, thus requiring you to input your PIN.

Penalty Fees

There are no directly related penalty fees with a debit card because of the nature of it. When you swipe a debit card to make a transaction, it is similar to writing a check, and the money is immediately deducted from your checking account. However, a word of caution is in order.

Banks are enjoying all of the punitive fees they can charge. They love it when you overdraw your checking account. Some are now allowing you to overdraw your account by approving debit-card transactions and ATM withdrawals even if there is not enough money in your account to cover the transaction. Do not assume that because your debit card works to give you money out of the ATM or make a purchase that you actually have money in the bank.

Fee-Free Debit Card

The way you make sure you never pay a fee for using your debit card is in knowing how to use it. First, your debit card should be a branded VISA or MasterCard. When you use this in a store, you have the choice to select either "debit" or "credit." Either way, that purchase price comes out of your checking account and will not go onto a credit-card balance. It is a debit card. Still you have this choice.

If you select "debit," you must input your PIN. If you select "credit," you will sign your name on the slip. The clerk has no idea if you are using a debit or credit card. His or her only concern is PIN versus signature. But it makes a difference for you. If you use your PIN, you are more likely to be charged a per transaction fee of up to $1 per use. It could go higher.

If you opt to give your signature instead, there will be no charge even if your bank charges a debit-card usage fee. Of course the merchants prefer that you use the PIN route, as the merchant's fee is considerably less than if you opt for a signature-based transaction.

Just keep in mind what's good for you and your goal to enjoy a fee-free debit card. It is not your responsibility to contribute to merchants' profit margins.

Stop the Penalty Fees!

By now you know how to not pay service fees for financial services. And now you want to know how to stop paying penalty fees? This is easy. Stop breaking the rules!

Stop bouncing checks; stop making late payments; stop pushing the limits on your credit cards. Stop allowing balances to revolve on your credit cards so that you are paying consumer debt.

If you are carrying a lot of debt, you may not be able to change the interest part of your equation overnight. But you can renew your resolve to get out of debt. Every month you will see that balance come down until you are free! Free of consumer debt, free of penalty fees, and free of fees that erode and nibble away at your money.

Chapter Nine

Home, Sweet Paid-for Home

... A home of our own is still the rock on which our hopes are built. Homeownership is a state of mind. It's your piece of the earth. It's where a family's toes grow roots. It's where the flowers are yours....

~ Jane Bryant Quinn, author *Make the Most of Your Money*

Buying a home is likely the single best way to build wealth on your ordinary income. But home ownership is about more than financial appreciation. Putting down roots and raising a family on land you know is yours offers emotional fulfillment and security too.

As wonderful as it is to buy your own home, you do not want to spend the rest of your life as a home buyer. You want to be a homeowner in every sense of the word. Paying your mortgage in full is your number-one goal as a homeowner and what I focus on in this chapter. As you are about to learn, you can own your home sooner than you ever dreamed possible, and save a lot of dough in the process.

The reason you want to work your way out of a mortgage is so that you can enjoy living "free" in retirement. Rent goes on forever; your mortgage payments eventually come to a stop, and if I have my way, that's going to be sooner than later.

But remember that interest on your mortgage and your property taxes are tax-deductible. This means that, for once, the government is putting money in your pocket by subsidizing the purchase of the house. Current mortgage rates are still low by historical standards, and buying a house at a fixed rate means you know what your housing costs will be in the future until your mortgage is paid off.

Buying a house is a kind of forced savings plan. Each month, a percentage of the mortgage payment goes to principal. It's a trivial amount early in the first years, but increases throughout the term of the mortgage. This is money on top of the increased value of the house each year, which is what makes this winning combination the best investment available to you.

Sweet Equity

Every mortgage has three important elements: market value, principal balance, and equity. Market value is the amount that house would sell for today. Principal balance is the amount you owe. Equity is the amount of money you would have in your pocket if you sold the house today, after the mortgage balance.

In general, a house in the U.S. appreciates 4 percent to 5 percent per year. Of course the figure varies from neighborhood to neighborhood and region to region, but it's a good rule-of-thumb. Do the math: If you bought a $200,000 house with 20 percent down—$40,000—and if it appreciates at 5 percent per year, the value increases $10,000 in the first year. That's $10,000 on a $40,000 down payment, a return of 25 percent.

Each month during the payback process, the principal balance goes down and the equity goes up. But this is the wonderful thing: The equity is fueled by two factors: appreciation (the home's value goes up just because houses generally become more valuable over time) and the shrinking mortgage. Each month you own a tiny bit more of the home. That is the definition of equity. Your equity continues to grow until that wonderful day when your mortgage is at $0 and your equity is at 100 percent.

Take It with You

You don't have to own the same home for your entire mortgage payback time. You can move your equity from one home to the next. When you sell, you use the equity from that house as the down payment on the next home. With each move you take more equity, making a larger down payment and requiring a smaller mortgage. The mistake would be to make only the minimum down payment on the next house and spend your equity on something else. That would require a much larger mortgage and put your final mortgage payoff date much farther into the future.

Provided you are careful to keep moving all of the equity from your prior home into the next home, your equity will continue to grow rapidly, and you will eventually own a home free and clear.

Rapid Mortgage Repayment

Perhaps you have heard of or have a "biweekly" mortgage-repayment plan. Your mortgage lender or a third party may have approached you to switch to this kind of plan. The basic principle is that by paying half of your mortgage payment every two weeks instead of all of it once a month, you can drastically reduce the amount of interest and repay the mortgage in far fewer years.

It's true. Here's an example: Let's say your monthly mortgage payment is $1,000. In one year you pay twelve of those payments—$12,000 each year. If you pay one-half of a payment ($500) every two weeks, or biweekly, you will make twenty-six half-payments in a year, or a total of $13,000, the equivalent of *thirteen* monthly payments. Therein lies the secret of the biweekly mortgage payment plan—making that additional monthly payment over a year's time.

A biweekly payment schedule typically reduces a mortgage payback time by five or six years, saving the borrower many thousands of dollars in interest. No doubt, a biweekly payment schedule is a painless and effective way to save a boatload of interest.

The theory is excellent but there is a problem. Biweekly payment plans offered by mortgage lenders are fraught with fees. Typically there's a conversion fee to change from a monthly plan to a biweekly plan. You may have learned this when your mortgage lender sent you a high-energy, excited letter inviting you to convert to a biweekly plan. It's true of course, but the problem is, lenders always charge fees to do this. There's a conversion fee of about $400. Then there's a $4 or $5 fee tacked on to each biweekly payment. If that doesn't sound like much, figure it out. It adds up. In fact, the initial fee plus the payment fees, if applied to your mortgage instead of boosting the lender's profit margins, could knock another year or so off your payback time.

There is an inherent yet often overlooked problem with converting to a biweekly plan: you're stuck. Once you convert, you must continue the biweekly schedule or be zinged with late fees. And if you want to go back to a monthly plan, there will be fees for that too.

Do It Yourself

You can do the same thing with your mortgage payback time and save all that interest too—without fees and without asking your lender for permission. It's simple. You can start now, and if in the future you are met with a season of financial challenge, you can pull back to your original lower payment schedule. You'll suffer no penalty or conversion fees. And you won't have to ask permission of your lender. Here's how:

Each month when you make your regularly scheduled mortgage payment write a second check for one-twelfth (1/12) of one regular mortgage payment. Using the simple scenario above, write a check for $1,000 for your regular mortgage payment. At the same time, write a second check for $83.33 (1/12 of $1,000). On this second check, write on the memo line: "principal prepayment only." Send both checks with your payment. You have complied with your lender's requirement of making at least one full payment each month and taken advantage of the fact that your mortgage does not have a prepayment penalty provision.

Do this each month, and by the end of a year you will have made the equivalent of thirteen monthly payments, twelve payments as scheduled with one full payment extra going to prepay the principal. Bingo! You have just accomplished the same action as a biweekly payment schedule on your terms—without fees. The nice thing about taking control of your own accelerated payment schedule in this way: you can stop and start up again at will. It's up to you, not the lender.

Pay Down or Pay Ahead

Whenever you send more than the amount of your regular payment you should write in the memo area of the check and also attach a note explaining what it is for; otherwise how will your lender know what to do with it?

Borrowers send extra money to their mortgage companies for two common reasons: (1) to pay down the principal balance, or (2) to make payments ahead.

When you send an additional payment or amount to pay down the principal balance, your loan balance goes down. But you still have to make the next scheduled payment.

Let's say you make your regular mortgage payment this month plus three extra payments. You enclose a note that the additional payments are to pay down the principal balance. You will still have a payment due in May, June, and July, as scheduled.

On the other hand, let's assume for a moment that you sent those three extra payments for a different reason. You are going to Europe for the summer and don't want to have to worry about making mortgage payments. It's just easier to make them now so you can forget it. In this scenario you want to pay the account ahead.

Attaching a note to the additional payments will tell the lender to apply these to the May, June, and July payments. You'll be back before the August payment is due.

If you are not clear about how you want those three extra payments handled, the lender might assume you want to pay down the principal balance. You head off on your trip assuming you've made your mortgage payments. Of course, you don't get the late notices because you're not around. You arrive home only to learn that your home is in foreclosure for failure to pay.

You cannot assume the mortgage company will automatically pay your account ahead if you do not send clear instructions. Nor can you assume they will know to pay down the principal balance.

Some lenders will simply return additional payments if they are not clear how they are to be handled. Others automatically apply additional sums to future payments, defaulting to the lender's benefit, which would be to pay ahead.

Do not staple your instructions to your check. Use a paper clip instead. And make sure you also abbreviate your instructions on the check itself. But don't leave it there. Follow up in a couple of weeks to make sure the transaction was handled per your instructions. If you get a monthly statement, just wait for it. If all you have are a stack of coupons, and your lender sends a statement once a year, make sure you call to verify that your account is being handled properly.

A Cautionary Note

You should not even think about prepaying your mortgage until you have amassed a respectable emergency fund equal to six months' living expenses, and have paid off all your unsecured debts. Prepaying your mortgage before achieving those goals is foolish, because when something unexpected happens, you'll keep running to credit cards—or worse, your home's equity—for a bail out if you do not have an emergency fund to fall back on.

Half the House

If there's a common mistake first-time homebuyers make, it is getting in over their heads. They commit to more house than they can afford. But they don't realize this fact because they allow a real-estate broker or mortgage lender to tell them how much they can afford through a process called prequalification. How do these people know? They look strictly at your current income and compare that to current market and economic conditions. However, your current conditions could change, and if you have a payment that stretches you to the limit, you could be in big trouble down the road.

I want you to consider a better way. Find out what you can afford to pay each month in principal and interest through the prequalifying process. Let's say for fun you can qualify for $2,000 payments, which will get you a $375,000 house with a 20 percent down payment for thirty years. But you don't want to pay for a house for thirty years.

So you tell the broker to show you homes in the $189,000 range (the median price for an existing single-family home in the U.S. at this writing, which in some areas wouldn't even buy a garage, but this is only an example, okay?) with $900 payments. It might be a smaller fixer-upper in a less desirable neighborhood, but that's just fine because you have a plan:

You are not going to make the required $900 payments each month. You are going to make $2,000 payments—the payments the lender said you could afford. Remember? Instead of taking thirty years, you will pay the mortgage in full in just eight years and avoid paying a ton of interest too.

You're still young. You have plenty of time to sell this house, apply the entire sale price toward the down payment on a nicer house that is (you guessed it) half the house you could qualify for. Repeat.

You'll own the next house in about five years this time around because you will have a larger down payment that required. Of course, this is an estimate because I am not clairvoyant, but the principle holds true.

This is such a smart way to become a homeowner because you opt for less house in the beginning of your homeownership career. And for your willingness to start small, you are rewarded handsomely because you pay far less interest in the long run, and become mortgage-free much sooner.

Refinancing

About the only thing trickier than figuring out if you should refinance your home's mortgage to take advantage of lower interest rates is addressing this dilemma in a couple of snappy, exciting, and terribly interesting paragraphs. But first, let's review some basic fundamental truths about a home mortgage.

Mortgages are meant to be paid off. The reason home mortgages in the U.S. are based on a thirty-year payback is so you will own your home free and clear before you retire. One problem with refinancing is that without weighing the long-term effects, borrowers reset the clock back to a thirty-year payback period.

There was a time when "burning the mortgage" was common practice. It was a noble, albeit common, accomplishment. Have you ever been invited to a mortgage burning party? My point, exactly. Making the last payment on a mortgage is a bit of a rarity.

To determine if you should refinance your mortgage, you need to look at the big picture, not only the monthly payment. A drop of two points in your interest rate could reduce your monthly payment by hundreds of dollars. If you only look at the payment, there's no question that refinancing is a good move. But you can't stop there. You need to look at the total payback on the proposed refinance and compare that to the total amount required to finish paying your mortgage at the current rate.

Let's say you have a thirty-year mortgage on $100,000 at 8 percent interest. Your monthly principal and interest payments are $734. After ten years of faithfully paying your mortgage payment each month, you have an outstanding balance of $87,872.

You get an opportunity to refinance that balance at 6 percent with new payments of $527. You're just about ready to go for the deal because you like the idea of having more than $200 each month for something else, when I come bursting into your life with a great big cautionary flag. Before you make your decision you need to look at the big picture: If you stay with your current mortgage, you will make 240 more payments of $734 for a total of $176,160. If you refinance, you will have 360 payments (refinancing typically restarts the clock) of $527 or a total payback of $189,720. Add to this the costs of refinancing (they vary greatly but could be several thousands of dollars for an appraisal, loan fees, recording fees, title insurance, and so on, and if added to the principal amount will also accrue interest), some of which may be required up front. There is some value to paying less each month, but rarely does that trump adding ten more years to your payback time.

Chances are high that the new lender offering the refinance will convince you to finance more than just the outstanding balance on your current mortgage. "Cashing out" some or all of your equity is in the lender's best interest but rarely yours.

Suggestions that you should take out money to add on or for any number of other homeowner improvements will be compelling. Many people take this opportunity to get their hands on cash to pay off credit-card debt, to pay for college tuition, or for some other life event. Before long the $87,872 you owed on your home becomes $100,000 or $200,000, or more.

You will make a serious error if you see your equity as cash to spend on what you want now. That would be to watch your precious equity go up in smoke and to take a giant step away from your dream of paying your mortgage in full so you are a real homeowner.

The promise of a low interest rate on the refinance makes this look quite inviting. I don't need to give you more numbers to prove just how costly a refinance can be under these circumstances, including using your equity. Not only will you actually increase your monthly payments, you'll extend the time it takes to pay off your mortgage. In the meantime, should you fall on hard times, you may have trouble making the much-larger payment. That opens the door to foreclosure and losing your home altogether.

Let me suggest a way that refinancing under the terms above could be highly beneficial. First, insist that you want to refinance only your outstanding balance, or in our example, $87,872. The temptation will be great to get your hands on some of your equity, but curb that urge. Your new payments will $527 as described above. Each month when you make this new payment, write an *additional check* for $207 directing this amount to be applied to "principal prepayment only."

You are paying the same amount you've been paying each month for the past ten years ($527 + $207 = $734). Nothing changes there. However, and this is the good part, you will have a total payback of only $134,327 (that's a savings of more than $55,000 in interest), and even better, you will pay off your mortgage completely in about fifteen years, not the twenty years you are looking at now. This is how refinancing can benefit you in a big way—not pump up the lender's bottom line and income stream.

Remember, always consider the total payback not just the new monthly payment when you evaluate a refinance. It is easy to figure this out if you have the right calculators. I used the "Loan Calculator with Amortization Schedule" and "Debt Investment Calculator" at *DebtProofLiving.com* in the calculations above. It was simple. These are two of the dozens of useful calculators my website members enjoy.

Variable vs. Fixed Interest

The illustration above assumed mortgages with fixed interest rates. If you have a variable interest- or interest-only mortgage, your motivation to refinance becomes more complicated. You need to refinance into a fixed-rate mortgage as soon as feasible.

If you got into the current mortgage because you could not handle the payment on a fixed-rate loan at the time, you should be in better shape now to do that. Because variable-rate mortgages are tied to indexes that reflect the current economic conditions, even if you have caps that keep the rate from increasing more than say 2 percent in a year, you are in a risky position. I suggest that you look toward refinancing only your current outstanding balance at the best fixed rate you can find.

Owning a home is a smart move for all kinds of reasons. Mortgage payments force you to save. You know you are building something for the future. You get deductions for taxes and interest and you can paint the rooms any color you like. But above all, homeownership allows you to look forward to the day you'll live mortgage-free. Play your cards right, and that day will arrive sooner than later.

Chapter Ten

Remember When
Talk Was Cheap?

Discipline comes through self-control .... Before you can control
conditions, you must first control yourself.

~ Napoleon Hill, author *Think and Grow Rich*

It is difficult to imagine life before wireless communication. Being just a speed dial away from friends and family gives a sense of security and convenience not many of us are willing to give up. It's the big bills we could live without.

More than 60 percent of all American households now have cell phones, the average monthly bill is $55, and only 61 percent of all pre-paid minutes get used. But this doesn't mean we've given up our land-lines. Nope, this pricey cell-phone phenomenon is in addition to what used to be the household telephone bill. Another bill, a new expense.

So have you looked at your phone bills lately? Maybe it's time to do that. Just stay calm. It's quite possible you can get the costs down to half the price. It's a matter of knowing your options, selecting the best plan, and then exercising personal discipline to not exceed your contract limits. That means the kids too—the connected generation.

The Phone at Home

Let's talk about your landline for a moment (the phone at home as opposed to cell phones). I can't believe I'm bringing this up, but given the number of households that still lease their phones from the phone company, may I suggest this is just horribly ill-advised? You are paying thousands of dollars for a $25 instrument. If your phone belongs to the phone company give it back, and then follow up to make sure the charge disappears from your phone bill each month. You can buy a phone just about anywhere for $20 or less.

Communication as a whole is a rapidly changing phenomenon. With the advent of voice-over Internet protocol (VOIP) and digital phone service through one's cable TV company, it is not reasonable for me to address each of these options, only to suggest that more options are waiting down the pike.

Before you dump your traditional landline, consider this: in most areas the emergency 911 system is tied to your home landline—your traditional telephone number. Giving up this line in favor of using your cell phone exclusively or setting up a VOIP system could jeopardize your safety.

When you dial 911 from your landline now, your address is immediately available to the operator, so emergency services can be immediately dispatched. Calling 911 from a cell phone or other communication source is not yet reliable enough to pinpoint your exact location.

However, by the time I complete the next paragraph that could have all changed, rendering the previous paragraphs hopelessly outdated. So consumer beware. Stay on top of what's going on in your area. And above all, compare costs. Do not contract for more service than you require, and be cautious about jumping on the bandwagon just because something is cool. If you don't need it, cool is not reason enough to pay for it.

Long-Distance Calling

I want you to consider dumping the long-distance portion of your landline phone service. Your long-distance service plan is likely to be riddled with "mystery fees." My experience is that no one really knows what these fees are for (just call customer service and ask—the explanations will be quite amusing) but they add up nonetheless. Try dividing the number of your long-distance minutes last month into the total amount you paid for long-distance calling, including all of those mystery fees. You may choke when you see your effective rate is 25 or 35 cents, or even higher, per minute. You can beat that price.

But first let's get back to kissing your landline long-distance service good-bye. You won't miss it, really. You have good and much-cheaper alternatives.

First, if you have a cell phone with prepaid long-distance, use it for your long-distance calling. Just make sure you do not go over your allotted minutes or rack up roaming charges. If you have unlimited long-distance calling on the weekends or during off-peak times, don't guess when those times kick in. Call to ask. Check your plan in advance to bone up on what you are paying each month and what the costs might be for going over (Ouch!).

Next, you need to purchase a prepaid long-distance calling card. This is the key to keeping your long-distance calling cheap. And I mean less than 3 cents a minute to anywhere in the U.S.

Prepaid long-distance calling card. The best prepaid phone cards are available at warehouse discount clubs (Costco, Sam's Club, and BJ's). A prepaid phone card is simple to use. You dial a toll-free number and follow the directions. Keep your long-distance card by your phone and you'll never be out of reach, but you will avoid spending a lot of money. On a personal note, our long-distance landline bill used to be in the $25-$30 range per month. Since we began using prepaid long-distance phone cards, we spend less than $50 *a year*, with minutes to spare.

As you appraise long-distance prepaid phone cards, look at the price per minute. Cards you buy in an airport are 50 cents per minute (or more)—a rate that is totally outrageous.

Wireless

Big bills, lousy coverage, poor customer service. If that sums up your relationship with your wireless (sometimes referred to as "cell" or "mobile")-service provider, you may be looking to switch companies—especially now that you can take your number with you. But hold the phone! There's lots to know before you haul off and make the big switcheroo into a new contract. You need information.

In wireless speak, minutes mean *air time*—actual time spent talking on the cellular phone. In the U.S. you rack up air time whether you place or receive the call. The air-time meter runs even when you make toll-free calls or directory assistance calls. The only exception: 911 calls.

Who Are You Anyway?

It's important that you know what kind of a user you are, based on your past calling history. Gather your statements for the past six to twelve months and take a look. If you've gone completely whacky with your phone usage in the past, this may not be a pretty picture. It's time to get a grip. Make an honest evaluation of your actual calling needs against what you've practiced in the past. Use the information to determine if you are a casual, frequent, or family plan user (see below). I cannot overemphasize how important it is to carefully match your expected calling patterns with a plan's quota of peak and off-peak minutes, as well as with its long-distance and roaming provisions.

It is possible that even the best family plan out there is still too rich for your financial blood if you are going over your prepaid minutes each month. Be realistic as you consider your future calling patterns. Remember, all of the charges that kick in when you go over your quotas add up to shock your socks off when you get the bill.

Three Types of Callers

These general caller characteristics will help you determine where you and each of your phone-carrying family members fit in:

Casual user. If you make no more than five hours of calls a month, which includes forty-five minutes of talking long-distance, or need a phone only for emergency situations, consider yourself a casual user. The new breed of children with cell phones falls into this category.

Frequent user. The caller who spends twenty hours per month on a cell phone with eighty minutes of that time long-distance is a frequent user.

Family user. If you have four cell phones in your family and all together you make more than thirty hours of calls in a month (some plans do not count the time you spend speaking to each other by cell phone), 160 minutes of which are long-distance, you will probably do best with a family plan.

Three Types of Wireless Calling Plans

Traditional prepaid. You pay for your minutes and airtime in advance. There are no contracts and no monthly bills; no activation fees, no deposits, no credit checks, no age limits, and no extra hidden costs. You cannot go over. When the time runs out, the talking stops.

Prepaid cell-phone plans once were reserved for those with lousy credit. Today they're ideal for kids who lack an adult's impulse control and access to cash. Industry watchers say it's the fastest-growing wireless segment.

On average, prepaid phone plans charge between 10 and 50 cents a minute, higher than traditional cell plans that offer unlimited night and weekend calling. The more minutes you buy at once, the lower your rates. Minutes typically expire after ninety days.

Hybrid prepaid. A wireless-phone plan that blends some of the best features of postpaid and prepaid phones. There are no credit checks, contracts, or early termination fees. But instead of having to track minutes and buy refill cards yourself, hybrid phones allow you to replenish your minutes automatically.

Postpaid. A phone plan where you pay for what you used after the fact—after you talked all month, after you've run up the talk time. A postpaid plan typically requires a credit check, a one- or two-year contract, and may be subject to age limitations, activation fees, and deposits. You are billed monthly and charged heavily if you go over the plan's limitations.

So How Do You Choose?

Traditional prepaid. Popular with chatty children and young adults with spotty credit, prepaid phones are a great option for the casual or for-emergency-only users. But this can be an expensive way to go for an active talker who requires many hundreds of minutes a month.

Even though all of the major wireless-service providers have rolled out prepaid options now, two companies dominate the prepaid wireless option.

1. *TracFone Wireless.* TracFone has the biggest digital coverage area in the U.S., with free voice mail, free caller ID, free call waiting, and nationwide long distance with no additional charge. How can that be when TracFone owns no cell-phone towers? Easy. They lease air time from local wireless providers. So wherever you are, you're automatical-

ly connected. You can't tell whose lines your calls are using, and it does-n't matter. What you want is seamless connectivity.

Even so, with TracFone you never receive a bill. Go to *Tracfone.com*. They are always running some kind of special deal to get the phone plus extra minutes at a discounted price. Pricing at this writing is as low as 10 cents a minute.

For the very casual user who wants a phone for only emergency calls, TracFone offers a one-year prepaid service plan with 150 anytime, anywhere minutes for less than $7.99 a month, paid annually, and that includes a new phone.

2. *Virgin Mobile.* Another pay-as-you go wireless phone company, you can call anywhere in the U.S., midnight or midday, weekday or weekend—and it's always the same airtime pricing: 25 cents per minute for the first ten minutes each day, 10 cents per minute after that. Virgin Mobile service means no contracts, no commitments, no monthly bills, no hidden fees. You have to spend $20 every ninety days (even if you have a air time balance remaining), and your account will stay healthy and active. Go to *VirginMobileUSA.com* or *VirginMobile.com* for details.

Because wireless technology, service providers, and plans change more often than most people change their socks, don't depend on any of this information to be correct at the moment you read this. Check with *MyRatePlan.com* to get up-to-the moment information on all three types of prepaid calling plans listed above. Simply click on "Prepaid Plans" under "Start with a Rate Plan."

Hybrid prepaid. Liberty Wireless offers a hybrid prepaid plan. It costs $39.99 per month for three hundred daytime minutes and seven hun-dred night and weekend minutes at this writing, which works out to about 4 cents a minute for total talk time, all prepaid. See *LibertyWireless.com* for more details and information on phones.

Postpaid. Louise got the shock of her life when she opened her first cell phone bill. How on earth could her $19.99 calling plan zoom to more than $300? Clearly a case of inaccurate decimal placement. Or was it?

It took only a few minutes with customer service for Louise to learn the sad truth: her needs and the dirt-cheap calling plan she signed up for were not even on the same planet. She failed to understand a few important details about cell-phone usage, or more accurately, wireless communication. Now she's stuck with a one-year contract.

Louise is not alone. Most cell-phone users know more about the cool features on their phones than they do about roaming charges, air time allotments, or home calling areas. Here are some terms to know about your plan:

- *Wireless phone.* Any phone that transmits signals through the air without a physical connection. A cell phone is one type of wireless phone. Also referred to as a mobile phone

- *Minutes.* In wireless speak, minutes mean air time—actual time spent talking on the wireless connection. In the U.S. you rack up air time whether you place or receive the call, although some plans now offer free incoming minutes. The air time meter runs even when you place toll-free calls or calls to directory assistance. The only exception is 911 calls.

- *Anytime minutes.* This is the air time included in your particular plan that you can use any time, day or night, during the month. Unless your plan includes a "rollover" provision, if you don't use your minutes, you'll lose them. Louise learned that her $19.99 plan included only 150 minutes of air time. Each minute of air time used over that number of minutes cost her 49 cents.

- *Home calling area.* This is defined by your service plan. If you make or receive a call outside the boundaries of your home area, expect to be charged long-distance and or roaming fees on top of air time. Louise had no idea her particular home calling area was so limited.

- *Roaming.* This is the price you pay for the ability to make or receive calls outside your home calling area. Roaming charges can get expensive. Louise paid 79 cents for each minute of roaming on top of air time and long-distance charges!

- *Long-distance rate.* This is the rate you pay per minute for calls you place outside of your home calling area. It can vary greatly from one plan to another and is charged on top of roaming and air time. Louise was charged nearly $1.50 per minute for calling long distance.

- *National long-distance.* If this is part of your plan, you can call anywhere within the fifty states without incurring additional charges. Beware: roaming charges may still apply.

- *Off-peak.* The part of the day defined by the provider when customers can expect to pay reduced air-time rates (with some plans off-peak air-time is not charged at all, or referred to as "free"), usually evenings and weekends. Louise's plan included 250 off-peak minutes. Foolishly she assumed that meant anytime after 5 P.M. She learned too late that her plan defines off-peak hours this way: weekdays from 9 P.M. to 7 A.M. the next morning, and all weekend from Friday 9 P.M. until Monday at 7 A.M.

- *Other services.* The fancy features offered by some phones and service providers these days. Text messaging, sending digital photos, email, Internet connection, call waiting, even voice mail can be add-ons charged separately.

- *Activation fee.* A one-time fee charged by many service providers. Louise got socked with a $36 activation fee.

- *Cancellation fee.* This is a charge ranging from $100 to $240 or more that you pay for canceling a phone contract.

Had Louise asked herself these few important questions prior to choosing a plan, she could have saved herself a lot of grief and a pile of dough:

- *At what time of day will I make most of my calls?*

- *On average, how long do I expect each call to last?*

- *How selective will I be in giving out my cell-phone number?*

- *Will I use my cell phone for long-distance calling?*

- *How often do I expect to travel outside my home calling area?*

While it was an expensive lesson, Louise got a second chance. Her provider allowed her to switch to a $39.99 plan that includes six hundred anytime minutes and five thousand off-peak minutes. She has a detailed map showing her home calling area. She'll also be careful to use her prepaid calling card from a landline for long-distance (3 cents a minute with her Sam's Club AT&T card) to avoid roaming and long-distance charges.

Service Providers

If you have a postpaid cell phone plan, pick up that phone right now and call your customer service. Ask this question: Am I on the right plan? If you are not using all the minutes you are obligated to purchase each month—or you routinely go over—it's possible you will be offered a better plan to fit your needs. Now that we are free to leave our service providers once the contract has been fulfilled and take our phone numbers with us, it seems that companies are more willing to accommodate customers in order to keep their business.

I had planned to insert a cool spreadsheet right here to give you a way to compare all plans and providers at a single glance. Then I discovered it would be about fifty pages long. Zzzzzz . . .

In the spirit of not trying to reinvent the wheel, I am happy to tell you about a company that offers a comprehensive online survey of cellular service providers, including each company's specific plans and complete details for each—with regular updates. You can even peruse the specific phones offered for each plan. It's not that scary. In fact, I'll take you by the hand and walk you through.

Go to *Telebright.com*, and click on "Consumer" under Rate Plan Comparisons. This takes you to a page where you input your area code and prefix for either your home or current wireless phone, then click on "Wireless." At the next screen, input your zip code, then click on "Plan," and up pops a chart showing all of the plans available in your area. Don't panic when you get many available plans. I got 166 on my initial search. Click on the option to see plans for all carriers.

The plans are now sorted according to price, with the cheapest first. Scroll down to find the area that matches your use (casual, frequent, family). Select up to five plans and click on "Compare." The site shows you these five plans side-by-side in all their detailed glory.

You will learn more about calling plans than you ever dreamed (or wanted) to know including, but not limited to, roaming charges, what hours are peak and off-peak, activation fees, long-distance charges, and on and on for each and every plan out there.

Clicking "Select" on any plan (don't worry, you don't have to buy to look) brings up details of the telephones available for that particular plan, including the specifications, price, add-on accessories, warranty, and so on.

While you could sign up with a plan right on the TeleBright site (make sure you are not still in an active contract period with your current service provider or you could end up with a very expensive penalty), you don't have to. You can take all of your newfound knowledge with you to the company's walk-in store. Or not. Use this site to research and comparison shop. You can learn more about what you have now or need in the future. Plans and details can change without notice and they will.

Remember: always select the plan first, then the phone. Don't get taken in by a promotional ad for a cool phone. You could get stuck with a rotten plan.

Chapter Eleven

Strategies for Big-Ticket Items

> *Living in debt is nerve-wracking, insomnia-producing, and*
> *family-wrecking. Just don't do it. There is nothing you can buy*
> *that feels as good as being in debt feels bad.*
>
> ~ Ben Stein

It's not every day we face the challenge (perhaps *trauma* is a better word) of buying a refrigerator, tires, carpeting, furnace, roof, or major car repair. Thank goodness for that.

I call these "Big-Ticket Items" not necessarily because they are large in size (although most are, now that I think about it), but rather because they have big price tags—generally $300 and higher.

These major purchases require major consideration to avoid making a major blunder. There's nothing like a hastily signed installment contract to make it seem as if you're living your life for double the price!

And how about that moment of angst after the new refrigerator is delivered and you discover the competition has the same model on sale for $400 less, including free delivery!

Slashing the cost of big-ticket items is about more than avoiding blunders. With the right information and general principles that follow, you can learn to acquire even the big things in your life for half the price.

In Search of "Secret Mart"

I'm no fool. I'm certain you anxiously turned to this chapter hoping for the location, Internet address, and toll-free phone number of a secret merchant who sells every home appliance, electronic item, brand of furniture, and choice of car for half price. Hey, while you're dreaming, why not throw in college educations and houses too? That would be great!

Of course, if there were such a resource, by now everyone would know about it. Such a vendor would put other merchants out of business and make the half prices at the "Secret Mart" the commonly accepted full price. Soon we'd be right back to where we are now. Suffice it to say it's not quite that easy.

Anticipate

Contrary to any past experience you may have had with big-ticket items, they should rarely, if ever, catch you by surprise. If they do, more than likely it's due to your failure to anticipate.

As much as you might want to believe that the refrigerator taking its last tortured breath two days before Thanksgiving was a case of bad luck, the truth is, if it is not still under manufacturer's warranty, you should have known. After all, refrigerators do not last forever. Most manufacturers these days, while loathe to admit it, build in obsolescence to their product strategy to reduce the time between repeat purchases. Expect fifteen years on a typical refrigerator if it was manufactured since the early 1980s. Beyond fifteen, you're on borrowed time. Anticipate.

Of course, at times all of us are unable to anticipate a big-ticket purchase requirement. I can't think of one at the moment (I am the eternal optimist after all), but none of us are clairvoyant or infallible. On those rare occasions you will bless the day you learned the principles of the big-ticket purchase.

Principles of the Big Ticket Purchase

Three-Year Rule

If not now, in time you will be in a position to pay for all of your big-ticket items with cash. Until then the three-year rule should prevail: Only buy a big-ticket item on credit if it has a life expectancy of more than three years, and only finance it for three years or less.

The purpose for the three-year rule is simple: you do not want to be caught in the trap of still paying for things long after they've been consumed or have lived their useful lives. Do not finance a big-ticket item for longer than three years. This is the tipping point, at which a durable item becomes less valuable than the amount still owed on it. It will be tempting to accept zero percent interest or low monthly payments for a longer term. But resist. You do not want to string this out past thirty-six months.

Match Quality to Need

It is not always wise to pay more to get the best quality possible—even if you can afford to do so. Though at times you are wise to pay for the most quality you can afford, the secret is to know how to match quality to need and then buy only that amount.

Determining how much quality you need is not always easy. There are many things to consider. In fact, you should always see the potential that a big-ticket item has two price tags: (1) the cost to purchase it, and (2) the cost to own it (i.e. repair, maintain, insure, fuel, store, and so on).

Do Your Homework

In December 1995 only 14 percent of Americans had access to the Internet. By December 2003 two-thirds of Americans had at-home access. By 2004 more people had Internet access in their homes than had cable TV. If you are not on the Internet, you probably need to put that into your near-term planning. In the meantime, find the closest library with Internet access and learn to maneuver online. There is no better, simpler, or faster way, in my opinion, to research consumer matters than online.

How does the item you're considering rate with the pros? While not the final authority, perhaps, I encourage you to consult *Consumer Reports* (*ConsumerReports.org*). This publication accepts no advertising and therefore can make unbiased assessments of everything consumer related. I suggest you check out their ratings before making a final decision on any type of appliance, electronics, or other big-ticket item. In fact, I will go so far as to recommend you get a subscription to this excellent publication.

While receiving the hard copy of the publication each month is an option, you may find an online subscription to *ConsumerReports.org* more useful, as you will have access to searchable back issues and reports. Their online research process is quite user-friendly.

On a personal note, I am usually surprised to learn that *Consumer Reports* does not frequently give its highest rating to the most expensive option. Imagine that—you do not always get what you pay for! Also I appreciate the way the publication's ratings are broken down to analyze all aspects of the item being tested and rated.

For example, I needed to make an informed decision on a vacuum cleaner recently. I came this close to buying a high-end model that I'd seen advertised on TV as having received *Consumer Reports'* highest rating.

I decided to check for myself and read the full report. Good thing I did. What I didn't learn from the ad was that this particular vacuum scored high in only one area of testing (picking up animal hair) but came in much lower in its overall rating. The highest-priced vacuum failed miserably in removing dust and microbes from carpet.

I have no pets, but I have carpeting, and this was important information. I changed my mind and opted for the vacuum that received *Consumer Reports'* overall highest rating—the Hoover Wind Tunnel. Remarkably it is not the most expensive model tested. In fact, I bought it for only $269 at Costco—half the price of the animal-hair, powerhouse model.

Consumer Reports is only one avenue of research available on the Internet. A site that allows consumers to give their opinions on everything you can imagine, *Epinions.com,* is also enlightening. At the very least it gives you things to consider that you might not have thought about.

It's likely that you will conduct your most practical research for a refrigerator, computer, or other big-ticket item with friends and family. Ask what they love or dislike about an appliance or electronic item. If you've never owned a side-by-side refrigerator, for example, it may come as important news to you that the typical frozen pizza will not fit into the tall-yet-skinny freezer configuration. Neither will a large appetizer tray or jumbo-sized turkey. You may learn that a bottom-freezer configuration typically features a pull-out drawer that makes searching for lost items much easier. Never underestimate the wisdom of someone who has actually owned an item you are considering for purchase.

Start early

When forced to make a snap decision on a big-ticket item, you are not likely to make the best decision. And worse, if it's a matter of urgency, you may be equally unprepared financially. Your decision could result in new debt. When it comes to big-ticket items, you need time. Anticipate when you will need to buy a car; figure out how old your household appliances are. While you want to do everything you can to keep them running, don't let their demise catch you by surprise. The more time you have, the better and more reasoned your decision will be. Time gives you the luxury of waiting for a killer sale. Time gives you the option to change your mind. Time is on your side.

Know the Policies

No matter with whom you do business, you need to ask several key questions before you make a final decision:

1. *What is your price guarantee policy?* Many merchants have a policy to match any competitor's price on the same item for up to a certain amount of time following your purchase. This is crucial and will protect you in the event you get that item home only to learn the store across town is offering the same thing at a much lower price.

2. *What is your return policy?* You need to know this before you make a final decision. You never know when you will need to return something for any number of reasons. Can you expect a refund or only store credit? What is the return time period? Store policies vary greatly, so make it your business to learn this information.

3. *What if this item fails during the warranty period?* You need to know if you will be required to carry your item into the store for repair or whether you will have to deal directly with the manufacturer. You need to know if repairs on large items will be performed at your home and if so how to arrange for this. Make it a habit to attach your sales receipt to the owner's manual and warranty. A handy way to file these documents is in a three-ring binder outfitted with plastic sleeve pages. You can slip the entire manual and documentation into a plastic sleeve so it is visible, searchable, and handy.

Make It Last

No matter what price you pay, you can effectively reduce the price further when you diligently maintain that big-ticket item. Push the envelope to increase the period of time before replacement. Simply rotating your tires will extend their useful life. Service the lawn mower at least once annually; run a gallon of vinegar through the washing machine every few months; turn the mattresses every three months; change the oil in the car as suggested by the manufacturer. And so on. You'll get longer life from items that cost a lot to replace.

Each additional year you get from your refrigerator is another year to save for a new one. Every mile you get out of your car represents a dollar you are not spending in interest to buy another car. That is money you can use elsewhere.

Compare Prices

A simple, albeit not necessarily exhaustive, way to compare prices on just about anything is to go online to *Froogle.google.com*. Type in the specific item and this search robot will list all of the matching references on the Internet, with current pricing. This search will even pick up items listed on eBay and other online auctions.

While not every store that carries this item will be listed (remember this engine is searching websites that sell products), in a matter of seconds you can get a good idea of the range of prices. Now you are in the ballpark with enough information to know a good price when you see it. You may need to get on the phone and call a few stores in your area. Ask a salesperson when this item will be on sale. Hopefully you will find a way to hold off until then.

Home Appliances

On Sale This Week ...

There is no need to waste time and gasoline driving from store to store looking for the best price. You may want to visit one store so you can actually see, touch, and measure the item you are researching. Then visit *SalesCircular.com* to click on your state and find what's on sale this week at Best Buy, Circuit City, CompUSA, Kmart, Office Depot, Office Max, Radio Shack, Sears, Staples, Target, Wal-Mart, and select local retailers in your area.

This site is updated weekly and combines the sales circulars of these merchants into a searchable format. It is quite amazing and a very useful tool. This site tracks only home appliances, electronics, computer hardware, and computer software for the stores listed.

Discount Warehouse Clubs

If you are a member of Costco, Sam's Club, or BJ's, consider that these three discount warehouse clubs often undercut all the competition on appliances, electronics, computer hardware, and software. However, they rarely carry a variety of models from the same manufacturer.

My experience is that *Consumer Reports'* highest-rated items are what you will most likely find at the clubs. You won't find all of Hoover's current models of vacuums, but you will find the one that got the nod from CR. The clubs also carry limited choices in mattresses, but do carry the brand most highly rated and for an excellent value. Furniture and home furnishings are limited, and a matter of personal taste. You will find a limited selection of refrigerators, freezers, washers, and dryers at the clubs. Tires, however, are an excellent buy at these clubs. In fact, you will have a difficult time beating their everyday tire prices. As always, consider your annual membership fee as part of the price when comparing club prices with non-membership stores.

You can conduct limited research on the discount club prices of big-ticket items at their respective websites. You do not have to be a member to search online.

Other Strategies

Floor models. Always consider making an offer on a floor model. It might show some wear, but if you can get the warranty intact and a big discount on the price, that should merit your consideration. It never hurts to ask.

Last year's model. Just like cars, appliance manufacturers come out with new souped-up models of refrigerators, dishwashers, ranges, microwaves, and washers and dryers with bigger price tags. Usually the only thing different is a bell or whistle.

Before agreeing to the current model, ask about last year's. Since your main concern is price—not resale value—the difference between last year's and the current model should be of little consequence.

Scratch and dent. It happens all the time. A new appliance or furniture item gets damaged in transit. The worse the damage, the greater the discount to get rid of it. But here's the great thing: unless the damage was so severe it affected the operation, the new warranty prevails.

If that gouge is on the side of the refrigerator that will not show, or the dent on the washer is of no consequence to you, let them give you an additional 40 percent off to take the problem off their hands. Many retailers have a special location where they send the scratch-and-dent problems, so ask where you can take a look at these items.

Energy Star. New appliances that consume energy, such as refrigerators, dishwashers, washers, and dryers, are rated by the government as to their energy efficiency. The Energy Star label (*EnergyStar.gov*) is the government's seal of approval to help consumers identify the most energy-efficient products on the market.

Energy Star labels will tell you how much energy in kilowatt-hours it will take to operate this appliance in one year. This is important, because paying less for an energy guzzler will cost a lot more in the long run. Remember, the price you pay for an appliance is only the down payment. An older refrigerator you get for free could be far more expensive than buying a new one that is energy efficient.

Furniture

If there's one thing you need to know about buying furniture, it is this: all prices are negotiable. Especially on new furniture. I am fairly confident that I can walk into any furniture store, point to any piece and ask, "Is this your best price?" Without flinching, the salesperson will knock 10 percent off like clockwork.

My philosophy is that if it's that easy to drop it by 10 percent, just imagine what might happen if I am willing to wait, persist, and walk away if necessary. An excellent tactic is to hand the salesperson a business card and say, "If you need to meet a quota in the next month or two, and you can help me get a better discount on this sofa or tell me when it will be on sale, give me a call." Now walk away. Leave. Go home and wait for the call.

Furniture Resources

Direct from High Point, N.C. Known as the Furniture Capital of the World, you can buy direct from some furniture manufacturers. If you live in the North Carolina area, you can order and pick up, however most of these merchants will ship. Many do not charge sales tax when shipping out of state, which may offset the shipping cost. It helps if you know the manufacturer and specific details about the items, including model numbers and style names. A good place to start if you are interested in getting a quote on buying furniture direct from the manufacture is *HighPointFurnitureSales.com.*

On a personal note, we purchased leather family room furniture directly from one manufacturer in High Point. The final cost, including shipping, was just under 50 percent of the price for this same suite at the furniture store in our area. It was a simple transaction and took no longer for delivery than the store quoted (most stores quote six to twelve weeks for delivery). I figure the delivery truck can drive to my house as easily as to a store's warehouse. It was a pleasant and simple transaction.

Gently used. There is a huge secondary market of furniture in this country. If you are willing to look, you will eventually find what you need. And you will find great prices. Goodwill and Salvation Army stores are a treasure trove for surprisingly high-quality furniture, provided you are willing to be patient and persistent.

Auction houses. You may have to look around to find a good auction house in your area, but when you do get ready for some amazing bargains. While it is likely the antiques will go for higher prices, other pieces that are considered used furniture typically can be purchased for rock-bottom prices.

Consignment. Furniture is the latest edition to the consignment store craze. Here you will find excellent-quality and pristine-condition used furniture, as well as home furnishings such as silver, china, and linens.

Prices in consignment stores will be higher than thrift stores, but still far less than new. Ask around; look in your local Yellow Pages under Furniture, Consignment. For the same money you would spend at IKEA or Sears, you may be able to pick up high-end, magnificent pieces for your home.

Estate sales. If you have the time and patience, you just might get lucky. Expect to find rooms of furniture offered in sets rather than individual pieces at estate sales. Typically those running the sale are not the relatives of the deceased, so don't feel bad about negotiating. It's all business. The people at the sale are simply hired facilitators.

Unfinished kits. If you are willing to do some of the work, you can save a lot by doing some of the tedious finishing. Unfinished furniture stores usually offer assembled but unfinished furniture which you can finish yourself, or for a small fee they'll do that for you. You can also purchase furniture kits that require both assembly and finishing. Now you will save even more. Check *ShakerWorkshops.com* and *Vandykes.com* (search "Furniture Kits") to find kits at reasonable prices.

Rental returns. Most stores that rent furniture (I am not advocating renting your furniture because that is such an expensive option) also sell returned pieces. If you're looking for some real steals, check this out. Simply call or go to a furniture rental store to inquire about their sales. Feel free to negotiate. Remember, they are not in the furniture storage business. Furniture that sits on their floor and in their warehouses does not earn money.

How to Buy a Mattress

If you want to drive yourself nuts, go shopping for a new mattress. You'll hear dozens of theories on coils, fabrics, stuffing, foam density, and warranties.

What I know about buying a mattress I've learned from the best: insiders now retired from the sleep-product industry.

Confusion factor. All of the major brands like Simmons, Serta and Sealy make decent mattresses, but if you plan to go from one chain store to the next comparing prices, forget it. The major brands change the names of the same mattress for each of the stores, so it is impossible to compare by make and model.

Shop by level. Each company makes "levels" of mattresses: Very cheap, decent cheap, good, and best. That's not what they call them, but you can tell by the pricing within each manufacturer's line of products. Expect several models in each price level.

Price matters. You get what you pay for in a mattress. A very cheap mattress is about 10 percent materials (foam, steel, padding) and 90 percent air. A mid-level mattress is about 40 percent materials and so on. The more material, the better the product and the higher the price. A high-quality mattress will be up to 90 percent materials, and therefore the heaviest. You can lift a mattress to determine its quality.

Weight matters. The heavier the sleeper, the heavier by weight you want your mattress. You will do just fine with a lightweight mattress in a guest room that is seldom used, or for your fifty-pound child. But for heavy adults, opt for the heaviest mattress you can afford.

No pillow top. A pillow-top mattress is a normal mattress with a layer of extra padding on top. It will wear out and flatten down long before the actual mattress will begin to show a dent. But it is sewn on permanently. You'll pay an extra hundred bucks for it ($200 if it has a pillow top on both sides). Buy a great mattress pad instead. Pay $40 and throw it away when it mashes down and get a new one. Your mattress will last for many years longer.

Take a nap. Once you've narrowed your selection to two or three, take a nap. Spend at least fifteen minutes on each of the beds you are considering. Comfort is key, so don't make a hasty decision.

Negotiate. At the very least you should get free delivery and removal of your old mattress.

Trust the clubs. Warehouse clubs like Costco and Sam's Club carry a limited choice of name-brand mattress sets in all sizes. Typically they're top of the line at cut-rate prices. But you won't have a salesman to consult (perhaps that's a good thing). You won't be able to take a nap either. However, I can say from personal experience, the clubs make wise choices. Trust them and you'll knock hundreds off your mattress purchase.

Computers

My best advice before buying a computer is to know what you need and then buy up a level or two. Go to various computer websites to educate yourself. Dell, Compaq, and Gateway are only three examples. I can't think of a big-ticket item purchase that requires you to match quality with need more than a computer.

If you are buying a laptop computer, plan on it breaking down. Laptops carried from place to place get beat up in their travels. Technical support and maintenance and the cost of an extended warranty are key factors when making your decision on a portable computer.

Desktop computers have a better reputation for service. We currently have about ten desktop computers and two laptops at

Cheapskate Central (my office in California). Over the fourteen years since I premiered my national subscription newsletter *Debt-Proof Living* (formerly *Cheapskate Monthly*), we've purchased no fewer than twenty-five computers. In all that time only two of our computers ever required service. You guessed it—both laptops.

On a personal note, while I don't believe Dell makes the best computer in the world, they offer, in my opinion, the best service. That is key in my decision making. I am currently doing my best to wear out my fifth Dell laptop computer.

To date I have had eleven keyboard replacements, the same number of touchpad replacements, at least a dozen monitors replaced, and more motherboards than I can count. Dell service even replaces the keys when I wear off the letters. None of this suggests that Dell makes an inferior product; I am hard on computers. I expect a lot, and so far Dell has delivered. I do opt for the best service plan available and pay for the extended warranty on the laptops. I cannot afford in my work to be without my computer. And when my laptop decides to rebel, a single phone call has a service technician knocking on my door no matter where I am in my travels, within twenty-four hours. I'm a big fan of Dell for their service. For my needs their product is more than adequate.

It's a Frantic Site ... but Worth a Look

If you are both diligent and patient, the place to learn about the best buys on computers, associated peripherals, and other electronics is *GotApex.com*. Let me warn you that this site brings new meaning to the term *sense of urgency*. Deals come and go quickly.

Contributors discover and post great deals and special offers that often add up to nothing short of spectacular. You'll feel that every deal you see is too good to pass up, and because it will expire in the next five minutes, if not sooner, you will feel compelled to buy right now. The secret is to remember why you're there and what you are looking for specifically, and then take a deep breath.

Extended Warranties

Recently I was standing in line in an office supply store. The customer in front of me purchased a $39 calculator. I couldn't help but hear the clerk offer her an extended warranty.

The woman hesitated then they went back and forth a bit. The saleslady was persistent suggesting it would be expensive to repair this $39 calculator. I had to look the other way and bite my tongue to keep myself from blurting, "Don't do it! Keep your nine bucks!" Clearly she couldn't read my mind, because she went for the bait and swallowed the hook, and the clerk reeled her in.

If you've ever wondered why retailers are so persistent in offering extended warranties, here it is: *money*. Now there's a real shocker. Extended warranties offer retailers a whopping 70 percent profit on average, as opposed to about 10 percent profit on the product itself.

Extended warranties benefit the company issuing the warranty more than the person buying the warranty. Companies would not sell extended warranties if that were not the case. Such warranties are rarely a good investment because these days most appliances and electronics are dependable.

The Problem

In general, here's the problem with extended warranties: They don't cover the most trouble-prone years of an appliance's life. If that item is going to fail, statistically it is most likely to do so either in the first six months or much later, long after an extended warranty is unavailable.

The time between six months old and five years old is usually the most trouble-free time or the appliance's "mid-term." Most manufacturers offer a one-year warranty on their appliances to cover any early failures, which in most cases is sufficient. Extended warranties are usually not offered for the entire life of the appliance, only that generally trouble-free mid-term period.

Exceptions

If you know a particular big-ticket item is notorious for failing during the initial three years, an extended warranty may be a wise choice. That is why I purchased extended warranties for both my treadmill and my laptop computers—both have high failure rates. And I'm glad I did, because both extended warranties have more than paid for themselves by covering big repair bills.

If you have had miserable experiences in the past with appliances breaking down, the peace of mind you'll get with an extended warranty may be well worth the price. But that's a decision you need to make on a case-by-case basis. Just keep in mind that unless it's a treadmill or laptop computer, the odds are heavily stacked against you.

Here's an Idea...

Instead of buying extended warranties, set up your own Repair and Maintenance account. Rather than handing your money to the retailers for extended warranties, pay that money to yourself into an account in your name every month. Never miss; never be late. That way, if you do need major repairs you have the money, and the interest.

On the other hand, if it turns out you never require major repairs (more likely), the extended warranty fund plus interest will be your profit, not the retailers'.

Chapter Twelve

Your Dream Ride
for Half the Price

Debt is so ingrained into our culture that most Americans can't even envision a car without a payment, a house without a mortgage, a student without a loan and credit without a card. We've been sold debt with such repetition and with such fervor that most folks can't conceive of what it would be like to have NO payments.

~ Dave Ramsey, Author and Radio Host

An automobile represents a major purchase. For most it is second only to buying a home. It is also the most dreaded of all consumer purchases and the one most likely to throw a major kink in your financial picture.

Big car payments can place you in financial jeopardy faster than just about any other consumer acquisition. Many people assume the only way to buy a car is with a big loan. And with cars getting more and more expensive and loan terms expanding to accommodate buyers' needs, the perpetual car payment is becoming a fact of life for many people.

This presents a serious dilemma. In the fourth or fifth year, a car is likely to require repairs but is not yet paid for. Who can afford the big car payment and the repairs? The conclusion for many is that it's time to get rid of the car, trade it in on a new model with a new loan for another six years, maybe seven. But since the car is not yet paid off, the shortfall rolls over into the next loan, resulting in an even bigger loan, bigger payments, and more payments.

It's easy to see how this perpetual-car-payment mentality takes over. "What's the use?" is most people's response. "We'll always have a car payment, so we might as well get used to it!" And with two or three cars per household, the cost of transportation turns into a financial nightmare.

Most expensive. The most expensive way to drive a car is to finance a new car and trade it in every two or three years for a newer car. While a zero-percent loan can make this an attractive way to go because the payment is less, the loan quickly becomes greater than the car's market value which makes that car "unsaleable."

Cheapest. The cheapest way to drive a car is to pay all cash for a late model, low-mileage, domestic model. Somewhere between these two extremes lie untold ways to lease or own an automobile, but not many options will afford you the freedom to own a car for half the price. Yet getting to that place is possible, provided you have a plan.

What Not to Do

I received the following letter from one of my newsletter subscribers:

> *After several years of trading our vehicles in and upgrading each time, we now have a gas-guzzling 2003 Chevy Trailblazer. The current market value on this vehicle is $19,510 wholesale (what we could get on*

a trade-in) and $22,930 retail (if we could sell it to a private party). We owe $33,335 on a 0 percent loan.

We pay $156 in gasoline alone each month. My husband doesn't think there is any way we can get out of this. We'd like to replace it with a cheap clunker that will cost less to operate. We have $1,400 in savings, and I'm just wondering if there is a way out of this, or do we just have to dig our heels in until we pay it off? We really regret all the bad choices we made and would be willing to drive something much cheaper.

Perhaps you have already figured out the poor judgment calls Alec and Tina (not their real names) made that landed them in this nearly impossible situation.

It started with a brand-new car financed to the hilt. I can only assume that they, like so many, made the mistake of considering only the monthly payments, not the total cost of the vehicle and, specifically, the full amount of the loan. I suspect they agreed to a long-term loan to get the lowest possible monthly payments.

Even before that car was paid off, they decided to upgrade (it's easy to get that new-car fever and a case of the "I wants" when you see other vehicles on the road and in the neighbors' driveways, or when your family expands), but they had a problem. The not-yet-paid-for car was worth less than the amount they owed on the lease or loan. But they really wanted the bigger, newer, fancier car.

New Cars Cause Fuzzy Thinking

A clever salesperson suggests they could easily drive home in the new car today, provided they can swing a higher payment. Here's where things get fuzzy. Alec and Tina are so enamored with the possibility of having the new car of their dreams for just a bit more each month that they don't fully consider the big picture (they forget to consider higher insurance costs, larger licensing fees, a bigger engine that eats more gas and a longer-term loan).

Let's say the car they want to trade-in has a value of $12,000, but they owe $13,500. The salesman says not to worry; he will pay off their car so they're free to buy the new one of their dreams. Wow! That's fantastic.

Of course what Alec and Tina mean by "pay off" isn't exactly what Salesman Sam has in mind. They're thinking "gift"; Sam's talking "rollover," which means adding on the $1,500 shortfall to the new loan, thereby extending their loan period by another year or longer.

But it's not even *that* easy. Because the salesman doesn't clearly disclose how this trade-in will work, Alec and Tina are unaware that in exchange for this gracious offer, Salesman Sam discounts the value of the car they are trading in, which only increases the shortfall.

Unsuspecting customers Alec and Tina are confused by all the numbers, so the salesman mercifully cuts to the chase and says they can drive the new car home today. He names the affordable monthly payment. What they don't realize is how many long years these payments will go on and how difficult it will be.

Of course, depreciation plays a role in all of this, knocking about 20 percent off the car's market value the moment they drive it off the lot.

Apparently Alec and Tina did this kind of car swapping more than a few times, to the point that they are now $11,000 in the hole. For all practical purposes, they are stuck, even with a 0 percent loan. They have a car they can't sell, big fuel bills they cannot afford, and payments of $555 a month for five more years. It's difficult to see how a 0-percent loan did them any good.

Still, things could be worse. They could have agreed to this deal with 5 percent or 6 percent interest, which would boost those monthly payments to $629 for another five years. And while I hate to bring up such a negative possibility, if Alec and Tina wreck this car, or it is stolen and declared a total loss, they will find themselves in a real pickle.

Standard collision insurance covers up to the current market value of the car, not the amount owed against it. Without "gap insurance" that specifically addresses this situation, and can be pricey, they could find themselves owing $12,000 on a car that has gone to the big junk-yard in the sky, with no way to replace it but by agreeing to take on yet another auto loan.

There is nothing like a bad car deal to put a major strain on any budget. Multiply that by two bad car deals running simultaneously and it can look like an impossible situation. Alec and Tina have three possible ways to get out of their bad deal. I'll explain them to you in a moment. But first I want to tell you how I know about all this by first-hand experience.

One Story Deserves Another

Harold and I leased our first car way back in 1978. Our good car was totaled in the middle of the night as we slept, while on vacation and far from home. It was a nightmare. We got the insurance check, which was the amount left once the loan was paid. It was nowhere close to what we would need to buy another car.

Believing it was just too risky to buy a used car, and because the money we had wouldn't make much of a down payment on a new one, we looked for other alternatives. Automobile leasing had just come into its own and was all the buzz. The theory was that by leasing you only pay for as much car as you drive. No down payment requirements, and your monthly payments are much lower.

It sounded plausible. To our amazement it was true. We leased a brand-new station wagon that would have been beyond our reach to buy. The payments were affordable, and the cash we had on hand covered the origination fees and lease payment for the first month. It was quite painless.

Still, even with our new car, we were in a mess because we needed a second car. We had the clunkiest of all clunkers as a second car and it had reached the tipping point, where we were sure the repairs and maintenance were costing more than it was worth. The idea of the auto lease stuck in our minds.

Why not lease another car? We couldn't think of a good reason not to and so we did. Now we had two brand-new leased cars. It was very nice.

But wait, it doesn't stop there! Before you stop reading and run off to lease a new car, let me tell you the rest of the story.

Leasing a car is really a long-term rental agreement, along with a promise to return the car in exactly the condition you got it—brand-new with absolutely no sign that you've ever driven it or that a kid ever sat in it, let alone launched a few soft drinks and an occasional coffee onto its fine upholstery. There are many provisions and hidden costs involved in leasing a car—buried in the fine print.

Auto leases include a huge penalty for each mile over the typical fifteen thousand you drive it per year. The lease agreement demands that you return the car at the end of the term in exactly the same condition as new—no scratches, dents, dings, or bruises; no wear on the upholstery; no stains on the carpet. Impossible? Why, of course. Just show me any three-year-old car in brand-new condition and I'll show you a car that has been sealed in a garage and driven only on Sundays for three years.

At the end of our two leases, we were up against a wall. We had no cash for down payments on two new car purchases; we had no money to buy used clunkers. But there was another problem. An auto lease contains something called "residual value," the amount the car must be worth at the end of the lease. And if it's not, the person leasing the car has to pay the difference. It's like being upside down in a car-loan deal (remember Alec and Tina?).

Then guess what! We found one of those clever salespeople who pulled a rabbit out of the hat and rolled all of the fees, penalties, and shortfalls from both of our leased cars into new leases for two brand-new cars! "And while we're at it, Mr. and Mrs. Hunt, why don't we get you into the cars you really want and will make you look good?"

And so we did. Several times, for a total of twenty-two years. What choice did we have? We were always behind the eight ball, having never saved enough money to own our cars. Our lease payments grew and grew to cover all of the rollovers. But oh, did we drive nice cars! We had the original Mazda Rx-7; a minivan; various imports, including a BMW; and a Cadillac the size of a yacht, to name just a few.

We finally got off the auto lease treadmill, but not without a good deal of effort. During the last year of the last auto I leased, we sold that vehicle and came up with the cash necessary to pay off the lease. I took a huge emotional leap and agreed to not have a car until we could get ourselves back onto firm financial ground. It was difficult at first, but my desire to stop $1,000 a month in auto expenses was quite motivating.

When Harold's last auto lease was over finally, we agreed that we would take the cash we had available ($4,000) and buy the best clunker we could find. We needed a car to commute to work (we work in the same office), but we also needed some kind of truck or utility vehicle for his work as a property manager.

We settled on a fairly beat-up Chevy El Camino in good running condition. I can't say the interior condition matched. In fact, it was just one step up from disgusting. I cleaned it with disinfectant and polished that car the best I could, and it still looked bad. But it ran and was paid for.

The car was fine. It was my attitude that needed adjustment. I'd had my own car since I was twenty-one. I enjoyed that sense of independence and being in control of the road. And the radio and the seat position. All of it. I didn't mind following my husband to work every day. I felt independent and modern. But all of that changed overnight. Thankfully our plan was to endure this sharing thing for only a few months.

But something funny happened. I soon discovered the joy of having a driver. I could sleep, read, talk, or do anything I wanted on the commute to and from work. No longer did I have to pump gas, wash a car, manage oil changes, or send in license fees. Our insurance dropped dramatically. Our driveway wasn't crowded. Having just one car simplified our lives.

After two years we treated the El Camino, by now a classic and quite collectible, to a new interior. We put in a new engine, new wheels, and tires. We were getting ready to have it painted when it was tragically stolen. In broad daylight, the clunker I loathed was snatched right out from under our noses. Several days later it surfaced, stripped to the bare frame. Gone forever.

Fortunately we'd been saving money each month in anticipation of buying another car someday. That money together with the insurance proceeds got us a new truck. To this day we still share one paid-for vehicle. Whether we will ever go back to two cars remains to be seen.

It took a great deal of effort, determination, and attitude adjustment to right all the wrongs we committed in the automobile area of our lives.

Rules for Buying a Car for Half the Price

Rule #1: Pay cash

The first rule for how to drive a car for half the price is to pay cash for it. Hang on. I know you may not be able to do that right now. Just be patient and I will teach you how. This principle is so important I will repeat it: pay cash for your car.

Rule #2: Opt for Late Model

Because new cars depreciate so dramatically (20 percent the minute it becomes a used car) your best economic bet is to buy a late-model, previously owned car.

Rule #3: Always Make Payments

I hope that got your attention! On the one hand I just told you to always pay cash for your cars. And now I am telling you to always make payments. Both principles are true.

You must adopt the attitude that as long as you intend to own a car you must anticipate the cost by making monthly payments to yourself. Unlike a home that appreciates, cars depreciate, so you must always anticipate a car's replacement. Anticipate your automobile needs by making car payments to yourself. Now you are always earning interest, not paying it. You make payments even when your car is fully paid for and even when you are fully satisfied with the car you are driving at the time. Why? Remember, cars depreciate and wear out.

If you are not always anticipating the next purchase you will find yourself rubbing elbows with Alec and Tina in the little cubicle outside the manager's office in some new car dealership.

Paying All Cash

I once heard a speaker say he wouldn't walk across hot coals for the fun of it. But if he could be shown how a short, painful walk would do away with a lifetime of worry, frustration, and the fear that comes with constantly being broke, then bring on the hot coals!

While the method that follows isn't exactly hot coals, it does represent a lifestyle change for a while. It's a short-term sacrifice to achieve something amazing that few people will ever achieve in their lifetimes: paying all cash for a car, and perhaps, if you choose, even a brand-new car. Eventually.

Let's say that tomorrow morning your car is destroyed beyond repair. You must have a car, and because you have no money saved, you opt to buy a brand-new car with nothing down. How much can you afford to pay each month for a car payment? Realistically. $200? $350 $600?

Okay, back to reality. Your car isn't destroyed, and you'll keep driving it for a while. But remember the amount you said you believe you could afford to pay for a car payment each month? Keep reading.

Open a special savings account somewhere convenient and begin immediately to make monthly payments into that account. Let's say your payments are $300 a month You pay $300 to yourself every month. That's right, to *you*. Be strict with yourself—rigid and unbending! No late payments, no slacking. In the meantime, and as you are making these big new payments, continue driving the car you have now for one more year, even if it is a real clunker. You can endure anything as long as you have a plan and you know it will end. Think hot coals.

Depending on where you've opened this account, you will begin earning interest, albeit a small amount, on the growing balance instead of paying interest on a conventional auto loan. At the end of a year, you will have accumulated $3,600 cash plus interest in your account in the Bank of You. Not bad!

Now sell your clunker. I don't know what you have or what it might be worth so let's say you can sell it for $2,000. Put that money with the $3,600 and buy the best car you can find for $5,600 all cash. By now you've become used to making $300 payments to yourself, so don't stop. It's becoming a habit, and a very good one at that.

At the end of another year, sell the current clunker for say $4,800 and put that money together with the $3,600 you have saved during the year by making those payments to yourself. Now buy the best used car you can find for your $8,400. And continue making those payments.

At the end of year three, sell the current car for say $7,800, and together with the new $3,600 from your savings, buy the best $11,400 car you can find. Notice: Your selection of good used cars is getting better each year. You have graduated from clunkers to much more respectable automobiles.

In year four, sell the most recent car for say $11,000, add the $3,600 accumulation, and buy a $14,600 used car. By year five, you have at least

$17,000 cash to upgrade to an even better car. By year six, you should have at least $20,000 cash to buy a car.

Keep repeating this once each year…upgrading, paying cash for a better car, and still a better car. As you become more adept, you will lose your fear of buying and selling cars.

Keep this routine of making payments first then upgrading once a year. Within five or six years you will have accumulated enough cash to buy a brand-new car—all cash. You will have more than $20,000, including all of the interest you have earned each year on your $300 monthly deposits.

Imagine your confidence and personal power, knowing you are not at the mercy of any salesman, bank, or finance company as you look for a car. You can negotiate because you have plenty of experience by now.

Buying a brand-new car will certainly be an option. But I predict you will pass. Why? Because by this time you will be so good at buying late-model, domestic, low-mileage cars for a fraction of the price of a new one, you will scoff at the folly of buying new and feeling that big 20-percent depreciation hit on the front end.

Still, you will have the option to do exactly as I promised: buy a brand-new car, for all cash. And who knows? You just might. But I guarantee you will be able to drive the car of your dreams for half the price.

A Used Car

Whether you call it "previously owned," "gently used," or "second-hand," the truth is, every car is used. The moment it leaves the lot with its first owner behind the wheel it must be sold as "previously owned."

So when we talk about a used car, we're talking about a large range—from used for a day to a car that's been owned for a decade or longer. It means one mile on the odometer or 100,001 miles. Here's the key to driving a car for half the price: make sure you are not the first owner. Let someone else take that 20-percent depreciation hit.

Buying a previously owned car can be a lot simpler than buying new if you deal directly with the owner of the used car. You make a bid based on what you are willing to pay, and either the seller accepts or rejects your offer. It's a lot more complicated buying a used car from a dealer.

Their Loss, Your Great Deal

For many people there exists an incalculable fear when it comes to buying a used car. It stems from the myth that when you buy a used car, you're just buying someone else's problems, or that the only reason a used car is for sale is because it harbors all kinds of monstrous secrets under the hood and is held together with bailing wire. That myth is far from the truth and a completely overblown assessment of the world of used cars!

In these days of 100,000-mile warranties, improved technologies, vehicle history reports, 0-percent offers on new cars, and state lemon laws, there exists a huge secondary market of high-quality, previously used cars. Far from "lemons" you will be pleasantly surprised at how many cream puffs you'll find from which to choose! And being the all-cash buyer you are soon to become, you will have even greater bargaining power. Your personal confidence will soar.

Low-mileage. Many low-mileage used cars are available in your price range. I know this because I hear from original buyers like Alec and Tina who on impulse made a bad judgment call. They need to get out of that new-car deal and are willing to do just about anything—including selling at a loss. I advise people to do that because they are in such an untenable position with huge monthly payments hanging over their heads. So their loss will be your gain.

Nothing is wrong with these cars; people simply got in over their heads with more payment than they could handle. They can't trade them in; they have to sell them. And no matter the age, it is now considered a used car. And if you're flexible about colors and options, used cars are readily available, provided you are patient.

Repairs rarely rival a payment. Assuming that a used car, because of its potential for repairs, is more costly than a new one is a fallacy, especially if that new car is financed. The same people who insist to me that they can no longer afford repairs of a couple hundred dollars a month on their current vehicle will sign up for sixty or seventy-two payments of $350 or more on a new one.

What these folks are unwilling to see is that the repairs would not have been $200 a month every month. Once the problems were fixed, they would have had many more months with no repairs at all, allowing them to save toward the purchase of another car. Learn from their mistakes.

Fear of the unknown. The problem for many of us is the fear of the unknown and having to rely on others to handle problems. We fear mechanics and emergency breakdowns. I understand all of that, but it's time to lose the fear. Knowledge is power, and power casts out fear. If ever you have a big-ticket item in your life, it's a car. And buying a used car makes it more worthy of your best attention and willingness to learn. You will be rewarded handsomely!

How to Buy a Used Car

Know What You Can Spend

Before you even look at buying a car, you must know exactly how much you can afford to spend. If you must finance part of the purchase price, now is the time to address this. What monthly payment can you handle? Keep in mind you will have to pay registration and titling fees, and many states charge use or sales tax. You will need a down payment in cash. Your credit union or bank wants to see you contributing part of the purchase price up front.

If you must finance part of the cost (but only if you must, and for this one last time, hear?), keep the payments to twenty-four months if possible, thirty-six only in an unusual circumstance. Don't accept dealer financing on a used car because you will pay far too much in interest and fees.

You want the shortest financing terms possible so you will have plenty of time to begin making payments to yourself for the anticipated replacement of this car. Remember, because cars are constantly wearing out, they can only depreciate.

If you have a credit score over 650, go online to Capital One Auto Finance (*CapitalOne.com*) or E-Loan (*Eloan.com*), apply online, and get approved within the hour. They will mail you a check, which you'll have the next day. If your score is below 650, apply through Auto Credit Finders (*AutoCreditFinders.com*) instead.

Current Valuation

Make a list of the features you need in a car. Match your list to the makes and models of cars that appear to meet your minimum standards. You can find this information for no charge at sites like *Edmunds.com* and *KBB.com* (Kelley Blue Book). In your car search, keep your eye on the local classified ads, sites like *AutoTrader.com*, and other similar publications in your community. Keep your ears open too. You want to be the first to know about a great car for sale.

A Reputable Mechanic

You need to know where to find a real, live automobile mechanic you can trust. Ask friends, family, and coworkers. You need a mechanic with a "lift" who is willing to put a car you are considering up on it so he (and you, if you are so inclined) can inspect the body and frame from underneath.

Make sure the car you buy has not been in a major wreck. The only way to know for sure whether a car has been seriously damaged is to look. Unless it was declared a total loss by an insurance company, there may not be a paper trail to alert you to serious damage. Once a car has been wrecked to the point the frame is bent, or there are visible repairs such as bars welded to hold two pieces together, or other signs that the frame has been "straightened," that's a car you do not want to own. Your reputable mechanic will give you a fairly reasonable assessment of the soundness of the car's mechanical parts.

Ask the mechanic to take it for a test-drive. Look in the trunk for evidence the paint color has been changed. Look for water lines that indicate it might have been in a flood. Checking out a potential car with a mechanic may cost you a few bucks, so narrow your search before you bring in a car to be checked. There are so many excellent cars available, you really shouldn't settle for one with major problems.

Car History Report

Every car has a serial number called a VIN (vehicle identification number). You will find this on a metal bar riveted to the dash just inside the windshield on the driver's side. From the moment it's manufactured until that car is finally crushed in a junkyard and sent to be recycled into a new car, there's a paper trail—a history of who has owned it and where it has been registered. As a consumer you have a right to look at any car's history report for a small fee.

A vehicle's history report will tell you all about the title on the car. If the car was ever in a major flood or totaled for any other reason by an insurance company, it will show up as "salvage." That is a word you do not want to see on the title of a car you own.

The history report will also give you an odometer check. If the numbers showing now on the odometer do not add up to the numbers on the report, you know there's been some odometer tampering going on. The report will show if this vehicle has ever been stolen or damaged in a fire. You'll know if it was ever leased, owned by a car rental company, or used as a taxi or police car. All of this information will help you make a good assessment.

More than just interesting, this is information you cannot afford to be without. Access to the Internet makes finding out a car's history simple, provided you are willing to pay for a report. You can go to *CarFax.com* and pull up the history on any automobile, provided you have the VIN. The cost of the report is less than $20 for one vehicle or about $25 for multiple reports if you are considering several cars and want reports on all of them.

The Test-Drive

On a test-drive you'll do more than just drive this car. You'll give it a thorough inspection. Every car gives you many clues if you pay attention.

Audio off. Drive this car in silence so you can hear any rattle, nuance and engine noises.

The doors. Do they open and close properly and line up evenly?

The finish. Are there bumps or dimples in the paint? These could indicate some major body work or "filling" has been performed. Is the paint color inside the trunk or hood the same as on the exterior?

Under the hood. Is the engine clearly new while the car is old? If there's been an engine swap, you want to know the details and reason for the changeover. You want this in writing with evidence of who did the work and what parts were used.

The interior. Look at the carpeting, especially under the seats, the floor mats, and under the dashboard. Look for water damage or substandard care.

When considering a purchase from a car dealer as opposed to a private individual, keep this in mind: generally, dealers make a much greater profit on a used car than on a new one. Does that tell you anything? Whether that means dealers typically pay too little on trade-ins or mark them up considerably for sale—or both is more likely—clearly there is room for negotiation. And in most cases, lots of room.

How to Buy a New Car

I find it ironic that most people who buy new cars do so because they are broke. I do understand, sadly. I remember what it was like to have no money to buy a used car. And with financing so attractive for new autos, that often appears to be the only alternative.

If you are broke but feel you can afford a hefty new monthly payment, I want to encourage you not to buy new. Surely you have other options (like driving that clunker for another year as discussed earlier).

Yet buying a new car is not always a mistake. At times it is reasonable: (1) if you can either buy it with all cash or with a fairly short financing period of no longer than three years, and (2) if you plan to keep it and care for it meticulously for a long time. A *very* long time. Only then can you recover the loss on the front end due to depreciation.

The important thing is to know how to buy a new car confidently so you're sure that you've paid the very least for it. That means you need to go to "school" before you show up at the dealership.

Depending on the deal *du jour*, it's possible to drive out in a brand-new car without making much of a down payment, if at all. Such deals come and go, and at this writing 0-percent interest offers are showing up again to stimulate new car sales. It's enticing, remarkably easy, and therefore seems advisable. But don't kid yourself. Those low- or nothing-down deals—even with 0-percent interest—have a five- or six-year loan attached. There's nothing like multiplying a monthly payment by sixty or seventy-two to hit you with a rude awakening. Think: Alec and Tina. They are dying under the weight of a 0-percent auto loan.

Your assignment, should you choose to buy a new car, is to know as much as the salesperson does about the car you want to buy. Know the car, available options, and the actual cost that the dealer pays the manufacturer for each and every one. Never forget where the power of the transaction resides: in the party with the money—you.

What You Need to Know to Buy New

Consider the following elements when buying a new car, and in this order of importance:

1. *Price.* You must know with certainty how much you are willing to spend. Contrary to what a salesperson may suggest, the monthly payment is not your primary concern. The most important thing you need to know about a car is the full price of that car. Carry a calculator with you and do not be intimidated from inputting the monthly payment and multiplying by the number of months in the term. This is the first price tag you must consider.

2. *Cost to operate.* Every car has two price tags: (1) the price to purchase the car, and (2) the price to drive it: registration, licensing, insurance, fuel, maintenance and repairs. This second price tag is often overlooked in the excitement of getting a new car. The salesperson doesn't care about this second price tag, but it should make all the difference in the world to you.

3. *Loan terms.* In the event you will be financing this purchase (one day you will be paying all cash, I have faith), the interest rate and loan term come next in order of importance. You will want to land a favorable rate to allow you to pay off this auto loan in thirty-six months or less.

4. *Monthly payment.* This monthly payment needs to fit comfortably along with all of your other monthly expenses—within 80 percent of your net income. Never allow a salesperson to make the monthly payment your top priority. Keep control of the conversation and situation, never forgetting that the monthly payment, while important, is well down the line of importance.

5. *Resale value.* While you want a car that will hold its value, reselling it should not be in your top priorities. It comes near the bottom of the list.

6. *Color and options.* If you have a choice of color, that's fine. But putting this any place except at the bottom of your list of priorities is unwise.

The (Somewhat) Meaningless "Dealer's Invoice"

New cars have a sticker in the window with the manufacturer's suggested retail price (MSRP). Of course this is what the dealer wants you to pay. It is the retail price of that vehicle with the options listed. You never want to pay this price and you never should.

You may have heard you should pay no more than $100 over "dealer's invoice," the amount the dealer paid the manufacturer for this car. This is also called the "wholesale price." There was a time when the wholesale or dealer's invoice on any given car was difficult if not impossible to discover. But that's changed. This information is readily available at sites like *Edmunds.com* and others. But this has become somewhat meaningless, because dealers and manufacturers have invented new ways to bury fees and charges in the dealer's invoice.

The dealer's invoice fails to reveal financial incentives for the dealer, and something called "dealer holdback." This amount can be 2 to 3 percent of the cost of the car, and the manufacturer retains it for a period of time until after the car is sold. If you were to pay $100 over dealer invoice, that dealer would pocket a great deal more than $100. In fact, by the time all of the incentives and holdbacks are taken out of the picture, the true "invoice" amount can be hundreds,even thousands, of dollars below the invoice amount that has been seriously padded with all kinds of incentives and holdbacks.

How to Find the Real Number

The secret is to discover the dealers invoice minus any holdbacks, national dealer incentives, and customer rebates. That is the most important number you need to know.

You can purchase a report with this information from Consumer Reports (*ConsumerReports.org*). Their New Car Price Report costs $12 for one vehicle and $10 for each additional vehicle requested. This detailed report will give you the closest possible number for the true amount the dealer paid for the car you are interested in buying. Now add the dealer invoice for factory-installed options. Ignore (and always say no to) dealer-packs, such as undercoating, rustproofing, pinstriping, upholstery treating, and other unnecessary items. Subtract any rebates to the dealer or customer (you can learn about current rebates at *Carsdirect.com*), add the $100, or a reasonable markup, add the destination charge posted on the official sticker and add state and local tax.

Whew! Now you have the magic number for this specific car. And you know the amount you are willing to pay for it.

Let's say the magic number is $19,100. Fix that number in your mind. Engrave it on your frontal lobe. Become a broken record and never allow a salesman or manager to deter you from what you want—to pay $19,100 for this car.

Three-Year Rule

If you must finance this new car, make sure that you can pay the loan in full within three years (thirty-six months). This is critical. You want at least three years once this loan is paid to continue making the same payments to yourself. This will insure that you are prepared to repair or replace this car. Don't get caught in the trap of having car payments and repair bills at the same time—or worse, having no savings to buy this car's eventual replacement. Now you have options to either keep this car until the wheels fall off (in which case you will still need that nest egg growing to replace it because it will have little if any resale value) or upgrade while it still has value.

Arrange Your Own Financing

Dealer financing is rarely the best way to go. You will do much better if you go to your credit union, bank or a site like *CapitalOne.com* first before you even begin to shop for a car so you are "prequalified."

When financing is not an issue, you can negotiate more aggressively with a new-car salesperson. Don't visit a showroom unless you are prequalified, and never discuss how you're paying until you've negotiated the price.

Best Time to Shop

You want to shop on a day when there are more salespeople than customers. Now you can take advantage of the pressure that manufacturers put on dealers and dealers put on salespeople. Dealers work on a calendar month and year. This makes the last day of any month a good time to show up, as well as the last day of the year, December 31. And if it happens to be raining or snowing, it's even better. Storms cut down on willing buyers. Arriving near the end of the day puts you at an even better advantage.

Consider Dealership Alternatives

Costco, Sam's Club, and BJ's offer excellent auto sales programs for their members—a great way to go if you dread the negotiation process.

The discount clubs have arrangements with local dealerships for no-hassle, no haggling pricing, which is about $150 over dealer cost. Members also are entitled to any manufacturer's rebates, incentives, or special financing offers. You can find a participating dealer and the specially trained Authorized Dealer Contact for your specific area at *Costco.com*. Click on "Auto Sales." As a Costco member you will meet with a sale supervisor and bypass all of the negotiating process. You'll be handed an invoice with the Costco member price —a truly simple transaction.

There are also some no-negotiation dealerships referred to as "car stores." There are no commissioned salespeople, only order takers. The prices of the cars are discounted from the manufacturer's suggested retail price (MSRP) and dealer cost. If you absolutely cannot bear the thought of learning more than a salesman knows or don't want to negotiate, this arrangement might be a good option. Still, hold firm against add-ons like dealer-installed options or accessories. And never discuss a trade-in until you have set the price.

Remember our friends Alec and Tina? Now that we're informed, let's revisit their predicament. They have three choices:

1. Sell the SUV for the best price they can get, and then get a signature loan from their bank or credit union for the shortfall (about $12,000). While not ideal, paying off a $12,000 loan is a lot better than $33,335. In this scenario they take the $1,400 they have in savings and buy the best clunker they can find to get them by for now. In the meantime they should save each month the difference between the lower payment on the $12,000 loan and the payment they would have been making on the Trailblazer. This will create a nest egg to upgrade to a better clunker.

2. Keep the SUV but double up on the payments. If either Alec or Tina can take a part-time job and devote that entire paycheck to making double car payments, their SUV will be paid off in two to three years. That increases the likelihood they will drive a paid-for car for quite a few more years. However, once paid, they need to continue sizable monthly car payments to themselves in anticipation of replacing the Trailblazer.

3. Their third and only remaining option is to keep going with the loan they have, drive defensively, and drive as little as possible. They do not want to face big repair bills while still making huge monthly payments. Avoiding this may be difficult because, face it, five-year-old cars need repairs. But by changing the oil regularly, driving as few miles as possible, and keeping up with other routine maintenance, Alec and Tina will improve their chances.

The Dreaded Automobile Lease

Leasing an automobile is, in this author's opinion, a stupid way to drive a car. Forget about it. Leasing a car is a restrictive long-term rental. The car is not yours, but you are required to maintain, insure, license, and repair it as if it were.

Lease payments on new cars are not "a lot less" than what the payment would be if you were buying it. And it's not always true that you can get into a lease with nothing down. Read the fine print. It is not atypical for an auto lease to require $2,000 to $3,000 up front.

If You Want Out

If you are currently in an auto lease, concentrate on doing all you can to keep the vehicle in pristine condition with as few miles as possible (even then, expect to pay some excessive-wear or overmileage penalties).

Discern the earliest time you can terminate the lease. Then ride it out. This information will be found in your lease document under "Early Termination." You might also try selling it privately. If you attempt to trade in a leased vehicle that is still under contract in order to buy a new car, you will lose the maximum amount of money possible. Don't ever think you can walk out ahead on a trade-in. No one ever has. No one ever will.

Chapter Thirteen

Disaster, Disease, Death, and Other Fun Topics

I've been through some terrible things in my life,
some of which actually happened.

~ Mark Twain

With the money we've spent on insurance since we married in 1970, Harold and I could have easily paid cash for a summer home. Or a Rolls Royce.

Our auto insurance tab alone over the decades is stunning. Having insured two sons from learning permits to being on their own, we know a thing or two about paying through the nose for adequate coverage.

It kills me to think we flushed so much money down the drain for all the types of insurance we've carried through the years. Oh, I'm grateful that we never had a fire, flood, burglary, or other crisis to trigger a homeowner's insurance claim. I'm relieved that the auto insurance claims we have filed over the decades have been relatively insignificant in the big scope of things. And I'm happy that despite all the life insurance premiums we've paid, I've never received a payment as a beneficiary to a life insurance policy. Still, I cringe when I total all the premiums we've paid out.

Hey You...in the Back, Wake Up!

I wouldn't blame you if you find the subject of insurance so boring, complicated, and beyond comprehension you're tempted to skip this chapter and take a nap. I hear you. But please don't. Like it or not, insurance is one of life's must-haves.

If you drive a car, you must have insurance. If you have a dependent family, you must have life insurance. If you have a pulse, you must have health insurance. If you own a mortgage, you must have fire and liability insurance.

You don't have a choice; but insurance should not cost a fortune. You can do some things to keep your premiums low while not compromising the coverage you need. The secret to having insurance is to have just enough—but not too much—and then to pay as little as possible for adequate coverage in the event you actually need it one day.

General Guidelines

Insure Your Basic Needs

Nothing is righteous about carrying too much insurance or having duplicate coverage. You could easily wind up insurance-poor if you listen to every insurance salesperson and attempt to remove every risk from your life.

Share the Risk

You share risks with your insurance carrier by accepting larger deductibles. The deductible is the amount of money you agree to pay toward a loss before your insurance kicks in. Increasing your deductibles lowers your premiums.

File Claims Reluctantly

If you make too many claims—or the wrong kinds of claims—you run the risk of losing your low rates through outrageous increases to your premiums. Or worse, having your policies cancelled.

If that's not bad enough, most insurers these days report claims of their policyholders to big databases. Originally set up to detect and discourage fraud, these secret history files are now being used by insurers to determine coverage and rates.

The way to protect your history and also save money on your premiums is to know when not to file a claim. Don't be too hasty to report a claim if (1) the damage is less than $1,000 and no one was injured, (2) the loss is the result of your negligence, or (3) the damage involves water and/or "mold." Take care of the problem yourself to keep from having relatively small incidents place a black eye on your insurance history.

It is far better to carry a higher deductible and file claims rarely than to pay big bucks for a low-deductible policy and then file everything imaginable in an effort to "get your money's worth."

Press for Discounts

All policies can be subject to discounts for a plethora of conditions or situations for which the insured qualifies. Some discounts are more well-known than others. Here's an example: a simple spark arrester attached to the top of our chimney lopped $14 from our annual homeowner's premium. In truth, it's a $2.50 piece of window screen to prevent an errant spark from shooting out onto the roof. We discovered the possibility of this discount on our own after reading an article in a consumer magazine. Asking our agent if this was a possibility for us sent him to some big book on a shelf in his office, and sure enough, such a discount was available.

Never assume an insurance agent will volunteer every possible discount for which you are eligible. You have to prod. Ask the agent to peruse the list of every possible discount available on your auto and homeowner/renters insurance policies, and then strive to become eligible for them.

Build a Good History

Grab a highlighter because this next concept is important: Maintain good credit and driving records. Your credit score together with your driving record have a significant bearing on the cost of your health, automobile, and life insurance.

Remember, insurance is all about assessing risk. If you have a low credit score and numerous moving violations and/or accidents on your driving record, you appear to be one who takes unreasonable risks. You may be seen as accident-prone and reckless with your finances and behind the wheel. Many industries see a person's credit report as a character reference. Because these two reports are so important, you need to monitor them yourself.

Know your state's laws with regard to how long speeding tickets, accidents, and other moving violations stay on your record. Do all you can to improve your credit score (*MyFico.com* has an education channel). Live as though your life is an open book. It is in more ways than you think.

Shop Around

Insurance companies are in fierce competition. Before renewing your policies, make a few phone calls. Other companies will jump at the chance to give you a quote. You gotta' shop around!

If you get a lower bid, call your company to report your finding. Give them a chance to keep you. If they are not willing to match or beat that premium, say you'll be making a change. Longevity with a company may earn you discounts in the future, so don't make your decision hastily. But it takes many years of discounts to come close to a significant premium reduction.

Here's the bottom line: do all you can to stay with your company and at the same time force them to be competitive with their rates before making a switch.

Automobile Insurance

You're just about to make a decision on buying a new car. But before you drive out in a fancy European sports number, call your insurance agent or log on to *Edmunds.com*. Find out what it costs to insure that gem. Check with the Insurance Institute for Highway Safety (*IIHS.org*) for the auto's safety ratings.

While you're at that website, and before you make your decision, take a look at the repair statistics. Here's a clue: domestic cars are cheaper to insure because they cost less to repair. Cars that are highly desirable among thieves are more expensive to insure. Your premiums will increase significantly if your car is on law enforcement's "List of Cars Most Likely to Be Stolen."

Boring Is Cheapest

As a general rule you will keep your auto insurance premiums down when you choose to drive a domestic non-luxury, non-sports car. Just another reason perhaps that self-made millionaires, according to the authors of *The Millionaire Next Door*, by Thomas Stanley and William Danko (Pocket, 1998) drive late-model domestic cars. They are cheaper to buy, cheaper to repair and maintain, and cheaper to insure.

Bone Up on the Law

While laws vary from one state to the next, all fifty states have laws regarding financial responsibility and automobile insurance. Basically, if you drive without insurance you break the law.

The website *InsuranceLaw.com* lists insurance requirements by state. Know yours. Check it against your current policy. If your car is financed, you have little choice in the amount of coverage you carry, but you can shop insurers. The lender will set the requirements for the amount of insurance you must carry.

Unless you drive in a carpool or use your car in the course of work (in which case you need additional coverage for your passengers), likely you have no reason to increase your coverage beyond those limits. If you own your car outright, you have more options regarding insurance.

If the car has a market value of $2,500 or less, experts say you should consider canceling the collision portion of your policy.

Low Income and Assigned Risk

Many states have insurance available for low-income or high-risk drivers who because of their records cannot get conventional insurance. This kind of insurance is known as "assigned risk." You can find out more about the requirements and eligibility requirements for your state at *Insurancelaw.com*.

Capitalize on Your Connection to the Military

If you have a connection to the military—even if it's through your father, uncle, a relative by marriage, active or retired—you may be eligible to purchase automobile insurance through USAA Insurance (*USAA.com*). Let's hope you do qualify, because it will save you a boatload of money.

This is the same member-owned company, in business since the 1920s, that offers banking services to the public through USAA Federal Savings Bank. However—and this is an important clarification—USAA insurance products are limited to those who can prove they have a qualifying connection to the U.S. military.

Based in San Antonio, Texas, USAA offers insurance for its members in all fifty states. You cannot beat the low prices and high-quality coverage for property and casualty insurance, life insurance, automobile, and disability insurance. USAA customer service is exemplary, as is their attention to time and detail if you should have to file a claim.

If you have even the slightest hope of qualifying, give USAA a call at 800-292-8302 to find out if you can possibly meet the eligibility requirements. They will be able to help you make this determination over the phone. Once you are a member of USAA Insurance, you're in for life, even if your military connection retires or dies.

Don't Duplicate

Insurance is expensive enough, so you don't want to inadvertently carry double coverage. If you have homeowners or renter's insurance, you may not need personal property coverage on your vehicle to cover personal items that might be stolen from the car. If you have AAA road-assistance membership, you don't need a similar kind of towing service on your car's insurance policy. When you have a good health insurance plan, you typically do not need the medical protection offered on your auto insurance policy. But if you do not have insurance, this coverage could pay your bills if you and your passengers are injured.

Pay Less Frequently

Check your last insurance statements. Are you paying $5 or $10 extra just for the privilege of paying monthly? That might not sound like a lot until you multiply by twelve and then by the number of years you've been making monthly payments. Find out how to drop that fee. If it means you must pay quarterly, semi-annually, or even once a year, do it. Even the little stuff adds up.

Be a Good Driver

This is way beyond simply not putting on makeup or chatting on a hand-held mobile phone while driving (don't do that either). The secret of good driving is self-discipline and concentration. Defensive driving means you stick to the speed limit. Stop at stop signs and red lights not just to prevent accidents but to avoid tickets too.

Moving violations are increasingly more expensive as cities and counties are more and more strapped for revenue. To add injury to the insult of a $250 ticket, expect your premiums to shoot through the roof; you'll be lucky if they don't cancel you altogether.

Traffic School

If you or anyone listed on your family policy gets a speeding ticket or other moving violation, enroll in a state-approved traffic school, if available. In California an errant driver can attend traffic school once every two or three years, depending on the county. The driver must still pay the ticket, the cost of traffic school, and the cost of missing work if that becomes necessary. But once he's completed the required hours, the ticket is removed from his record. It disappears so it is not reported to the insurance company.

As expensive as a ticket and traffic school may be ($300 or more depending on the offense), it's considerably less than the cost of a premium increase. You will have to pay for the ticket anyway. You might as well get the ticket forgiven, if at all possible. Sitting for eight long hours in traffic school is something you will not want to repeat, so that becomes a deterrent to future tickets.

Qualify for Discounts

Non-smokers typically get discounts on auto insurance. Got a degree? At least one major auto insurer has determined that degreed drivers are more cautious and therefore less prone to filing a claim. They give a discount for that.

Companies give good student discounts for youthful drivers who stay in school and get good grades. Some states offer defensive driving courses for which insurance companies offer attendees a nice discount. Insure all of your cars with the same company, get a discount. If that company also has your home insurance, expect a double discount. You may get a discount if your car is outfitted with ABS braking system or other safety specifications.

In addition, the type of vehicle you buy could greatly affect your premium. A flashy red sports car usually costs more to insure than a mid-sized sedan. This is also true of vehicles on the most-stolen list.

Increase Your Deductible

The deductible is the amount of money you have to pay before your insurance company begins paying the rest. According to the Insurance Information Institute, the difference between an automobile insurance premium with a $200 deductible and the same coverage with $1,000 deductible could be 50 percent or more.

You'll pay for minor incidents anyway to protect your insurance history, so you might as well get a discount for that. Raising your deductible to $500 and eventually $1,000 is wise, provided you have that $1,000 in the event of a catastrophe.

Choosing to have a high deductible brings its own reward. You'll be more cautious and less willing to take risks when you know you'll have to come up with that first $1,000.

Drop Collision and Comprehensive

Collision is the part of your auto policy that pays for damage you do to yourself or your own car in an accident. Comprehensive insurance covers damage done by a force other than another car and driver, such as hail, fire, flood, flying squirrels, and so on.

If you have a newer car, you are well-advised to carry collision and comprehensive with a high deductible. If your car is financed, you have no choice; you must carry collision. However, once your car gets to the age and condition that if mishaps occur you're not likely to get it fixed—opting to replace the car instead—drop the collision and comprehensive coverages. Use the difference in premium to boost your new car fund.

Shop Around

Once each year when it's time for your auto insurance to renew, take an hour or so to call several insurance companies or go online. If companies you contact can't beat what you have, you will gain confidence in knowing you've got the best rate.

If they can beat your rate, call your current company with the details of that lower quote. If they won't match it, go with the lower rate. But chances are they will match it because they don't want to lose a good customer. And if you do make a switch, you've just saved yourself some money. Not bad for an hour or two of your time.

Insure Your Health

Health insurance is another of life's must-haves. Be grateful if you have a group plan through your employer. That remains the cheapest form of health insurance.

If you are self-employed or work for a company that does not offer a health insurance plan as a benefit, perhaps you've called to get a quote for an individual health insurance policy for you and your family. It's enough to give you a heart attack. But you are taking an intolerable risk if you go without health insurance altogether. While you might believe you are saving money, it's a risk you cannot afford.

The risks of no coverage are too great. It's not just the money. People without health insurance die sooner because they receive less preventive care and are less likely to have major diseases detected early. Medical bills are a factor in one out of five personal bankruptcy filings—the direct cause in one out of ten. You dare not be without health insurance. You can, though, take steps to reduce the cost of health insurance:

How to Cut the Cost

High-deductible policy. A high deductible policy ($2,500 per person is not out of the question as a last resort), sometimes referred to as "catastrophic insurance," is meant to be there in the event of a big health crisis that requires expensive treatments and hospitalization. You'll have to pay for all office visits, prescriptions, and other routine health maintenance, or what insurers consider the little stuff. For this arrangement you will get a very affordable premium.

You may assume that with a huge deductible it's as if you don't have insurance at all. But this type of coverage has a hidden benefit: it will entitle you to pay the lower insurer-negotiated discounts with hospitals and doctors. If you have no insurance, many health providers will actually charge you more than the amount an insured person pays for the exact same procedure.

Here's an example: An individual HMO policy from Blue Cross with $500 deductible could cost a twenty-five-year- old single person living in Los Angeles about $287 a month. But change that to a $2,500 deductible and the premium drops to $55. You have coverage for the catastrophic possibilities, but the monthly premium is about as low as they come.

Call Sam. Sam's Club has added individual personal health insurance to its line-up of member services. The policies have high-deductibles (like $1,500 per person per year), but come with prescription coverage and a relatively low premium. Learn more at *SamsClub.com* or call 888-799-8000 to get a quote.

Health Savings Account. An HSA is not something you purchase; it's a savings account into which you can deposit money on a tax-preferred basis. An HSA allows you to save pretax dollars to pay for the high deductible ($2,500 in the example above) if the need arises and other out-of-pocket medical expenses not covered by your insurance, such as dental and vision care.

Along with an HSA you must purchase a high-deductible health plan, one that will cover you should your medical expenses exceed the funds in your HSA. You can learn more about HSAs at *Treas.gov.* Another site, *HSAinsider.com,* will answer your questions about this beneficial cost-savings tool and help you locate an insurer too. (The Blue Cross HMO reference above is only one of many companies that offer such a plan.) Simply select your state then "Find."

Some insurers will offer you the insurance policy and the HSA in one package so you will not have to open a separate account. Other insurers offer just the insurance policy, and you will have to find a bank or other trustee to open your HSA. The two largest trustees for HSAs are MSA Bank (*MSAbank.com*) and First MSA (*FirstMSA.com*).

Join the Farm Bureau. You don't have to be a farmer to join the Farm Bureau in your state. Everyone is eligible to apply for membership by paying a nominal annual membership fee. Members are eligible to receive the many benefits and services available. One of these services is health insurance. As an example, residents of California are eligible to join the California Farm Bureau Federation (*CFBF.com*) The annual membership dues vary according to county of residence. CFBF members are eligible for health insurance through Nationwide (*NHPCalifornia.com*). To find the Farm Bureau for your state, simply do an Internet search for "Farm Bureau" plus your state.

By way of example, a single parent with two dependent children has health insurance coverage as a member of the Tennessee Farm Bureau (*TNFarmBureau.org*) with a reasonably low deductible and prescription coverage too. At this writing her premium is less than $250 a month; membership dues are about $25 a year.

Become a small group. In some cases, two people are enough to qualify as a small business "group." Costco (*Costco.com*) for example has teamed up with quality insurance carriers in a handful of states (parts of CA; HI, NV, OR, WA) to offer its Executive Business Members great health plans. Your "group" can enjoy quality health benefits at a group price with competitive rates. At the Costco website, look for "Business Services" then "Health Insurance" for more information and details. The health insurance plan offered by Costco qualifies as a high-deductible plan with which you could pair an HSA.

Trade associations. Depending on your profession and interests, there may be trade groups to which you belong or are eligible to join that offer group health insurance to its members. For example, the National Small Business Association is such an organization for self-employed or small-business owners, and the National Writer's Association offers health insurance as a member benefit.

Alumni and business associations often work out insurance deals with an insurance company, which includes a discount for association members. Ask your association's director about any such deals.

Insure Your Life

The secret to cutting the cost of life insurance is to make sure you have the right amount and the right type of policy. If you don't need life insurance, you'll save a bundle by simply getting rid of it. Just because you are alive docs not mean you need life insurance.

Do You Need It?

The purpose for life insurance is to replace your income, should you die, for those who are financially dependent on you. This would include minor children, perhaps a spouse, and possibly elderly parents in the event you now provide for their care and financial support.

Life insurance is not to make someone rich in the event of your sudden demise (in select situations, life insurance is used as an estate planning tool, but this is rare). Life insurance assures that those people who are dependent on you now will not fall into financial peril if your paycheck were to suddenly disappear.

If you are single, your children are grown, your spouse has an independent source of income and would not be thrown into financial ruin without your income, or you are independently wealthy, you most likely do not need life insurance. If you do fall into those categories and you do have life insurance, you may be overinsured, meaning that you are paying for something you may not need.

How Much?

If you determine that you need life insurance, the general rule of thumb is that you need eight times your gross annual income. That means if you earn $50,000 a year you should have at least $400,000 in life insurance. Theoretically, this is an amount on which, when invested carefully, your dependents could live without worry for three to four years—the time it would reasonably take for them to get on their feet and on with their lives. That is the purpose of life insurance, not to turn your heirs into wealthy people who will never have to work again.

Term Insurance

Pure, single-purpose life insurance is called "term insurance." If you die your beneficiary receives a check for the face value of your insurance policy, called the "death benefit." If you need life insurance, you want to buy only term insurance.

Term insurance is cheap compared to "whole life" insurance, which has cash value and combines a death benefit with an investment feature. Whole life insurance is expensive, complicated, and not advised for the person looking to cut the cost of life insurance without sacrificing the benefit.

Refinance

If you have a multiple-year policy (many life insurance policies have the premiums fixed for ten, fifteen, or even twenty years with a guarantee that the rate will not increase during that term), you are not obligated to keep it for that long. Rates for term insurance have dropped remarkably over the past decade, so it is possible to replace your current policy with a new one with a much-lower premium. Don't assume that because you're older now, insurance will cost more. If you find a better deal, grab it first, make sure the policy is in effect, and then cancel the older, more-expensive coverage. Make sure your current policy doesn't lapse until your new coverage is securely in place. Keep paying on the old policy until the new one is issued.

Coverage through Employer

Don't assume you have the best rate because you get it through your employer's group provider. In fact, this is usually the most expensive way to buy life insurance because the premiums are based on the persons in the group with the highest risks.

Shop Around

A good broker has access to many companies and can find you the best deal. Or you can shop quite conveniently at sites like *Insurance.com, Intelliquote.com,* and *Accuquote.com.* Compare all of the rates. With some companies you may qualify as "preferred" or "preferred plus," while other companies see you as having a more risky profile. If you are a member of Sam's Club (*SamsClub.com*) you may be eligible for rates 20 percent lower that the typical policy. Have a military connection: Don't forget you are eligible for coverage through USAA.

Lock In Coverage

Once you locate the cheapest rate, try to lock it in for a long time, twenty or thirty years. You will then have guaranteed-level premium coverage at that rate for as long as you need the insurance, even if rates increase in the future. However, keep in mind that you are not locked in for the full term. You can leave at will in favor of a better deal you might find in the future.

Insure Your Home and Possessions

Going without insurance on your home is, in my opinion, simply not an option. At the very least, you need enough fire insurance to satisfy the requirements of your lender if you have a mortgage. But beyond that you need some amount of insurance to cover the contents and also liability insurance to protect your financial assets. In addition, some regions of the country require specific "disaster-related" insurance. Know what is required where you live. You can save money on homeowners insurance in a number of ways.

Go for the Discounts

I know I am repeating myself, but let me simply remind you to make sure you are getting credit for every possible discount available for which you qualify. This keeps more money in your pocket. Anything that reduces your risk of having a claim may be rewarded with lower premiums.

Review Your Policy

I venture to say that most policyholders don't really know what their policy says, what it covers, what it excludes, or the myriad of disclaimers that limit their ability to be compensated in the event of an insured tragedy. Fortunately companies are making policies more reader-friendly, but don't expect this to be a light summer read. Slog through it—every single paragraph.

Insure Your Home, Not Your Dirt

While your home and its contents are at risk of fire, theft, and other perils, the dirt on which it sits is not. When deciding how much insurance you need to buy, do not count the value of the land. In some areas that can be 30 to 50 percent of the home's value.

Increase Your Deductible

Because you are not going to look to your homeowners insurance for small loses you can handle, there's no sense paying for the ability to do that. Opt for the highest deductible you can reasonably imagine covering. If you take a $500 deductible, your premium should drop by 12 percent. But you'll experience major savings if you can see your way clear to accept a $5,000 deductible—35 percent or more!

Use the Same Company

By placing your homeowner and auto coverages with the same company, you will get another discount. The longer you stay with the company without filing a claim, the bigger that discount will be.

Add an Umbrella

Consider adding an additional personal or "umbrella" liability policy to beef up your coverage as a homeowner or renter. Umbrella liability insurance is so named because it acts like an umbrella, sitting on top of your auto and homeowner's liability policies to provide extra protection. (Even if you don't own a home, remember that you still need renter's insurance to cover both your liability and your personal property.)

Use It and Lose It

While this principle holds for every type of insurance, for some reason it is especially egregious with your home's coverage. As odd and patently unfair as it may sound, the best way to get your premium increased- or cancelled altogether, is to even appear that you might have a reason to make a claim. This is another reason to carry a very high deductible to cover only the major stuff and then take care of the smaller stuff yourself. Calling your agent to ask if you are covered for water damage or mold could result in a cancellation, even if you do not have a problem or ever file the claim.

Don't Smoke

Non-smokers get discounts on homeowner's insurance. Most house fires involve cigarettes, so when someone in the home smokes, the likelihood of a fire increases significantly. Smokers put themselves, their families, and their homes at greater risk than Non-smokers.

Improve Your Security

Insurance companies offer handsome discounts to policyholders who go the extra mile with preventive measures. Install deadbolts on all outside doors and automatic security lighting on the outside of your home. A security system may net you an even greater discount. If you're shopping for a system, find out which one(s) your insurer recommends to get the best discount. Install smoke and CO_2 detectors and change the batteries every six months religiously.

Know Thy Water Heater

Make sure you know how old your water heater is and its life expectancy (add a couple of years to the warranty period to get a good idea). A rusted-out water heater can result in a flood, especially if it happens when you are out of town. Replacing it before it rusts through is one way to make sure you don't have to file a claim, which is about the best way to keep your premiums as low as possible.

Maintain, Maintain, Maintain

Water lines on washing machines, dishwashers, toilets, and sinks wear out with time. Replace them routinely, every couple of years. If you're going to get flooded it will likely be the result of a hose blowout—when you're not home, of course. Keep your roof in good shape; don't allow faucets to drip or toilets to leak. Live with the same care and consciousness you would if you had no insurance. And in the event that big disaster hits, you'll have your opportunity to place a substantial claim.

Finally, opt for an annual premium payment schedule if your company tacks on service fees for collecting more often and review your coverage once a year. You don't want to unwittingly be paying more to insure items you sold years ago.

Chapter Fourteen

Travel and Family Fun

*This is no longer a vacation. It's a quest. It's a quest for fun.
I'm gonna have fun, and you're gonna have fun!*

~ Chevy Chase, as Clark Griswold in *Vacation*

If you make one mistake in your quest to live your life for less, let it not be the elimination of family fun and entertainment. You need to keep your life in balance and find ways to do the things you love for a lot less money.

I've seen this happen so many times: A person or couple experiences a kind of financial epiphany after reading a book or attending a seminar: *We have to stop spending money!*

The sentiment is certainly sound, provided they mean spending money they do not have. But too many do the equivalent of saying they will never eat again, after they've polished off a Thanksgiving Day meal and are so stuffed they cannot move. At the moment, the thought of *ever eating* is unimaginable, and the commitment to not eat again is high. But of course, it's not reality.

Someone who makes a new financial commitment after making too many money mistakes does the same thing. They make a list of everything now banned from their lives for as long as it takes them to get out of debt. They hang their RDRP (lingo for my *Rapid Debt-Repayment Plan*, a visual road map for how and when they will be debt-free) on the 'fridge right next to a list of "no-mores"—no more eating out, movies, trips, clothes, gifts. The list goes on and on.

I understand. Once you make a U-turn on the road to where you are headed (financial trouble) and now seek the road to solvency (financial freedom), you get this burst of determination to make double payments, triple if possible. You are so motivated, you just need to think of a few more things to eliminate.

Just like that, these overly zealous folks move from one out-of-balance situation to another. Their new austerity plan lasts slightly longer than the plan to never eat again. Both are unrealistic and totally unreasonable. They've set themselves up to fail, and so they do.

I've seen thousands of people turn their lives around, get out of debt, and go on to become affluent. And I've seen many try and fizzle. Those who make it follow a specific plan and stay in balance. They give, they save, and they see some kind of entertainment as essential in their lives even though they are in debt. All these elements provide balance and make the journey bearable.

Don't expect this chapter to be an exhaustive treatment of all the ways you can save on travel, or every possible way a family can have fun together. My intention is to stimulate your creative juices and build your confidence by giving you good, solid advice on how to find cheap travel, how to save money on movies, and some other neat ideas for your next family vacation.

Air Travel: Same Flight, Different Fares

The flight should have been less than three hours. But bad weather forced us to circle high above tornadoes threatening the Dallas-Fort Worth airport for another two hours. Finally the pilot announced we were heading to Austin before we ran out of fuel.

The people around me began chatting, and conversation turned to how much each of us paid for our round-trip ticket on this extended flight. Everyone pulled out ticket receipts for a group comparison. The lowest was $188, the highest, $876. As I recall, the high fare belonged to my seat mate. Mine was $188.

How can six people occupy identical seats but pay six different amounts? It's something called "fare basis." One airline may have as many as twenty different fare bases (also called "published fares") for each of the seats on any given flight. Clearly my $188 was at or close to the bottom on that particular flight, while my neighbor was at the top, paying full-fare coach. I booked my flight well in advance and met the requirement at the time to stay over Saturday on this nonrefundable ticket. His ticket may have been purchased at the last minute with a refundable provision.

Here's the important thing to know about airline fares, using my $188 seat as an example. Logically, if everyone in coach with me on that flight had booked their seats when I did, we would all get that $188 fare. But that's not the case. More likely, there were only two $188 seats on that entire flight. But of course that flight could be advertised at the $188 rate followed by lines of fine print about restrictions.

Not only are published fares complicated, they constantly change. A conservative estimate is that if you consider all of each individual airline's published fares, it takes thousands of updates in a single day to keep all data current. No wonder I can search six different times in one day and come up with six completely different results. But have no fear, there are ways to discover the lowest fare for the trip you wish to take.

It takes time and effort to assure that when you travel you pay the lowest possible price for your seat under the least restrictive terms and the best conditions. There is no one-stop-shopping when it comes to travel. You cannot count on one resource to be the only place you find the lowest fares and best deals.

If there's one area of life that requires serious homework, it's traveling for half the price. But you will be paid handsomely for your time and effort.

Every airline has a long list of "published rates" that change often. Let's use travel between Los Angeles and New York City as an example. Many airlines fly that route, and one airline alone could have twenty different published rates for the same seat in coach, each rate with different conditions. And possibly each flight has only a few seats at the cheapest published rate.

Determine the Lowest Published Rate

You can search many ways for airfares and you'll get a wide variety of results. But without knowing the lowest published rate so you can compare your results, you'll waste a lot time and get confused. So the first thing you need to discover is the lowest published rate for the route you want to travel. You can search for this rate in two ways—by phone and by the Internet.

By phone. Call the toll-free reservations number of an airline you know that flies the route you want to travel. Tell the reservations agent you are not sure of the dates you want to fly (even if you have a good idea). Ask the agent to bring up the list of published rates for the route you have in mind and to please scroll down to the bottom to tell you the cheapest rate and its terms. This will be an unusual request, but the information is not confidential. Be friendly and cordial. If this agent is not cooperative, kindly end the call, and then call back to speak to someone else.

Once you have identified the lowest published rate, ask the agent to check the dates you wish to fly to see if that fare is available. Easy as that. If you like what you hear, book it. If not, you now have a valuable bit of information (the lowest published rate) to continue your search.

Online. Go to the online travel agency *Travelocity.com*. In the box labeled "The Best Priced Trip," fill in *only* the "From" and "To" fields. Do not put in any dates, even if you know the dates you wish to fly. Now click on "Flexible Dates," then "Search Flights."

This will give you a broad range of published rates from many airlines, starting with the cheapest. Here's an example at this writing: Round trip rate between Orange County (close to Los Angeles) and Newark (close to New York City) for $183 on the low end to $1,005 on the high end. Clicking on "Rules" for the $183 fare shows these conditions: fourteen-day advance purchase, no refunds, and a requirement to stay over a Saturday—and only on selected flights. Aha! That sounds like that airline's lowest published rate.

But alas, just because a published rate of $183 exists for at least one seat on one flight for that route on that airline doesn't mean there's a ticket available at that rate. (Ah, the wild and whacky world of airline ticketing.) But there could be, and that's where the fun begins—finding it.

Next click on "Select" to see the flights that have a seat available for this fare. If you find the fare for your dates, book it here or call the airline directly to avoid the booking fee. But keep in mind, you may have stumbled onto a "Webfare," and the agent may not have booking access to it.

In Search of Cheap Seats

Online travel agencies. The Internet allows you to play travel agent at sites like Expedia, Travelocity, and Orbitz. What makes these "travel agencies" and not online search engines is that they actually sell the product. You pay them directly, not the airline or hotel or rental car agency. They are paid a commission by the travel entity in the same way a more traditional travel agent is paid.

As you check each of the online agencies, expect different results. One might turn up information the others do not for the same flights. Just keep comparing what you find to the lowest published fare you already found. It's possible you can find that low fare online and on a flight unavailable if you talked with the reservations agent first.

One advantage of online agencies is their package deals. Typically these include a rental car and or hotel room. These agencies run travel specials all the time, which may warrant your consideration. If you are truly flexible and looking to book a vacation, check their last-minute deals. You never know what might surface. But make sure you have your bags packed. They are truly last-minute deals.

Hint: If you are booking at the last minute, you might beat the best round-trip price available by booking the same itinerary with a hotel room thrown in. Many times a tour company like Pleasant Holidays will offer a package deal that includes round-trip airfare plus seven nights in a nice hotel. And the price is considerably less than the round-trip ticket purchased alone from the airline. Even if you can't use the hotel room, you'll get the round-trip ticket for much less.

Travel search engines. Unlike online agencies where you actually book and purchase travel products (airline tickets and hotel rooms), search engines just look for online published Web fares. These sites are like little robots that run all over cyberspace grabbing fares for your consideration. No robot is perfect, so it's not a bad idea to run your search on several engines.

SideStep (*SideStep.com*) is a good travel search engine, with an option to download its free software to your hard drive (you can opt to access this information from the SideStep website). The process takes literally seconds, and you'll get an icon on your toolbar. SideStep will turn up many options with small regional airlines, including one-way fares that are very competitive.

BookingBuddy (*BookingBuddy.com*) and Mobissimo (*Mobissimo.com*) operate much the same as SideStep but with no downloads required.

Booking Buddy lets you compare all of the results from Expedia, Orbitz, Travelocity, Hotwire, Priceline, and 1-800-Cheapseats. You can also search each of the airlines websites from *BookingBuddy.com*.

Every travel search engine has its own unique features and as such can turn up different results. It takes little effort to run a search on each of them just to confirm you're getting the best rate for your particular need at the time.

Airline websites. All airlines have websites now where you can search and book online. And they like it when you do, because you save them a lot of money. Expect booking bonuses in the form of frequent flyer miles only when you book directly at the airline's website. The bonus miles will show up in your account once your travel is complete.

Most airline websites provide complete flight schedules online as well as schematics for the seating arrangements in their fleet of aircraft. The more you know before you book a flight, the better experience you will have.

Name-your-price sites. Priceline (*Priceline.com*) offers a travel option where you name a price you'd be willing to pay to get from point A to point B. Once you name your price, Priceline checks with major airlines to see if they would be willing to sell you a seat for that price.

This may be a good alternative for travelers with time and flexibility. The problem is, you must pay for your ticket before you find out specifics (like the time of day you will travel, how many stops you have to make, or how long a layover is required to reach your destination). Once again, you have a much better chance of getting the price you want if you go in with a good idea about the lowest published rate for the itinerary you need. At least you'll know if you're in the lowest possible ballpark.

Priceline will prompt you if you've come in so ridiculously low there is no way your bid will be accepted. For what it's worth, I scoffed at their promptings one time and landed the price I offered.

Priceline is a good alternative for that last-minute flight you need to book. If you are just two or three days out, the airlines are pretty sure how many empty seats they'll have on any specific flight, so selling one for at least something generally makes sense. But remember, the restrictions are formidable.

Ticket consolidators. These companies buy big blocks of tickets from major airlines for resale. And they buy them from obscure airlines you've never heard of as well as the biggies. Consolidators (*CheapTickets.com* is one of the recognized names on the Internet) are limited in what they can offer because they do not buy tickets on every flight.

Buying from a consolidator can, therefore, be risky, but the attractive price can ease the pain. It sure can't hurt to check to see what is available that fits your need.

Because consolidators offer the best deals on international travel, it would be worth your time to check a site like *AirlineConsolidators.com* and also the Sunday paper for ads on really cheap fares. Again, read the fine print. Know what you must give up in terms of cancellation, change, and on board amenities for that dirt-cheap ticket.

Discount warehouse clubs. All of the big three—Sam's Club, Costco, and BJ's—offer their members vacation packages, such as cruises and other travel deals. Check current offerings at their respective websites: *SamsClub.com, Costco.com.* and *BJs.com.* Their prices are competitive and typically devoid of many of the fees you would pay when booking through a traditional travel agent or cruise operator.

Travel agents. Think of a travel agent as the place you get a first or second opinion for long trips that have complicated connections, multiple city travel, and especially travel abroad. A travel agent will not likely be of great benefit in getting the best deal for short, quick trips.

These days a travel agent has to be really good at finding great deals to stay in business. Over the years, the travel agency industry has been beaten down by the travel industry, which has greatly reduced the commissions they pay. And because a travel agent is a commissioned sales-person, you can bet you will not hear about any deals that do not pay a commission. Can't say I blame the agent. Still, that is not reason enough for me to pay more through a travel agent than I will to book the fare myself.

Frequent flier clubs. Join every club for every airline you fly. There is no cost to join and even if you believe you will never fly this partic-ular airline again, who knows? Once you've accumulated enough miles to earn a reward, use them to buy expensive tickets, not fares on deep discount.

Value the free ticket at the price of a standard excursion fare, which at the time of this writing is about $400 to $500. That means one mile is worth about two cents. Getting them for free is a good thing. But one caution: purposely charging things on a credit card in an effort to earn more miles is really stupid if those charges go on to create debt. Paying 16.99 percent interest each month on dollars for which you earned 2 cents toward a reward ticket makes no sense.

Creative Ticketing

If you are willing to spend the time and get creative there are clever ways you can save even more money on air travel.

One-way trip. Buying a round-trip ticket even though you need to fly only one way may save you money, because typically a one-way tick-et is expensive compared to a more-competitive round-trip. Of course, the return portion of the ticket will be lost when you are a no-show, but you spent less money.

Split ticketing. Booking an end-to-end combination is a clever way to cut the cost when a nonstop flight is more expensive than a connect-ing or direct flight. The way to do this is to split your itinerary into two separate round-trips. This will give you the option to use two different airlines to get the best deals on both.

When researching your itinerary through one of the online travel agencies, use the "Multiple Flights" option. For example, instead of inputting Boston as your origin and Honolulu as your destination, select multiple flights to open a third window that will allow you to type in three locations—Boston, San Francisco, and Honolulu. The results will show you the airline(s) that fly this route and connecting services in San Francisco.

Hotels

Finding bargain rates on overnight accommodations is easier than ever, thanks to online travel agencies and other sites, such as *Hotels.com*, that double as researching assistants.

Like airlines, most hotel and motel chains operate excellent websites that allow you to search and book online as well. But following a few guidelines will insure that you get the best deal possible.

Before booking a hotel, assess your needs. A family on vacation has different needs than a business traveler attending a convention in the heart of a big city. A new breed of establishments that are a cross between a motel and hotel may fit your needs and your budget more readily than a full-service fancy hotel complete with bell people to tip, valets to tip, room service with added service charges, dry cleaners, restaurants, and a steep parking fee added onto the daily rate.

Chains like Courtyard, Homewood Suites, Embassy Suites, and Holiday Inn Express (there are many others) offer excellent accommodations without all the add-ons you neither need nor want. These chains do not have bellmen or valets. They do, however, include in the price of the room some kind of small kitchen with a refrigerator and often a stove or microwave, breakfast in the lobby, free parking, high-speed Internet, and so on.

Which number to call? Do your research online, but when it comes to actually booking the reservation, do not call the chain's 1-800 central reservations number. You'll be tempted to do this because it is a free call, but don't yield to temptation. Calling that operator who books rooms for hundreds of locations will get you the rack rate and that's it. Don't book it through the website either. Pay for the call to the exact location's front desk to negotiate your price and book your reservation.

Rack rate. This term always makes me laugh. What it means is the full price of a hotel room—the price quoted on the company's website. Never pay the rack rate. There is always a discount for which you can qualify.

Time to call. Try not to call during the rush hours of early morning or late evening. Front-desk personnel are up to their eyeballs in guests checking out and checking in. Try 10 P.M. after things have settled down. At least one travel expert insists that calling at 4 .P.M on a Sunday is the best time to get a great rate. Top management is likely not working on Sunday afternoon, and the front-desk clerks need to sell rooms. You are more likely to get the lower rate.

The price of a hotel room is always negotiable. In fact, there could be twenty or more different rates for the rooms in a single establishment. There are corporate discounts, family discounts, discounts to members of organizations like AAA, AARP, Mobile and Chevron Clubs, just to name a few. Start by asking which discounts might apply. You discovered the rack rate when you visited this company's website, so you know where to start. If you cannot get a rate you like, excuse yourself and call a competitor.

Know your add-ons. The price you are quoted will be for the room itself. Most hotels do not mention the occupancy and sales taxes, which can be excessive. Bring it up. Ask what that will be exactly. Is there an additional charge for parking? Is breakfast included in the rate?

In-room phone. Beware. Some hotels charge as much as $3 for each local call plus 10 cents a minute when that call goes over three minutes. Place a direct long-distance call from your room or dial up your laptop modem through the room phone and leave it on for a few hours, and you're likely to add on the cost of an entire night's stay.

One of the first things you should do when you get to the room is read the phone-call pricing policy. It should be posted close to the telephone. Are local calls free? Is there a charge to dial a toll-free number? This is one of those hidden profit centers for the hotel.

If you have a cell phone, use it. If you do not have a cell phone, use the pay phone in the hotel lobby along with your prepaid phone card that you carry with you at all times. If local and toll-free calls are free from your room, use your prepaid phone card in your room for all non-local calls.

Minibar. If there's a fully stocked minibar in your room, look out. There could be a $3 minisoda and $16 bag of cashews in your future. You can nip this potential problem in the bud if you ask the bellman who delivered your bags to your room to empty the minibar and inform the front desk. Now you have a refrigerator in which you can keep drinks and food items you purchase from the deli or store down the street.

Rental Cars

If you are not careful, all the money you saved on the airline ticket and overnight accommodations will disappear in the rental-car bill. Do not let the thought of renting an automobile throw you into an emotional tailspin. A highly commissioned salesperson sits behind the desk, so remember that everything you hear is geared to getting more of your money from your wallet and into her pocket. It's a friendly competition, and you need to win this one.

Call your insurance agent first. If you know you will be renting a car, do yourself a favor and call your personal automobile insurance agent ahead of time. Find out what coverage you have that applies to renting a car. Typically your collision and liability insurance covers you in any car you drive. Beyond that, ask about something called "loss of use." The rental agent will bring this up, so be prepared. If you were to wreck the rental and they hit you with a charge to cover the loss of revenue they suffered while the rental was being repaired, would your insurance pay for this? It should, and if your agent is unsure and defaults to the position that it probably does not, do not settle for that. Make sure he reads the policy and tells you for certain one way or the other. Then read it for yourself to verify.

Plan to be badgered about insurance by the rental agency when you reserve the car. If your insurance covers everything, be strong. Just say no.

Which number? Just as when booking your hotel room you called the location directly, avoid the car-rental company's toll-free numbers. Call the exact location where you will rent the car to get the best rate and the best car. And if there's an agency at the airport and another downtown, call both to compare rates. Don't be afraid to ask for an upgrade once a low rate has been offered. Saturday morning is a good time to call if you need a car the following week. Most weekly renters return cars on Friday night, so what appeared to be an empty lot yesterday could show a glut of cars on Saturday.

Daily rate. You will be quoted daily rates when you research and eventually book a rental car. But don't get too excited. That is not the true rate, only the base rate. Many things that can push that daily rate through the sky. So brace yourself and know what's coming. Be prepared with the right answer to the questions you will be asked.

Fuel charges. Brace yourself for this method of customer fleecing. If you do not return the car filled to the brim with fuel (allow for time to find a cheap station before returning), you run the risk of paying $4 or more a gallon, and they will charge you for a full tank of gas even if you use only a partial tank. It's just too confusing, too expensive to buy fuel from the car-rental company. Always opt for returning the car full of gasoline, and then don't forget to do so before you return the car.

Add-on charges. Ask ahead of time about the add-on charges. You will be shocked to see the taxes, surcharges, airport fees (even if the rental agent is not located at the airport), city fees, a charge to wash the car, and on and on. Companies do not always disclose these fees, but you want to know what they are before you agree to the rental contract.

That original daily rate that was so attractive can double right before your eyes if you are not careful and willing to speak up. Some add-ons are unavoidable (taxes and government-mandated surcharges) but others can be negotiated, like the fee to wash the car or the massive insurance-coverage options.

Extra driver. Many companies will charge you an additional $5 or more a day if you plan to allow a second driver. You dare not say no to this option and then allow someone else to drive the car. Just be aware of this possible charge. Some companies do not charge additional for an extra driver, so you need to ask up front.

Drop-off charges. Returning a car to a location other than the place you picked it up can be expensive. Know exactly what this will be before you choose such an option. As much as hundreds in "drop-off" charges can be tacked on, so beware.

Twenty-four-hour clock. If you rent a car for one day but lose track of time and return it 24.5 hours later, you may be hit with an additional day's rental charge. Ask about this before you agree to the rental. You want a company that gives a generous grace period of at least an hour and then charges a partial rate per hour thereafter.

Independent rental agencies. Visit *CarRentalExpress.com* where more than three hundred independent car-rental agencies are independently rated by consumers. At this site you can also compare the rates of the national agencies.

Online travel agencies. Travelocity, Hotwire, Expedia, and Priceline are online travel agencies that book car rentals. At Priceline you can name your own price as you would the price of an airline ticket. Keep in mind, and I know I run the risk of being redundant, but this is important. The price quoted is only the daily rate devoid of all of the taxes, fees, and surcharges that will be added.

Book together. Often when you book an airline flight through an airline directly, its website, or with an online travel agency, you will be offered an option to add on a rental car or a hotel room. This might be a good deal, but you'll only know if you have done your homework and know how to compare those rates.

Fun on Family Vacations

Free Factory Tours

Free factory tours can make for great vacation fun, especially when the company manufactures something kids like. Free samples can't hurt! You may not have to travel far to take one of these fun field trips. There may be tours right in your own city.

Here's just a sampling of free tours available in different parts of the country:

Mrs. Grossman's, Petaluma, Calif. This is the sticker company kids and scrapbookers know and love. Mrs. Grossman's prints fifteen thousand miles of stickers every year! Your family can see what's behind the fuss on a free factory tour of the bright and colorful printing plant. The tour begins with a video narrated by the owner's dog Angus and concludes with a free sticker-art class and a gift bag stuffed with stickers. A gift shop sells all of the company's seven hundred sticker designs. Reservations are recommended. Call 800-429-4549 or log on to *MrsGrossmans.com* for details.

Tillamook Cheese, Tillamook, Ore. Visitors are treated to a free tour, showcasing the entire cheese-making process from cow to mouth. Interactive kiosks provide nutritional information for kids of all ages. As visitors reach the end of the tour, they are treated to samples of Tillamook's famous cheese. For more information and tour times, go to *TillamookCheese.com.*

Eli's Cheesecake World, Chicago, Ill. Eli's Cheesecake World is the only place where you can see Chicago's favorite dessert actually being made. It's fun and educational to watch Eli's bakers busy at work. Visit the sixty-two-thousand-square-foot state-of-the-art bakery and enjoy a slice of Eli's rich, creamy cheesecake! Call ahead for reservations at 773-205-3800. More information at *EliCheesecake.com*.

U.S. Bureau of Engraving and Printing, Fort Worth, Tex. At the new Western Currency Facility, adults and kids will love learning all about U.S. paper currency. Best of all, you can actually see billions of dollars being printed as you walk along an enclosed walkway suspended over the production floor. Before or after your tour, enjoy two floors of interactive exhibits showcasing the history of currency and the intricacies of the printing process. Other features of the Visitor Center include a theater film, a gift shop, and a vending and rest area. The tour and fabulous Visitor Center opened April 2004, and is free to the public. To schedule a tour, please call 817-231-4000 or toll-free 866-865-1194; visit *MoneyFactory.com* and click on "Locations and Tours."

Dozens of other great factory tours are located in every state. Find a list by state at *FactoryToursUSA.com*.

Museums

Living-history museums. At least two thousand living-history museums around the country bring the past to life and offer learning as a joyous adventure. Spring and summer are the best times to visit because they offer many special children's programs and family events. Many can be seen in an afternoon, while others might require the entire weekend. I suggest you start with a virtual visit. Go to *ALHfam.org,* the site of the Association for Living History Farms and Agricultural Museums, which covers every area of the U.S. and Canada. You can take a virtual tour of wonderful places like the Jamestown Settlement in Williamsburg, Vir., the Henry Ford Museum in Dearborn, Mich., and Conner Prairie in Fishers, Ind., to name just a few. You can find hours of operation, entrance fees, and the programs they currently offer.

Children's museums. There are over 250 children's museums in the U.S., most of them offering free admission one day each month. The

Association of Children's Museums (*ChildrensMuseums.org* or 202-898-1080) will give you specific information on all of the children's museums in the U.S. including free days.

Washington, D.C. A trip to our nation's capitol is not only interesting, historical, and educational, but the majority of museums and tours around the city are free.

Movies

Movies are a big part of many families' entertainment—an activity that can sabotage even the best-laid plans to stay within a spending plan. Pay full price for one movie in a first-class movie theater these days, and a family of four sharing a family-sized popcorn is likely to spend $50! But you can reduce that high price without giving up the entertainment and pleasure of watching a great movie together.

Buy Tickets in Bulk

By mail. You can get a discount when you purchase tickets in bulk for all Regal Cinemas, United Artists, and Edwards Theatres. Go to *RegalCinemas.com*, click on "Gift Certificates" and then on "Gift Store." You can choose from two levels of tickets.

1. VIP Super Saver tickets are not good during the first twelve days of select new releases. Minimum purchase of fifty tickets is required. Tickets carry a surcharge of $2.50 if redeemed at any Manhattan, New York, location or for any IMAX/giant screen feature. No expiration date. $5.50 each.

2. Premiere Super Saver tickets are accepted for any movie at any time, even opening night of blockbuster films. Minimum purchase of fifty tickets is required. Tickets carry a surcharge of $1.50 if redeemed at any Manhattan, New York, location or for any IMAX/giant screen feature. No expiration date. $6.50 each.

Costco members. You can purchase Regal's Premiere Super Saver tickets as described above, $34.95 for five tickets (that works out to $6.99 each) plus shipping and handling at *Costco.com*. Under "Personal," search for "Movie Tickets."

Rentals by Mail

For the person or family spending a great deal each month to attend or rent movies, this may be a way to cut that cost of that entertainment.

Netflix. You can rent an unlimited number of DVDs for a monthly flat rate of $17.99 to receive three DVDs at a time, or $11.99 a month to receive two DVDs at a time (maximum four rentals per month). As soon as you send them back, they send you the next three on your list. That includes all postage and handling fees both ways. There are no late fees or due dates, no contract to sign, and you can cancel at any time. Keep three DVDs at a time as long as you like. You can choose from over twenty-five thousand titles. For more information go to *Netflix.com*.

Blockbuster. Following Netflix's lead, Blockbuster has broken into mail-order movies by offering a similar plan, with a monthly flat rate of $14.99 for three DVDs at a time, no late fees or due dates. Average turnaround time: two to three days; see *Blockbuster.com* for more information or to join.

Caution: Because you pay a flat monthly fee for all the movies you can watch, keep in mind that if they sit around unwatched for too long, you run the risk of not watching enough movies to make it worth the cost.

On Loan

Public library. Most libraries offer current movies on VHS and also DVDs for loan, in the same way you check out books. There may be a slight charge, but many libraries lend for free. Even if you pay $2 per movie, that's far less than any other option.

Chapter Fifteen

Your Satisfaction Guaranteed

Consumers need to know how to write letters of complaint, petition or appeal, in order to get what they fairly deserve.

~ Ellen Phillips, Author *Shocked, Appalled and Dismayed!*

When you've spent so much time and effort to get the best price, the last thing you expect is to get ripped off. You need to exercise the same level of care and diligence that got you the great deal in the first place. Make sure you protect your consumer rights so you enjoy full satisfaction from the goods and services you buy. The law is on your side when it comes to customer satisfaction.

Are you ever frustrated with customer service? Have you ever been cheated, taken to the cleaners, or hung out to dry by a retailer or service provider? Nothing is quite so frustrating as working hard to be a good steward of your money only to discover you are dissatisfied with the purchase. To be a savvy consumer you need the know-how and confidence to make sure that no matter what, no one ever gets your hard-earned money without your permission.

But first, let me tell you a story. Cheapskate Central (my office in California where we publish the national subscription newsletter *Debt-Proof Living*, formerly *Cheapskate Monthly*) is a bustling, busy place. We ship loads of parcels every day, and nearly all of our mail goes by U.S. Postal Service. However, when we have large shipments, we call UPS. Because we don't ship regularly by UPS, we do not have a corporate account. We pay the driver at pickup, something we've done for years.

Some months ago we began getting annoying past-due notices from UPS. A call to customer service to point out that we have no account and always pay in advance fell on deaf ears. The next notice we got said we'd been turned over to collection for failure to pay two outstanding invoices.

We made copies of our paid receipts, together with copies of our cancelled checks for both of the shipments in question. That did absolutely no good. UPS Customer Service would not deal with us since they'd turned our situation over to collection. Collection personnel were rude and completely unimpressed with our proof of payment.

After several months of this ridiculous runaround, my staff's collective frustration reached a fever pitch. It was time for me to move into action. I went to the UPS website, clicked on "Investor Relations" and found the names of the top executives and the Board of Directors, complete with titles and corporate mailing address.

I wrote a letter to the president. I began, *Dear Sir, I am shocked, appalled, and dismayed...*

I proceeded to outline our situation and the steps we had taken in an attempt to solve the problem, naming names and giving dates. Next, I told the president specifically the way I would like this matter resolved and the date by which that needed to happen. I was not rude, but assertive and professional. I did not ask for anything unusual or inappropriate. I wanted the matter to be resolved, all negatives removed from our record and a letter stating that we did not owe UPS any money.

I attached copies of the supporting documentation and sent it. I hoped that my displeasure with UPS would be subtly emphasized when my package arrived via FedEx.

Within a week, not only did we receive a personal phone call of apology, we also received a letter of assurance and evidence that no negative marks were associated with our company. Then UPS went one better. They enclosed a generous check to cover the cost of—you guessed it!—our FedEx charges. I was in a forgiving mood. The matter was settled exactly as I requested, and we continue to ship by UPS.

When things don't go right with a product or service, you have the right as a customer to expect some kind of adjustment. That might be a refund, replacement, or apology. But that's not likely to happen without you taking the initiative.

Making Your Voice Heard

Sometimes you just have to complain! The secret is to do so with such style and grace that your opponent is prompted to act—not out of duress but because you present a compelling case and make it possible for him to remediate the circumstance with dignity and grace.

Just the facts. While the details are fresh in your mind, write down what happened. Include as many details as possible so you don't have to rely on your memory.

Start easy. Make at least one good-faith attempt to reach a resolution at the customer-service level. Don't threaten; simply state your case and the resolution you expect. Take notes. Keep a paper trail that includes names of the people you speak with, including their titles and phone numbers.

Be nice. No matter your method of communication, do not make threats or use foul language. Wait until your anger subsides. Stay calm; keep it professional.

Write to the top. If you cannot reasonably resolve the issue, head straight for the top. Find the name and address of the highest level person in the company—the president or CEO. Don't waste your time working up the ladder. Go to the company's website or call the corporate office to find the name and mailing address of the president.

State your case. Be very clear on what the problem is, what you have done to attempt a resolution and exactly how you want this resolved.

Use strong language. Words like shocking, appalled, egregious, outraged, and reprehensible get their attention. Use these words if they fairly describe your situation.

Know what you want. What will make you feel better and relieve the bitter taste you have in your mouth for this company? Explain this to the president in clear and precise terms.

Name the date. Give a specific date two to three weeks hence by which you expect this matter to be resolved. Be sure to follow up if that date comes and goes with no response.

Keep it brief. Don't go on and on for many pages. Get to the point, delete all unnecessary words. Use exclamation marks and other emphases with extreme caution, if at all. Let your choice of words deliver the tone you desire. Try to keep your letter to a single page.

Proofread. Some of us can't see our own spelling and grammatical errors. Find someone willing to proof your finished letter. There's nothing like poor grammar and typos to detract, devalue, and dilute your message. Keep working at it until your letter is impeccable. Now the president will take your matter seriously.

Attach documentation. Make copies of the items that support your claim and prove your situation. Do not send original receipts, claim tickets or photos. Keep those originals in a safe place.

Make it easy to respond. Be sure to give the president an easy way to reach you. Give your name, address, phone number, and the best time to reach you.

Be bold. Use bold and CAPS when you type the following in the lower left area of the envelope: FOR IMMEDIATE AND PERSONAL ATTENTION!

Get a signed receipt. You have many options to send your letter. It's best if you select a method that gives you a signed receipt. Certified U.S. Mail with return receipt (available at any post office) is the cheapest option; FedEx or Express Mail will get greater attention.

Expect results. Corporate heads are not happy when they're pulled into customer service issues. And rightly so. It's embarrassing for management to discover their subordinates cannot keep customers happy. Imagine how frustrating that is for the guy at the top.

Say thank you. Assume the best and thank the president in advance for his or her attention and for resolving this matter for you.

Promise to reconsider. The president's motivation to respond to you is to keep you as a customer, not an enemy who spreads bad reports about the company. State in your letter that this is your desire as well, but only when you receive a positive outcome.

Keep copies. In most cases, contacting the top dog will put an end to your troubles. But just in case you have to take this matter further by lodging a complaint with a federal agency, consumer group, or worse— hiring an attorney—you will need evidence of your attempts to resolve the issue. You'll have a much easier time if you keep careful copies of everything.

Go higher if you must. You can file a complaint with the Federal Trade Commission (FTC) against any company. Go to *FTC.gov*, click on

"For Consumers" and then on "File a Complaint." Or file a complaint by phone: 877-382-4357.

Your state's attorney general will likely have a hotline and or toll-free number and page on the state government's website. Look these up and read the frequently asked questions. You may have the opportunity to make your complaint online if you feel that is appropriate.

Need Help?

Ellen Phillips is a professional letter writer who has recovered millions of dollars for her clients (mostly individuals, but she will write ghost letters for corporations as well as government agencies who need that special touch) who were not satisfied with the goods or services they purchased. This woman knows how to get results, and you can learn these secrets in her book *Shocked, Appalled, and Dismayed!* (Vintage, 1998).

Common Complaints

Dry cleaners. The International Fabricare Institute (800-638-2627; *IFI.org*) has a testing facility and investigates consumer complaints against its members.

Telephone/wireless services. The Federal Communications Commission (888-225-5322; *FCC.gov*) oversees complaints about problems with interstate calling, unauthorized charges, and switching services from one carrier to another.

Insurance. Go to your state's website or general information phone number and find the contact information for your state's insurance commissioner. Making a formal complaint will undoubtedly create a stir and give you the attention needed to solve your dispute.

Credit cards. While many agencies police banks and credit-card issuers, the Federal Reserve Board is the best all-purpose place to start. The FRB is required by law to forward your complaint to the appropriate agency that oversees the issuer of your particular credit card. Prepare for major bureaucratic red tape. Send your written complaint to: Federal Reserve Board, Division of Consumer and Community Affairs, 20th Street and Constitution Avenue NW, Washington, DC 20551; FRB.*gov.* Or call the Federal Depository Insurance Corporation (FDIC) toll-free, 877-275-3342; *FDIC.gov.*

Chapter Sixteen

Rules to
Live By

Hope is not a strategy. It takes much more than hope to improve your financial situation. You're also going to need support, information, tools and motivation. In short, positive impact comes only from action.

~ Michael D. Milner, *MoneySpot.org*

I have a quirk, a kind of brain glitch that annoys me to no end. I cannot easily distinguish left from right. My brain locks up and gives me a "Page Cannot Be Displayed" message.

Of course, I blame this on Mrs. Sailor. It goes back to that day in first grade when she called on me to answer a simple "left or right?" question. I froze. I did not know the answer. This is not good for a child who fears eternal damnation for even the slightest infraction. Worse, I didn't know how I would ever figure it out. No one else in the class had a problem with left and right.

My six-year-old reasoning concluded that the class learned "left from right" on a day I was home sick. I would go thirty-five years attributing my problem to a missed lesson.

Imagine my relief the day I learned the whys and wherefores of my personal struggle and a few simple exercises to make things better. If I'd only had the courage to say I didn't understand and to ask for help back then, I might have spared myself a lot of grief.

Perhaps you feel this way when it comes to managing your money. It can't be that difficult, everyone around you seems to handle their money just fine. It's as if you were out sick the day everyone else learned the rules of personal finance.

I have just the relief you need—Ten Simple Rules of Personal Finance to live by. If you will take these to heart, make them your own, and exercise them daily, I promise this will make things better. You will save yourself a lot of grief.

It's only too late if you don't start now.

Ten Simple Rules of Personal Finance

1. Know where your money goes.

The act of carefully tracking your spending will give you the power of truth about what's real in your life versus what you imagine. Keep track. Write it down, every day.

At the end of the month make a simple analysis. Your spending quite naturally falls into categories. Add up how much you spent on groceries, meal replacements, gasoline, utilities, clothes, and so on, right down the line. If you spent it, count it—even if you paid with a check or credit card. It's sometimes frightening to see spending in the big picture. A few dollars here and a couple more there do not give a clear picture of where all the money goes. Seeing it in black and white will empower you to make wiser choices.

2. Give away 10 percent of your paycheck.

You have two enemies that will do all they can to make sure you do not live below your means, that you spend all that you have and hope to have. The first is *greed*. The antidote for greed is *giving*.

Greed is that voice whispering in your ear that insists you are entitled to have anything you want. Greed keeps you from being satisfied. Giving away some of your income brings balance to your life.

Giving connects you to something greater than yourself; it takes your eyes off your situation. Giving is the tangible expression of gratitude and proves the condition of your heart. Giving easily defeats your enemy called greed.

Wealth is a great thing to have, also a great thing to share.

3. Save 10 percent of your paycheck.

Your second financial enemy is *fear*—fear of poverty, fear of running out of money, fear of losing your job, or any number of money-related fears. The antidote for fear is *saving*. Diligently save 10 percent of your paycheck—over and above any contributions you are making to retirement plans—always and without fail. This is the way to build a Contingency Fund equal to six month's income stashed away (see my book *Debt-Proof Living* for specifics on how to grow your Contingency Fund, where to keep it, and when to use it). It will be there to carry you through times when your income stream is cut off. And that will happen sometime in the future. Get prepared.

4. Tell your money where to go so you won't wonder where it went.

You receive a finite amount of money. Whatever the amount, it is not enough for you to be foolish. You need to plan your spending. I know that sounds curiously like a "budget," and if that word creeps you out, don't use it. Just sit down and have a talk with yourself.

How much do you spend for your house payment or rent? Okay,

that's a start. Move on to that big monster called *food*. How much of your money do you plan to spend on groceries? Meal replacements? Clothes? Gasoline? Insurance? Entertainment? If you've been tracking your spending, you have the exact information you need to decide where next month's money will go. If you haven't started, look at your checkbook, credit-card statements, and so on. You're a creature of habit, so you can expect the past to repeat itself unless you say it's time for a change. It's your money, so do yourself a favor and decide how you will spend it. You dare not leave it to chance.

Make a simple plan ahead of time—and then have the personal discipline to follow it. This will make all the difference.

5. Cap your spending at 80 percent of your paycheck.

The secret for living below your means is making the conscious effort to put a cap on your spending. Living on 80 percent of your take-home pay requires discipline, financial maturity, and effort to find every way possible to pay less than the full price for everything from food to clothes, insurance to transportation, and more.

6. Do not debt. If you're in it, get out.

You may find it odd to use the word *debt* as a verb. But it works well to describe the act of paying for something with credit and then allowing it to become a revolving balance subject to double-digit interest.

Start with your credit-card debt. Create a payback plan. Hang your plan on the refrigerator so you see if often. If you are making only minimum payments, nearly all of it represents profit for your creditors. You need that money—it needs to stay in your life, not their pockets. You need to get out of debt! And you can. But you'll never achieve that until you stop adding to the balances. That's what I mean when I suggest you stop debting.

Get out all of your unsecured debts and line them up so the smallest is at the top. Do whatever you can possibly manage to pay it off as quickly as possible. Then take that monthly payment and add it to the next debt in line. That's the way to get out of debt fast.

If you could use more intensive help with this, check out my Rapid Debt-Repayment Plan. You can find a free demonstration of how it works at *DebtProofLiving.com*. The plan in its entirety is in my book *Debt-Proof Living*. It is a remarkable plan, in my humble opinion. Once you see how it works I predict you will know two things for sure: (1) that you can get out of debt, and (2) exactly how to do it.

7. Buy what you need and want what you have.

Allowing yourself to want what you don't have is a terrible waste of energy. Find contentment in wanting what you do have. When you need something, buy it, and then make the conscious choice to be content. Do not shop mindlessly, wandering around shopping malls hoping to find something.

You cannot have it all but you can have enough. Trying to have it all only leads to misery, because if you live for having it all, what you have is never enough. Having more and more only leads to dissatisfaction and disappointment. Having enough means choosing when to stop. At that point, one experiences fulfillment and the satisfaction of having enough.

8. Never confuse saving with spending less.

When you buy something on sale you are not "saving" money. You are only spending less. Spending less is a good thing and the whole point of this book. But that is not the same as saving. If you were actually saving money when you bought a $1,200 cashmere coat on sale for $75 (Wow! How did I miss that sale?), you would've stopped at the bank on the way home from the mall and deposited the $1,125 you did not spend into your savings account. Now you have saved something. Most of the time you are only spending less.

9. Do not try to impress others.

When you live to impress others, you allow them to make your decisions for you. The truth is, no one really cares. Instead, live by your values of honesty and integrity. And never pay retail.

10. Above all, anticipate.

Have you ever forgotten to pay the rent? Probably not. That's because it happens every month. You get used to it. You anticipate when it is due. But how are you with anticipating other expenses—things that don't happen regularly each month? I'm thinking of tires for the car, back-to-school clothes for the kids, a new refrigerator, a big insurance bill, or the cost of a family vacation. Doesn't seem the same, does it? But those kinds of expenses are most likely to throw you off track. The unexpected and irregular expenses catch us off guard and send us running to credit cards for a bail out.

Failure to plan is expensive. Choosing to anticipate is the way to head off the big financial blows, because you are buying a commodity more precious than money: time. Time to make decisions and to find the best price. Your goal is to always make that half the price!

Afterword

When our boys were small, they loved to play a game at the arcade, "Whack-a-Gopher."

It's a tabletop affair with plastic gophers hiding out of sight. You get a great big rubber mallet, and when you hit the Start button, a gopher pops up. You have to "whack!" it hard to get it to go away, but just as you do, another pops up, so you have to "whack!" that one; another pops up more rapidly, and soon it's a battle of whacking fast and hard enough to get them to go away before another pops up. I cannot think of a better illustration for the way some people manage their money.

They spend all they have, use as much credit as they can find, and then start whacking. Because they're not prepared for the future when something unexpected happens, it's like a gopher popping up. They scramble, looking for what bill can go delinquent for a while so they can "whack!" this emergency or that unexpected expense. But as soon as they do, something else pops up. As soon as it's put down, another pops up, and soon it's happening so fast there is no way to keep up. It's exhausting.

Cutting your expenses will only give you a heavier mallet. It will not take care of all the "gophers" in your life. You need to get rid of your gophers by saving for the future, paying off debt, and then anticipating your expenses—all of them.

A good money manager has a plan to anticipate irregular and even unexpected expenses. A good money management plan brings balance and sanity to your life. It keeps expenses under control and allows your income to catch up and even exceed the amount of money required to live. Once that happens, you will find yourself in the enviable position of consistently living below your means easily and on purpose.

I'd Rather Have the Money, Bob!

Did you see us? Harold and I were on TV with Bob Barker. Before you run to check your TiVo I'd better tell you this was a while ago. Try 1971.

We were plucked from the live audience of that old favorite *Truth or Consequences* along with two other couples. Ours was a kind of "newly-wed game" stunt. They put the guys in a soundproof booth, and we ladies had to predict how our husbands would answer questions.

Of course we won. And a mighty nice prize it was—$50 and a blender. We already had a blender, so I remember thinking I'd rather have the money. We could have walked away with $85 cash.

To this day, watching Bob on TV still brings back fond memories. Still, whenever someone wins the Showcase with $35,000 of all kinds of stuff to clutter his or her life, I can almost hear what the winner is thinking, *I'd rather have the money, Bob!* But instead, the winner gets all the stuff, and has to pay taxes on the full retail value to boot. (We got off easy ... not much tax due on $50 and a blender).

Every day you should suggest that same thing to yourself—I'd rather have the money!

Let's say you see a great new pair of shoes you simply cannot resist. They're on sale ...this won't last, and it's such a great deal. No matter how you pay for them (cash, credit, check), it's a done deal. You've got the shoes, they've got your money.

Here's where your thinking gets all messed up. Your choices, you believe, are to either 1) have the shoes or 2) not have the shoes. One is a happy outcome, the other negative, or so you believe.

How would your decision change if the salesman had the shoes in one hand and the $50 cash in the other? Would you take the shoes or the money?

That is exactly the choice you have with every purchase. Either you get the [fill in the blank] or you get the money. Either you buy the shoes or leave $50 in your bank account.

If you could see your lifetime earnings in one big pile of money and watch how each spending decision diminishes the amount you get to keep, I have a feeling you would take your decisions more seriously. You'd opt to take the money more often than the stuff to clutter your life, and in so doing move yourself that much closer to living your life for half the price!

Time to Say Good-bye

Well, look at this, will you? We've come to the end of our journey. My work is done, but yours has just begun.

But don't worry; I'm not going anywhere. I want to stick around to encourage you on your quest to live your life for half the price. But more than that, I want to hear about your progress and all the discoveries you make for new ways to keep more of your money. And please accept the gift I have for you—a six-month online premium subscription to my newsletter *Debt-Proof Living* (formerly *Cheapskate Monthly*). See page 307 for complete information and instructions to sign up.

As you can imagine, I get a lot of mail and while I cannot promise a response, you can be sure your letter will be read, considered, and thoroughly enjoyed. Brace yourself for this email address. It's so long that when I get your message, I'll stand and applaud your diligence for having typed it so flawlessly:

Mary@LiveYourLifeForHalfThePrice.com

I can't wait to hear from you. Thanks in advance!

Appendix A

I promised to share some of my favorite fast and easy recipes with you and here they are, in no particular order. Nothing in this Appendix will take a lot of time, culinary skill or money. And of course by now you know the bonus, right? You will save time and money.

The First Supper

If you're not used to cooking meals at home, here's a good one to start with.

Blasted Chicken. Preheat oven to a very hot 450 F. You'll need one whole, thawed 3 1/2 pound chicken; salt and pepper. Remove giblets from cavity to be used another time. Rinse the chicken inside and out; set in a baking dish (on a rack if you have one that fits your baking dish), breast side up. Do not tuck in the wings or tie it shut. Sprinkle liberally with salt and pepper all over the outside and inside. Bake at 450 degrees for 45 minutes. Don't peek or you'll blow the results. Remove and allow the chicken to sit for a few minutes. Cut apart with big kitchen shears or a sharp knife. Hint: If your chicken is just slightly larger, bake a few minutes longer. But do not exceed 3 3/4 pounds or the bird will not cooked thoroughly on the inside before the outside turns to charcoal.

Notes: The high temperature will sear the bird quickly and this is the secret to keeping all of the juices sealed inside. You may experience splattering and smoke coming for your oven because of the grease that is hitting the sides of the oven and also the fat in the bottom of the baking dish.

You can alleviate this somewhat by placing two slices of bread in the bottom of the baking dish under the rack. This will create a kind of sponge and keep the grease from splattering so much. I do not use any precaution, however. I just let the chicken splatter and spit at will. Every time I make Blasted Chicken I am reminded to run my oven's self-clean option, later.

Sensational Rice. While your chicken is blasting (you will be quivering with excitement because this is just so much fun but do not give into your urges to open that over door), remove the outside layers from one onion and chop it into small pieces. Heat two tablespoons vegetable oil in a skillet and sauté the onion over medium heat until soft.

Add 1 cup raw rice (any type *except* pre-cooked or Minute Rice). Continue sautéing until the rice begins to brown, stirring constantly (about 10 minutes). Be careful not to burn. Quickly add 1 1/2 cups canned chicken broth, chicken broth from your freezer if you have any, or two chicken bouillon cubes plus 1 1/2 cups water.

Add 1/2 to 1 teaspoon salt according to your preference, and pepper to taste. Bring to a full rolling boil. Cover, leave on the burner and turn the heat off. Leave covered for about 20 minutes. Serves 4-6. Hint: If you start the rice as soon as you put the chicken in the oven, both will be done at the same time.

Tip: Serve Blasted Chicken and Sensational Rice with a simple tossed green salad and warm bread. This is a meal sure to please even the pickiest eater. You could fix this meal once a week for the rest of your life and never tire of it, it's that great. It's quick, easy and healthy. And did I say cheap?

I make this meal to serve six for less than $5, and I do it all the time. (I just checked and I have 7 chickens in my freezer ... oh, how I love my stockpile.) My family, friends and office staff think I'm a gourmet genius. Please. Don't blow my secret.

Quick and Easy Stir-Fry

Step 1. Set your wok or a heavy skillet on low heat. While it's heating, get about one pound of protein ready and place within easy reach of the skillet. You can use shrimp (raw and peeled or canned, drained), fresh scallops, boneless chicken cut into strips; any type of red meat sliced thin or cubed tofu. It can even be left-over chicken or beef (just reduce the cooking time if the meat is precooked).

Step 2. Place the protein in a bowl. Pour 2 tablespoons of soy sauce over the protein. Toss so all of the pieces are coated.

Step 3. Cut one onion into about 16 wedges. Set to the side.

Step 4. Prepare vegetables. Cut about two cups of any combination of sliced carrots, celery, scallions, mushrooms, bell pepper, zucchini; snow peas stringed, and canned water chestnuts and or baby corn, drained well. Basically use any vegetables you have on hand. You need only small amounts. Do not commit vegetable overload.

Step 5. Place the onion wedges and vegetables on the counter close to the skillet. Peel and mince 1 tablespoon each fresh ginger and garlic and place alongside the vegetables.

Step 6. In a small dish combine 2 teaspoons cornstarch with 2 tablespoons cold water or chicken broth. Stir until smooth and place close to the other ingredients along with 1 cup stir-fry sauce (available in the supermarket Asian aisle) and cooking oil.

Okay ... let's check. Are all of your ingredients lined up and within easy reach? You're ready to go! Turn the skillet high and turn on the exhaust fan. Quickly pour in 1 tablespoon oil to coat the bottom of the pan. Follow with half the protein. Stir constantly for about two minutes, moving the small pieces of protein that cook quickly. Remove to a plate and stir-fry the remaining half of the protein, removing when done.

Pour another 2 tablespoons oil into the skillet and follow quickly with the onion wedges, all the while leaving the temperature on high. Stir and cook the onion for about one minute. Add the minced ginger and garlic and continue to stir. Quickly follow with no more than 1 cup of vegetables and continue to stir-fry (err on the side of less rather than more). After about 2 minutes remove these items from the skillet to the protein plate. Continue cooking the vegetables in small batches until done. Do not over cook.

Return all of the protein and vegetables to the sizzling hot skillet. Add the stir-fry sauce a little at a time until everything is nicely coated. You don't want this to turn to soup, so go easy.

Stir in the cornstarch mixture and continue stirring until the sauce thickens and everything is coated with this glaze. If it gets too thick add a little water or chicken broth and continue to stir. You're done! Serve immediately over steamed rice. Serves 4 to 6.

Three Packets and a Roast

One beef roast (chuck, London broil,
round—you name it)
Three packets of dry mix:
Brown Gravy dry mix
Italian Dressing dry mix
Ranch Dressing dry mix

Place beef in the slow cooker (no need to brown). Tear open these three packets and pour contents over the raw meat: Pour one cup of water over the top. Cover with lid, cook on low for 8-10 hours for a very large roast, fewer hours if smaller, or on high for 5-6 hours. Check for doneness after 4-5 hours because time will vary depending on the cut of beef, size and so on.

The regular price of these packets of dry mix is ridiculously high. But good news: They come on sale often, and you'll find coupons for them as well. You know the routine.

Hint: If your slow cooker is large-(6- to 7-quart capacity) you can cook a very large roast or two large London broils to serve a big group and have leftovers too. Simply double up on the packets of dry mix and increase water to one and one-half cups.

Optional: Add cut up potatoes and carrots during the last hour of cooking; frozen peas during the last 10 minutes. Expect beautiful, rich, dark brown gravy and the best pot roast ever.

Variations:

Three Packets and a Cluck: Substitute a whole chicken for the roast plus these three packets: Chicken Gravy dry mix, Ranch Dressing dry mix and Italian Dressing dry mix. Follow instructions above for the Roast. Cooking time may vary, so check for doneness after 3-4 hours.

Three Packets and an Oink: Substitute a pork roast and these three packets: Pork Gravy dry mix, Ranch Dressing dry mix and Italian Dressing dry mix. Ditto.

Designer Muffins

Tired of high-fat, high-cost fast-food breakfasts? I've got a fantastic solution: Quick and easy Designer Muffins. With a little improvising, you can make and serve scrumptious muffins in a variety of flavors to make use of (and use up) ingredients you have on hand. Use this basic muffin recipe to get started then refer to the options that follow.

Orange Muffins

1 1/2 cups all-purpose flour
1 teaspoon baking powder
1 teaspoon baking soda
1/2 cup buttermilk
1 egg
1/4 cup honey
2 tablespoons butter
2 tablespoons applesauce
1/2 cup chopped oranges

Preheat the oven to 400 F. Lightly coat a 12-cup muffin tin with non-stick spray. In a large bowl, combine the dry ingredients and mix well. In a medium bowl, combine the buttermilk, egg, honey, butter and applesauce. Mix well. Stir the wet ingredients into the flour mixture, add the oranges and stir to combine. Fill muffin tins 3/4 full. Bake for 12 to 15 minutes or until a toothpick inserted in the center of a muffin comes out clean. Yield: 12 muffins.

Variations:

Instead of all-purpose flour. Use a combination of flours such as whole-wheat flour or cornmeal. You can also substitute up to 1/2 cup cooked rice or bran cereal for an equal amount of flour.

Instead of buttermilk. Use low-fat buttermilk, soy milk, regular or nonfat sour cream, whole or skim milk, regular or nonfat plain yogurt, orange juice or apple juice.

Instead of honey. Use maple syrup, granulated sugar, brown sugar, molasses or frozen apple juice concentrate (may increase up to 1/2 cup if you like a sweeter muffin).

Instead of butter. Use reduced calorie butter, oil or margarine.

Instead of applesauce. Use any pureed fruit or nonfat plain yogurt.

Instead of chopped oranges. Use chopped apples, mashed

bananas, dates, drained and chopped canned fruits, blueberries, raspberries, cranberries, raisins, pumpkin puree, mashed cooked sweet potatoes, shredded carrots or zucchini, nuts or shredded cheeses. As long as you stay under 1/2 cup, the wetter ingredients won't throw off the wet-dry balance of the recipe.

Save yourself time and make double or triple batches of your favorite muffins to freeze and reheat later. Bake and cool the muffins, freeze them on a baking sheet, then quickly transfer them to tightly sealed plastic bags. They'll keep frozen for up to two months without losing flavor. Thaw muffins in the refrigerator overnight then reheat individually in the microwave on high power for one minute or until steaming hot.

Muffin Mix

Keep a batch of this dry muffin mix in the pantry and you'll be able to turn out hot, homemade muffins in just 20 minutes flat!

> 5 cups all-purpose flour
> 1 cup whole wheat flour
> 1-1/2 cups sugar
> 1 cup instant nonfat dry milk powder
> 1/4 cup baking powder
> 2 tsp. salt
> 1 tablespoon cinnamon
> 1/2 teaspoon ground cloves

Mix in large bowl and store in air tight container. To bake muffins, place 2 cups mix in a large bowl. Add 2/3 cup water, 1 slightly beaten egg and 1/4 cup oil. With a fork, mix until dry ingredients are just moistened. Fill paper lined muffin cups 1/2 full. Bake at 400 degrees for 10-15 minutes or until muffins are puffed and pass the toothpick test.

Muffin Mix can be kept in the pantry well sealed for up to six months; longer when stored in the refrigerator.

Master Recipes

Master Recipe for White Rice

Forget the instructions on the back of the bag unless you want scorched or mushy rice. Instead, learn how to make perfect rice every time.

Sauté 1 cup raw white rice in two tablespoons oil in a sauce pan over high heat until the kernels are well-coated and turn bright white, 3 to 4 minutes, stirring constantly. Add 1 1/2 cups water. Bring to a rolling boil, stirring just to blend the ingredients. Cover, leave on the burner and turn the heat to the very lowest setting.

Leave undisturbed and covered for 15 minutes (do not peek!). Remove from the burner (still do not peek) and wait for 10 minutes or so while you are getting the rest of the meal on the table. Now remove the lid, fluff with a fork, season with plenty of salt and pepper to taste.

This recipe multiplies well, but as you increase the rice you decrease the proportion of water. For example: 2 cups of rice with 2 3/4 cups of water. Tip: Make a big batch of rice, allow to cool then put 1-2 cups into individual freezer zip-type bags. Refrigerate. Now you have future meals partly made and ready to go.

Master Recipe for Brown Rice

Making brown rice is not as simple as white. Brown rice, to be satisfying with its nutty, gutsy flavor and more texture, needs to be slightly sticky and just a bit chewy.

The foolproof way to make brown rice is in the oven. Preheat oven to 375 F. Spread 1 1/2 cups brown rice (long, medium or short-grain) in an 8-inch baking dish. Add 2 teaspoons butter or vegetable oil and 1/2 teaspoon salt to 2 1/3 cups boiling water. Pour over rice.

Cover the baking dish tightly with a doubled layer of foil. Bake rice 1 hour, or until tender.

Remove baking dish from oven and uncover. Fluff rice with a dinner fork, then cover dish with a clean kitchen towel. Allow to stand 5 minutes. Uncover and let rice stand 5 minutes long, serve immediately. This amount serves 4-6. You can double the recipe, prepare in a 9 x 13 baking dish with no increase in cooking time.

Perfect Pasta

Bring a large covered pot of water to boil. Drop in a pound of pasta (more or less, whatever amount you desire). Stir. Replace lid and turn heat off. Do not peek until at least 10 minutes have passed.

Check doneness by eating one piece of pasta. If it sticks to your teeth when you bite into it, return lid to the pot and allow to sit for 5 minutes longer. Check again. It should be done perfectly, not mushy but not too chewy either. Pour into a colander to drain. Rinse with cold water. Once cool, you can put 1-2 cup portions of cooked pasta into zip-bags and store in the refrigerator if you cook for one or two people. Or larger portions for a larger group. Either way you'll have pasta for the week (you should use cooked pasta within a week for optimum flavor and texture).

For a hot dish, simply drop the contents of a bag of pre-boiled pasta into a pot of boiling water to freshen and heat it. After 30 to 60 seconds, pour into colander to drain. You're ready to top with a sauce, toss with butter and Parmesan cheese or any other way you enjoy pasta. Or use it cold in a pasta salad.

Chicken and Beef Broth

Because you will be cooking chicken and ground beef a lot you are going to end up with lot of chicken and beef broth or "stock" (it's an automatic thing, nothing you have to allow time for—it's just going to happen).

The last thing you want to do is to throw it out. But to freeze home-made stock or broth in big containers will not be good, either. Once frozen it will be useless to you because you won't be able to thaw just a small portion that you need. The solution: muffin tins.

Whenever you have stock or broth left from recipes or techniques that follow, pour it into muffin tins and freeze. Once frozen, pop out the frozen portions and store in a large zip-type bag. Now you can remove one or two as needed without thawing the entire amount. You will be using this to make rice, soups, gravies and sauces. Cooking with homemade broth and stock is so much better than canned stock or even bouillon cubes. Cheaper too.

Master Biscuit Mix

(Compare to Bisquick)

5 pounds all-purpose flour
2 1/2 cups dry milk
3/4 cup double acting baking powder
2 tablespoons Cream of Tartar
3 tablespoons salt
1/2 cup sugar
4 2/3 cups (2 pounds) solid vegetable shortening

Sift dry ingredients together. Cut in shortening until mix looks like cornmeal. Store at room temperature in a large sealable container like Tupperware for up to six months. Makes 30 cups mix.

One dozen biscuits: 3 cups Master Mix, 3/4 cup water. Blend and knead a few strokes. Roll out and cut biscuits with a round biscuit cut-ter, or into squares or diamond shapes. Bake 10 minute at 450 F.

Dumplings: Use the same measurements as for biscuits. Drop into hot liquid of choice. Cook 10 minutes uncovered and an additional 10 minutes covered.

One dozen muffins: 3 cups Master Mix, 1/2 cup sugar, 1 egg, 1 cup water. Mix water and egg; add dry ingredients. Add optional items such as blueberries, chocolate chips, nuts and so forth, as desired. Bake in muffin cups for 25 minutes at 450 F.

Four dozen drop cookies: 3 cups Master Mix, 1 cup sugar, 1 egg, 1/3 cup water, 1 teaspoon vanilla, 1/2 cup nuts or chocolate chips. Bake 10-12 minutes at 375 F.

Nine-inch round coffee cake: 3 cups Master Mix, 1/2 cup sugar, 1 egg, and 2/3 cup water. Blend all ingredients and pour into a greased 9-inch cake pan. Cover with topping: 1/2 cup brown sugar, 3 tablespoons butter, 1/2 teaspoon cinnamon. Optional: Add 1/2 cup nuts or raisins to the topping mix. Bake for 25 minutes at 400 F.

18 medium pancakes: 3 cups Master Mix, 1 1/2 cups water, 1 egg. Blend only until barely incorporated. Prepare pancakes or waffles as usual.

Eight-inch square gingerbread: 2 cups Master Mix, 1/4 cup sugar, 1 egg, 1/2 cup water, 1/2 cup molasses, 1/2 teaspoon each cinnamon, ginger and ground cloves. Beat egg together with the water and molasses. Mix well with dry ingredients until all are incorporated. Pour into greased 8-inch square cake pan. Bake 40 minutes at 350 F.

Eight-inch square cornbread or muffins: 1 1/4 cups Master Mix, 3/4 cup cornmeal, 1 egg, 1 tablespoon sugar, 1/2 cup water. Mix all ingredients until fully incorporated. Pour into greased pan or muffin cups. Bake 25 minutes at 400 F.

Shortcake: 2 cups Master Mix, 2 tablespoons sugar, 1/2 cup water. Mix all ingredients and bake in a greased 8 x 8 pan, or roll out and cut into individual cakes to be placed on a cookie sheet. Bake 25 minutes at 400 F, or a few minutes less for individual shortcakes, until they just begin to brown.

Note: You can use Master Mix in any recipe calling for Bisquick, making sure you substitute water for milk if the recipe calls for milk.

Cake Mix Cookies

You can make cookies from any flavor of boxed cake mix. Just add 1/2 cup of oil, 2 eggs, 1 tablespoon water and 1 to 2 teaspoons of any flavor of extract to the dry mix. Mix well with an electric mixer, roll into 1-inch balls, flatten onto an ungreased cookie sheet and bake for 8-10 minutes at 350 F.

Get creative with the flavor choices. For example, 2 teaspoons lemon extract with a yellow cake mix makes Lemon Cookies. When cooled dust them with powdered sugar. Or add 2 teaspoons of vanilla extract to a white cake mix for a delicious sugar cookie. How about 2 teaspoons of mint extract and a chocolate cake mix? Add white chocolate chips to a strawberry cake mix for a unique result. This cookie dough, once mixed, can be frozen for baking later. Just roll into a "log," cover tightly with plastic wrap and then slice what you need and bake.

Whacky Doodle Beef

Once I made a terrible mistake. I froze 10 pounds of ground beef. That big block of frozen burger languished in my freezer for what seems like years. What was I thinking? I should have browned it first then frozen it in usable portions. But browning beef is such a messy job!

Just when I knew I would never make that same mistake again, I came upon another cheap ground beef opportunity. The expiration date was nearing and my supermarket needed to get rid of ground beef. Ten pounds! I almost walked by. Then I decided to try something different, albeit a little weird.

I put the entire 10 pounds of raw ground beef into my big stock pot. I added enough water to cover and set it over high heat to come to a boil, no cover, no salt. After about 5 minutes I gave it a stir to break up the big clumps, which were few. The hot water was doing all of my work for me-no splatters, no mess. When all of the pink color disappeared I knew it was done, even though it had not reached a rolling boil.

I placed my large colander into a big bowl in the sink and poured the now cooked beef into the colander. I did this in batches because my colander would not hold all of it at once. This drained off all the liquid into the bowl including the fat, leaving uniformly fine-textured ground beef in the colander. No clumps! I could have done the same thing scooping the meat from the stock pot with a large sieve, transferring the drained beef into a large bowl. When done draining I put the beef broth in the refrigerator. Later I skimmed off the fat and poured the beef broth into muffin tins and placed them in the freezer. Once frozen these individual portions of frozen broth can be popped out and placed in a large plastic zip-type bag and stored in the freezer.

I measured about 1 1/2 cups of cooked beef (the equivalent of about 1 pound of raw ground beef) into each gallon-size zip-type freezer bags, pressed out the air and zipped. I laid each one on the counter to flatten it thin then stacked them like sheets of paper and popped the stack into the freezer.

Because my bags of beef are so flat I can use them frozen—no thawing required. I take one of these flat frozen packages of ground beef from the freezer, whack it on the side of the sink to break it into pieces, unzip and pour the contents into a non-stick skillet. It's ready for all uses. Here's the best part: This method removes the fat, leaving the ground meat virtually fat-free.

Create Your Own Designer Cuisine

Ever feel like a kitchen klutz? Wish you could take that odd assortment of stuff in the pantry, refrigerator and freezer and make something delicious without a specific recipe and without having to run to the market? Well, grab your whisk and shout for joy! Thanks to this foolproof, 5-Step plan you can create fabulous, original, homemade, delicious and nutritious entrees designed By You, using the items you have on hand.

Step 1: Combine 1 8-ounce carton sour cream, 1 cup milk, 1 cup water, 1 teaspoon salt and 1 teaspoon pepper with one item from Group A (omit sour cream and milk when using tomatoes).

Step 2: Stir in one item from each of Groups B, C, D, and E.

Step 3: Spoon mixture into a lightly greased 13- x 9- x 2-inch baking dish.

Step 4: Sprinkle with one or two choices from Group F.

Step 5: Cover and bake casserole at 350 F, for 1 hour and 10 minutes. Uncover and bake 10 additional minutes. Yield: 6 servings.

Group A:

1 - 10 3/4-ounce can cream of mushroom soup, undiluted

1 - 10 3/4-ounce can cream of celery soup, undiluted

1 - 10 3/4-ounce can Cheddar cheese soup, undiluted

2 - 14 1/2-ounce cans Italian-style diced tomatoes, undrained

1 - 10 3/4-ounce can cream of chicken soup, undiluted

Group B:

2 - 6-ounce cans solid white tuna, drained and flaked

2 cups chopped cooked chicken

2 cups chopped cooked ham

2 cups chopped cooked turkey

1 pound ground beef, browned and drained

Group C:

2 cups uncooked elbow macaroni

1 cup uncooked rice

4 cups uncooked wide egg noodles

3 cups uncooked medium pasta shells

Group D:

1 - 10-ounce package frozen chopped spinach, thawed and drained

1 - 10-ounce package frozen cut broccoli

1 - 10-ounce package frozen Italian green beans

1 - 10-ounce package frozen pea pods

1 - 16-ounce package frozen sliced yellow squash

1 - 10-ounce package frozen whole kernel corn

Group E:

1 - 3-ounce can sliced mushrooms, drained

1/4 cup sliced ripe olives

1/4 cup chopped bell pepper

1/4 cup chopped onion

1/4 cup chopped celery

2 cloves garlic, minced

1 - 4 1/2-ounce can chopped green chilies

1 - 1 1/4-ounce envelope taco seasoning mix

Group F:

1/2 cup (2 ounces) shredded mozzarella cheese

1/2 cup (2 ounces) shredded Swiss cheese

1/2 cup grated Parmesan cheese

1/2 cup fine, dry breadcrumbs

Sample combinations:

Chicken Casserole. Cream of chicken soup, broccoli, rice, chicken, Parmesan cheese and bread crumbs.

Ham Casserole. Cream of celery soup, Italian green beans, wide egg noodles, ham, garlic and two portions Swiss cheese.

Turkey Casserole. Italian-style diced tomatoes, spinach, medium pasta shells, turkey, onion, garlic, mozzarella cheese and bread crumbs.

Vegetarian Casserole. Italian-style diced tomatoes, yellow squash, rice, olives, four portions celery, four portions bell pepper, garlic, Parmesan cheese and bread crumbs.

Now it's your turn. Enjoy!

Make Your Own Mixes

They're convenient and tasty, but have you ever considered the high cost of your favorite prepared mixes and spices? In less time than it takes you to run to the market to pick up a box of Rice a Roni or Shake 'N Bake, you can make it yourself, and save a bundle in the process.

It's difficult to say for sure what these recipes will cost by comparison because there are so many variables, but I can assure you it's pennies, not dollars!

Beef Gravy Mix

1 1/3 cup instant non-fat powdered milk
3/4 cup instant flour (like Wondra or
    Shake & Blend)
3 tablespoons instant beef bouillon granules
1/8 teaspoon ground thyme
1/4 teaspoon onion powder
1/8 teaspoon sage
1/2 cup butter or margarine, room temperature

3 tablespoons brown sauce for gravy
(like Kitchen Bouquet)

Combine milk powder, flour, bouillon granules, thyme, onion powder and sage. Stir with a wire whisk to blend. Use a pastry blender or 2 knives to cut in butter or margarine until evenly distributed. Drizzle brown sauce for gravy over mixture. Stir with wire whisk until blended. Spoon into a 3-cup container with a tight-fitting lid. Label with date and contents. Store in refrigerator. Use within 4 to 6 weeks. Makes about 2 2/3 cups beef gravy mix.

To use: Pour 1 cup cold water into saucepan. Use a whisk to stir 1/2 cup beef gravy mix into water. Stir constantly over medium heat until gravy is smooth and slightly thickened, 2 to 3 minutes. Makes about 1 cup gravy.

Dry Onion Soup Mix

3/4 cup dry minced onion
1/3 cup beef bouillon powder
4 teaspoons onion powder
1/4 teaspoon crushed celery seed
1/4 teaspoon sugar

Combine all ingredients Store in tight fitting container. About 5 tablespoons of mix are equal to one 1.25-ounce package. Onion Dip: Combine 5 tablespoons mix with one pint of sour cream.

Like Rice-a-Roni

2 cups uncooked rice (not instant or Minute Rice)
1 cup of broken vermicelli pasta pieces, (find this in the pasta aisle)
1/4 cup dried parsley flakes
6 tablespoons instant chicken OR beef bouillon powder or granules
2 tsp. onion powder

1/2 teaspoon garlic powder
1/4 teaspoon dried thyme

Shake or stir dry mixture well.

To Use: Place 1 cup mix and 2 tablespoons butter or margarine in a heavy saucepan with 2 1/4 cups water. Bring to a boil. Cover and reduce heat. Simmer for 15 minutes or until rice is tender.

Taco Seasoning Mix

2 teaspoons instant minced onion
1 teaspoon salt
1 teaspoon chili powder
1/2 teaspoon cornstarch
1/8 teaspoon crushed dried red pepper
1/2 teaspoon instant minced garlic
1/4 teaspoon dried oregano leaves
1/2 teaspoon ground cumin

Mix all ingredients together well. Store in tightly sealed bag or container.

To make Taco Filling: Brown 1 1/2 pounds lean ground beef in a medium skillet over medium-high heat. Drain the fat. Add 1/2 cup water and 2 tablespoons Taco Seasoning mix. Reduce heat and simmer 10 minutes, stirring occasionally. Makes filling for 8 to 10 tacos.

Cook's Note: This recipe multiplies well, but should be used within six months.

Chicken Gravy Mix

1 1/3 cups powdered milk
3/4 cup Wondra instant flour
3 tablespoons chicken bouillon granules
1/4 teaspoon sage or poultry seasoning
1/4 teaspoon onion powder

1/8 teaspoon black pepper
1/2 cup salted butter or margarine, room temp.

Combine all ingredients in a bowl. Use a pastry blender or 2 knives to cut in butter until evenly distributed. Mix well and store in a 3-cup tightly covered container in the refrigerator. Use within 4 to 6 weeks.

To use: Pour 1 cup cold water in saucepan. Using a whisk to blend, stir in 1/2 cup mix. Stir constantly over medium heat until gravy is smooth and slightly thickened, about 2-3 minutes. Makes 1 cup gravy.

Country Gravy Mix

1 cup all-purpose flour
2 teaspoons garlic salt
1 teaspoon paprika
1 teaspoon ground black pepper
1/4 teaspoon poultry seasoning
1/2 teaspoon salt

Mix all ingredients well and store in a tightly sealed container. Note: The best country gravy is made in the skillet with drippings that remain after frying chicken or sausage. However, you can substitute unsalted butter for the drippings.

To make gravy: Discard all but 2 tablespoons of the frying oil (or melt 2 tablespoons unsalted butter) in the skillet. Over low heat stir in 2 tablespoons of the Country Gravy Mix. Stirring constantly, cook about 2 minutes. Whisk in 1 cup chicken broth, scraping browned bits off bottom of skillet. Stir in 1 cup milk and bring all to a boil over high heat, stirring constantly. Reduce heat to low and simmer for about 5 minutes. Serve immediately with chicken, mashed potatoes or biscuits. Yield: 2 cups gravy.

Family-Friendly Finger Foods

In less time than it takes you to get into the car and drive to the store to pick up a box of coating mix for chicken, you can make your own at home for half the price, or less. In fact you can make this fabulous mix in five minutes flat. And if that's not enough, you'll get three bonuses for your effort:

1. A much better price—the real stuff costs $.69 an ounce (or $11 a pound!) on a good day.

2. You'll know what's in it and have the ability to adjust the salt to your taste, and be able to pronounce each and every ingredient.

3. This is so much better than its store-bought cousin. If your kids don't agree, I'll eat my shakin' bag!

First you need to make this coating mix.

Shake It, Bake It

4 cups dry bread crumbs
1/3 cup vegetable oil
1 tablespoon salt
1 tablespoon paprika
1 tablespoon celery salt
1 teaspoon ground black pepper
1/2 teaspoon garlic salt
1/2 teaspoon minced garlic
1/4 teaspoon minced onion
1 pinch dried basil leaves
1 pinch dried parsley
1 pinch dried oregano

Combine all ingredients in a large re-sealable plastic bag. Seal bag and shake all ingredients together. Store in a sealed container for up to six month in the pantry, longer in the refrigerator.

Remove the amount you need and store the balance in a tightly sealed container or bag in the refrigerator. You will need about one cup of coating mix for a 3 pound chicken cut up, or 6 to 8 pieces.

Now you're ready to make the chicken strips or nuggets (the only difference is the shape you cut the chicken).

Chicken Nuggets

2 pounds boneless, skinless chicken breasts,
cut into 1-1/2 to 2-inch pieces or 1-inch strips

1 1/2 cups Shake It, Bake It coating mixture

Preheat oven to 400 F. Moisten chicken pieces with water. Shake off excess water. Place coating mix in a plastic bag. Shake 3 or 4 pieces at a time with coating mix. Discard any remaining coating mix. Place chicken pieces in a single layer in a foil lined 15x10x1-inch baking pan.

Bake 10 to 15 minutes or until chicken is cooked through. Serve with ranch dressing or the dipping sauces that follow.

If you prefer a more traditional fried chicken, you're going to love these chicken fingers. The secret is the buttermilk marinade.

Breaded Chicken Fingers

6 boneless, skinless chicken breasts
cut into 1/2 inch strips
1 egg, beaten
1 cup buttermilk
1 1/2 teaspoons garlic powder
1 cup all-purpose flour
1 cup seasoned bread crumbs
1 teaspoon salt
1 teaspoon baking powder
1 quart oil for frying

Place chicken strips into a large, resealable plastic bag. In a small bowl, mix the egg, buttermilk and garlic powder. Pour mixture into bag with chicken. Seal, and refrigerate 2 to 4 hours.

In another large, resealable plastic bag, mix together the flour, bread crumbs, salt and baking powder. Remove chicken from refrigerator, and drain, discarding buttermilk mixture. Place chicken in flour mixture bag. Seal, and shake to coat.

Heat oil in a large, heavy skillet to 375 F. Place coated chicken in hot oil. Fry until golden brown and juices run clear, or about 7 minutes. Drain on paper towels.

Sweet and Sour Dipping Sauce

2 cups water
2/3 cup distilled white vinegar
1 1/2 cups white sugar
1 (6 ounce) can tomato paste
1 (8 ounce) can crushed pineapple, drained
3 tablespoons cornstarch

In a medium saucepan over medium heat, mix together all of the ingredients. Cook, stirring occasionally, 15 minutes, or until mixture reaches desired color and consistency.

Honey-Mustard Dipping Sauce

1 1/2 cups mayonnaise
1/4 cup prepared Dijon-style mustard
1/2 cup honey

Mix all ingredients in a medium bowl. Chill in the refrigerator at least two hours before serving.

Asian Dipping Sauce

1/4 cup soy sauce
1/2 teaspoon sesame oil

1 clove garlic, minced
1 teaspoon green onions, chopped
1 tablespoon water
2 tablespoons hoisin sauce
1/4 teaspoon minced fresh ginger
1/2 teaspoon white sugar

In a small mixing bowl, combine all ingredients. Mix well, add additional hoisin sauce to thicken mixture to your desired consistency if needed. Yield 1/4 cup sauce. Recipe multiplies well.

Cover the sauce, and refrigerate for 1 to 2 hours to allow flavors time to blend. Heat before serving.

Appendix B

In the previous chapters we've talked about how to cut the cost of life's big expenses. But if you're not careful all you don't spend on the big stuff will disappear on "small spending." Nevertheless, and as space permits, I want to share a few resources with you—in random order, with no particular theme or category in mind.

Home Roasted Coffee

If you love good coffee but hate paying $11 to $16 a pound for high-quality coffee beans of marginal freshness, have I got great news. You can drink the best and pay half the price. The secret? Roast your own coffee beans. It's cheap, it's fun and you'll be the envy of your friends and family. Try it a few times and you'll have a new hobby.

While there are several methods for roasting, the easiest is to do this outdoors in a popcorn popper, specifically a West Bend Poppery II air popper. If you don't have one stashed in your garage from years gone by you can pick these up at garage sales and on eBay for just a few dollars. Here's the least you need to know that will get you roasting as soon as your beans arrive.

Plug in the machine. Measure and pour 3/4 cup green beans into the chamber. Place the top including the butter melting dish in place. The beans will stir themselves, you do nothing. After a few minutes you will hear the "first crack." The beans won't "pop" out like popcorn, but simply make a slight cracking noise from the heat building up inside them. You will notice the beans starting to turn brown if you lift the butter dish and peer into the chamber. Replace and allow to continue roasting.

After about five minutes from the start you will hear the "second crack." Now you are at a light (City) to medium roast. If you wait up to about 6 minutes (one popper will vary in temperature from another so the time may vary as well) you will have a full-bodied dark French roast—my personal favorite. At this state the beans begin to smoke which is why you must roast outdoors. The fragrance does not smell at all like coffee, by the way. But you will enjoy it.

Once you reach a dark roast you must immediately unplug and pour the beans into a colander. Actually you need two (I use a colander and a sieve) so you can pour the beans back and forth between the two to cool them quickly. If you've gone for a dark roast they will smoke up a storm as you quickly cool them and that's just fine. (You will know from the smell if you've gone too far and truly burned the coffee in which case don't give up. Just toss it out and roast up another batch.) That's it. Done.

Roasted beans should be allowed to mellow for at least two hours before grinding. Store beans in a tightly sealed container. Grind the beans in your coffee grinder as you would any beans you purchase from the supermarket or coffee shop.

And now for the good news: Green beans start as low as $3.65 a pound (at this writing), depending on the origin and variety. I'm a creature of habit and have become very fond of the La Minita Tarrazu coffee beans from Costa Rica. The price of all coffee beans fluctuates according to world market conditions, but to give you an idea I've never paid more than $6 a pound for this high quality coffee, usually less. And when the price is right I order 25 to 50 pounds at a time.

If you find a good cup of coffee to be one of life's extraordinary joys, just wait until you make it from beans you've roasted yourself. It's very much like the difference between a vine-ripened tomato from my garden and one of those barely-pink excuses for a tomato in the grocery store.

It takes an entire growing season to have luscious tomatoes and they last for such a short time. But coffee? I can have it every day year round. And I love serving really good coffee to my family and friends too. There's just nothing to compare. That fresh coffee beans roasted at home are so economical makes it just that much more delicious!

Coffee Resources

U-Roast-Em (URoastEm.com). This is my favorite no-frills green coffee bean source. Owner Jim Cameron stocks an impressive line up of beans from around the world. The prices are excellent with customer service to match. You'll find good information and personal attention at this site. You can purchase a single pound of beans, a discount if you order five pounds at a time. However you'll get better discounts if you order twenty-five pounds at a time. Not to worry: Green beans have a very long shelf life—up to a year, provided they are stored in an ordinary kraft paper bag, cotton cloth or burlap bags. Coffee needs to breathe so moisture cannot condense around it, so don't lock it up in an airtight vault, tomb or cedar chest. Direct sunlight is not good either.

Once roasted, coffee beans should be used within two weeks. Once ground, coffee should be used immediately.

Sweet Marias (SweetMarias.com). You will find terrific information in the library at this site. Also offers equipment, supplies and green beans, but prices are typically higher than U-Roast-Em.

West Bend Poppery II. This particular hot air popcorn popper is no longer manufactured but used models are plentiful. You may have one of these air poppers stashed in the garage, a distant reminder of your college dorm days. Or look for this the next time you scour thrift stores or go "garage saling." For sure you can find this particular air popper on eBay. You will want to keep your coffee roasting popper for that purpose only. It will get quite grungy in time, although still very useful.

Other: Theoretically you can roast coffee in any vessel that gets very hot. A Whirly-Pop popcorn popper works well as does a cast iron skillet. I've used both but only outdoors on the side burner of my barbecue grill. Both must be stirred manually and watched carefully. In my opinion, while you can roast more coffee at a time, the stir method is not as reliable or easy as the air popcorn popper.

Fabric

You might find fabric to be an odd mention. Yes you might, until you discover that I am a lover of fabric. A sewer and quilter too. So of course you would expect me to have a couple of secrets up my sleeve. If you know your fabrics, I can direct you to some bargain resources.

The Fabric Shack (FabricShack.com) carries a very extensive line of name brand, first-quality fabrics: Moda, Bernatex, Hoffman, Nathan, Robert Kaufman, RJR, P&B to name a few. While retail prices for high quality yard goods vary from one region to another, I can count on this store to routinely price the items I want at up to 50% off my best price locally. The service is excellent, fabrics are delivered with the greatest of care and customer service is first class.

144 Quilt Shops. Imagine visiting all 144 of the very best quilt shops in the U.S. at the same time. That's what you have if you go to *QuiltShops.com*. My favorite search on this site is to use the word "Sale" followed by whatever I'm looking for. For example, at this writing I searched "Sale flannel" and came up with 1,392 bolts of flannel on sale! Because I selected "thumbnail" as my view option I have a swatch of each and every bolt on my computer screen for my consideration. Of course that's far too many to comprehend so I can narrow my search by adding "green." As I consider each possibility I can also check out that particular quilt shop. I might find myself in Montana or Connecticut. Even if I do not make a purchase, I stay current on what's hot, what's not, competitive prices and how my local quilt shop stacks up against the competition nationwide. I often find exactly what I need on sale for 50 percent off, or more. Of course shipping and handling are a factor to be considered whenever buying by mail order.

Phoenix Textiles (Fabric.com) is another of my mail order favorites. But think of this as a gigantic warehouse where you'd better be wearing comfortable shoes because you're going to be there for a while. You'll have to dig for treasure, but when you find it expect the price to be worth the effort. Lots of name brands, home decorating and upholstery fabrics; quilt, craft, and apparel fabrics. There's always a large selection of $2 per yard fabrics, sometimes even cheaper! The service here is reliable, but don't expect a lot of attention to detail when it comes to packing your shipment. But who cares when the price is so right?

Hancocks of Paducah, Ky (Hancocks-Paducah.com). Not to be confused with the chain of fabric stores, Hancocks, Hancocks of Paducah is the largest fabric store in the world. At least that's how it appeared to me when I visited several years ago. It is so huge and well organized I was paralyzed with excitement. They have an excellent website with online ordering, a great catalog that is released quarterly and top-of-the-line customer service. Regular prices are consistently 25 percent less than retail in my local quilt shop for the exact same high quality fabric.

Books

Let me say I approach this paragraph with mixed emotions. On the one hand I write books for my livelihood. My husband enjoys eating so he encourages me in every way he can! And this only works for us if people actually *buy* my books. On the other hand I must say I hope you did not pay full price for one you now hold, or any others for that matter. There are several ways you can get books at deep discounts.

Amazon. Many of the books available at *Amazon.com* can be purchased "used" for considerably less than the cover price. You will see this option right at the book listing.

Half.com. Exactly as you might imagine, this is a website where you can find books for half the price. Expect previously owned books with exact condition clearly disclosed. Remarkably you can find current bestsellers. You can also sell your gently read books at *Half.com.*

The downside at *Half.com* is that since the site is a kind of a clearinghouse for many small individual sellers, you need to be patient. Don't expect next day delivery the way you might (for an additional fee) at a site like *Amazon.com* or *BN.com.* Buy hey, at half or less, the price is right. One caution: Watch the shipping and handling charges. If you opt for "media mail" delivery (cheap!) your book will arrive (someday) via the slowest method the US Postal Service can arrange. If you upgrade you might unknowingly negate what you've saved. Just pay attention.

Library. Not every book you need to read is a book you need to own. There is no better place for you to find those books than at your local public library. And while you're there look around and see all that you do not want to miss.

Not only can you borrow books, videos and audio books, you can read your favorite magazines, newspapers, attend a book signing or join a reading group. All libraries are now equipped with computers and Internet access. If you don't know how to use a computer, most will even teach you how to do that, how to get online and up to speed with life in cyberspace. Libraries have printers you can use (there may be a nominal charge for the paper) to print your work or pages from the Internet.

Have you checked your library's website lately? Be prepared for a treat. More than likely you can search the library's catalog and even make a reservation for that hot, new bestseller. Can't find the book you need? Request the librarian to get it for you through the interbranch lending program. Or if it's a new title request they add it to the library's collection with your name first on the list to borrow it.

Dansko

Okay, if the brand is not immediately familiar to you, skip ahead. This is for those who are hooked on a brand of shoes from Denmark. You may know that the Dansko website showcases styles, features, colors, size and so on—then directs you to a retailer or "etailer" to actually purchase the product at full retail. However, the very observant person will notice at the top of the homepage at *Dansko.com* these beautiful words: "Shop the Outlet." Click on that and you will go to the Dansko online factory outlet where they sell "seconds" (there is a very clear description with closeup pictures of what this means). This is an authentic factory outlet. You can purchase directly from Dansko at discounts of 30 percent off and up.

Laundry Detergent

Someday I'm going to write an entire book on laundry—that's how much I love the subject matter. But until then, let me tell you how to cut the cost of laundry detergent by far more than half the price. Why would you want to do this? To avoid spending $15 or more each month on laundry detergent is about as good a reason as any! After all, who really cares what detergent you use if the results are satisfactory?

Make your own. Yes, you can make your own laundry detergent and it is quite good. Unless you add perfume, however, you are not going to love this for its fragrance. And if you demand a lot of suds, this is not for you. But if it's cost effectiveness that grabs your attention, this is a viable way you can get your laundry detergent down to around three cents a load.

> 3 pints water (6 cups)
> 1/3 bar Fels-Naptha soap, grated
> 1/2 cup Super Washing Soda

1/2 cup borax
2 tablespoons glycerin
2 gallon bucket
1 quart hot water
Hot water

Grate the bar of Fels-Naptha as you would a chunk of cheese (just make sure you wash that grater well). Mix the grated soap in a medium sized saucepan with 3 pints of water, and heat on low until dissolved. Stir in Washing Soda and Borax. Stir until thickened, and remove from heat.

Pour one quart hot water into a two-gallon bucket. Add soap mixture and glycerin and mix well. Now fill bucket with additional hot water and mix well. Set aside for 24 hours, or until mixture thickens. It will have a slight jell consistency.

Use 1/2 to 3/4 cup of mixture per load, depending on the hardness of your water (the harder your water, the more detergent). Note: If you need suds to prove your detergent is "working," this is not the recipe for you. This is a non-sudsing, fragrance-free laundry product. The dirty water in your laundry tub will be all the proof you need that this works. Ideal for front-loading machines that require low-sudsing detergent.

Can't find?

Fels-Naptha Laundry bar. Look for this in the laundry aisle of your supermarket. It looks quite old-fashioned, wrapped in parchment paper. Manufactured by the Dial Corporation, *Dialcorp.com.*

Super Washing Soda. Also in the laundry aisle. It comes in a 55-ounce yellow box. Do not substitute baking soda. For more information see *TheLaundryBasket.com.*

Borax. One brand name is 20 Mule Team® Borax, also found on the laundry aisle of most supermarkets.

Glycerin. Available in drug stores and pharmacies, you'll get a much better buy at a craft store—about $2 for 8 oz. Look in the soap making aisle.

Can't find? You can purchase all of these products online at *SoapsGoneBuy.com* or call 877-796-9498 after 5 P.M., Central Time.

Shampoo

Come on...'fess up. You feel guilty using $.99 shampoo because it's really bad for your hair and the $24 variety at the salon is so much better especially for chemically-treated hair. Right? Wrong!

Some cheap shampoos are wonderful and some $24 varieties have all the gentleness of a can of scouring powder. Price has nothing to do with quality.

All shampoos regardless of the brand are 80 to 90 percent water. The rest is detergent with a pathetically few drops of fragrance and other additives and preservatives. There are basically two kinds of detergent: Anionic (harsh) and cationic (gentle). The only part of the shampoo bottle that's regulated by the Food and Drug Administration (FDA) is the list of ingredients. Manufacturers can and do make any claim they like on the unregulated portions of the label. Sometimes the hype has some merit, often it has none.

Pay no attention to anything on that bottle or packaging except for the list of ingredients. Water (or some fancy name for good old H2O) will always be the first ingredient. Next comes the detergent. Examples you can expect to find:

Ammonium Lauryl Sulfate - very harsh

Ammonium Laureth Sulfate - harsh

Sodium Lauryl Sulfate (SLS) - still harsh

Sodium Laureth Sulfate (SLES) - mild, great choice

TEA (or MEA) Lauryl Sulfate - gentle, good choice

TEA (or MEA) Laureth Sulfate - gentle, good choice

Shampoos often contain antistatic and detangling agents and also thickeners, humectants (moisturizers) and conditioners. But these items are in such small quantities it's almost a joke. Besides, the detergent washes all of it down the drain when you rinse.

You will find several popular shampoo brands contain the mild and gentle detergents, i.e. Herbal Essence.

If you clip the shampoo coupons from your Sunday newspaper and then watch for shampoo sales in your grocery store, you will never pay more than $1 a bottle again.

Finally, don't go for the lather. Use only a quarter-size amount of shampoo—that's all it takes. Interestingly, the "rinse and repeat" instruction you read on every shampoo bottle goes back to a marketing campaign one manufacturer came up with to increase sales. It does that alright. You can make your shampoo last twice as long if you simply do not repeat.

Conditioner

With some of the money you don't spend on shampoo, buy a quality conditioner. Unlike the shampoo that gets washed down the drain, the quality of conditioner does make a difference.

Resources

Chronological Order

Following are the resources cited in the preceding chapters in the order they appear.

Chapter 2

Debt-Proof Living, by Mary Hunt; DPL Press, 2005.

Chapter 3

Visa USA Marketing Brochure
www.usa.visa.com/business/accepting_visa/qsr/qsr_benefits.html

MasterCard Merchant Brochure
http://www.monstermerchantaccount.com/monsa.html

Dun & Bradstreet
http://www.dnb.com/us/

Mvelopes
http://cheapskatemonthly.mvelopes.com

Microsoft Money
www.microsoft.com/money

Intuit's Quicken
www.Quicken.com

FICO Credit Scores
www.myfico.com

Online auction sites
  www.onsale.com
  www.ubid.com
  www.overstock.com
  www.bidz.com

www.bidville.com
www.ebay.com
www.craigslist.com
www.auctions.yahoo.com

Shopping Robots
www.froogle.google.com
www.shopping.com

Ebay Tutorial for Sellers
eBay.com/university

Chapter 4

Price Books
www.organizedhome.com
www.moneyspot.org
www.stretcher.com
www.grocerybook.com
www.cheapcooking.com/pricebook.htm
www.practicalsaver.com

Coupon Companies
www.valassis.com
www.smartsource.com

Grocery List Services
www.thegrocerygame.com
www.couponmom.com

Coupon Organizers
www.virtualcouponorganizer.com
Real World Grocery Savings (e-book), by Kara Rosendaal;
PracticalSaver.com, 2004.

Supermarket Alternative
www.aldi.com

Community-Supported Agriculture (CSA)
www.NAL.usda.gov/afsic/csa

Chapter 5

"How Much Do Americans Pay for Fruits and Vegetables?"
http://ers.usda.gov/publications/aib790/aib790.pdf

"5-a-Day for Better Health"
www.5day.com

Slow Cooker, to find best price
www.froogle.google.com

Recipe Sites
www.about.com
www.crockpot.com
www.crockpot.cdkitchen.com
www.allrecipes.com

Cookbooks

Desperation Dinners! by Beverly Mills and Alicia Ross;
Workman, 1997.

The Rush-Hour Cook's Weekly Wonders by Brook Noel;
Champion Press, 2003.

Quick & Healthy Low-fat, Carb-Conscious Cooking by Brenda
Ponichtera, R.D.; ScaleDown Publishing, Inc., 2005,

Saving Dinner by Leanne Ely; Ballantine Books, 2003,

Online menu services
www.e-mealz.com
www.savingdinner.com (Menu Mailer)

Chapter 6

Meal Replacements
www.entertainment.com
www.jackinthebox.com
www.bk.com
www.chickfila.com
www.mcdonalds.com

www.kfc.com
www.elpolloloco.com

Entertainment Meals
www.restaurant.com
www.couponmom.com

Chapter 7

www.StyleMakeovers.com

Color Me Beautiful, by Carole Jackson; Ballantine Books, 1987.

The Pocket Stylist, by Kendall Farr; Gotham, 2004.

www.dansko.com

www.ebay.com

www.ouac.com

www.oshkoshbgosh.com

www.sears.com

Chapter 8

www.creditunion.coop

www.checksinthemail.com

USAA Federal Savings Bank
800-531-2265; www.usaa.com

ING Direct Worldwide
800-ING-DIRECT; www.ingdirect.com

No-Fee Credit Cards
www.cardtrak.com

Chapter 9

Online Calculators at www.debtproofliving.com
    Loan Calculator with Amortization Schedule
    Debt Investment Calculator

Chapter 10

Prepaid Wireless Services
    www.tracfone.com
    www.virginmobileusa.com
    www.virginmobile.com
    www.libertywireless.com

www.myrateplan.com

www.telebright.com

Chapter 11

Consumer Reports Magazine; www.consumerreports.org
www.epinions.com
www.froogle.google.com
www.salescircular.com
www.energystar.gov
www.highpointfurnituresales.com
www.shakerworkshops.com
www.vandykes.com
www.costco.com
www.samsclub.com
www.bjs.com
www.gotapex.com

Chapter 12

www.capitalone.com

www.eloan.com

www.autocreditfinders.com

www.edmunds.com

www.kbb.com

www.autotrader.com

www.carfax.com

www.consumerreports.org

www.carsdirect.com

www.costco.com

Chapter 13

www.myfico.com

www.edmunds.com

www.iihs.org

The Millionaire Next Door, by Thomas Stanley and William Danko;
    Pocket, 1998.

www.insurancelaw.com

www.usaa.com; 800-292-8302

www.samsclub.com; 888-799-8000

www.treas.gov

www.hsainsider.com

www.msabank.com

www.firstmsa.com

www.cfbf.com

www.nhpcalifornia.com

www.tnfarmbureau.org

www.costco.com

www.insurance.com

www.intelliquote.com

www.accuquote.com

Chapter 14

Online Travel Agencies

    Travelocity; www.travelocity.com

    1-800 Cheap Seats; www.1800cheapseats.com

    Hotwire; www.hotwire.com

    Expedia; www.expedia.com

    Ortitz; www.orbitz.com

Travel Search Engines

    www.sidestep.com

    www.bookingbuddy.com

    www.mobissimo.com

    www.priceline.com

    www.cheaptickets.com

    www.airlineconsolidators.com

www.samsclub.com

www.costco.com

www.bjs.com

www.hotels.com

www.carrentalexpress.com

www.mrsgrossmans.com; 800-429-4549

www.tillamookcheese.com;

www.elicheesecake.com; 773-205-3800

www.moneyfactory.com; 817-231-4000 or 866-865-1194

www.factorytoursusa.com

www.alhfam.org

www.childrensmuseums.org; 202-898-1080

www.regalcinemas.com

www.costco.com

www.netflix.com

www.blockbuster.com

Chapter 15

www.ftc.gov., 877-382-4357

Shocked, Appalled, and Dismayed!, by Ellen Phillips; Vintage, 1998.

www.ifi.org; 800-638-2627

www.fcc.gov., 888-225-5322

www.fdic.gov., 877-275-3342

Chapter 16

www.debtproofliving.com

Appendix B

www.fabricshack.com

www.QuiltShops.com

www.hancocks-paducah.com

www.fabric.com

www.amazon.com

www.u-roast-em.com; 715-634-6255

www.sweetmarias.com

www.half.com

www.bn.com

www.dansko.com

www.dialcorp.com

www.thelaundrybasket.com

www.soapsgonebuy.com 877-796-9498

Books

Ely, Leanne. *Saving Dinner,* Ballantine Books, 2003.

Farr, Kendall. *The Pocket Stylist*, Gotham, 2004.

Hunt, Mary. *Debt-Proof Living All-New Edition*, DPL Press, 2005.

Jackson, Carole. *Color Me Beautiful,* Ballantine Books, 1987.

Mills, Beverly and Alicia Ross. *Desperation Dinners!,* Workman, 1997.

Noel, Brook. *The Rush-Hour Cook's Weekly Wonders,* Champion Press, 2003.

Ponichtera, Brenda, R.D. *Quick & Healthy Low-fat, Carb-Conscious Cooking*, ScaleDown Publishing, Inc., 2005.

Phillips, Ellen. *Shocked, Appalled, and Dismayed!,* by Ellen Phillips, Vintage, 1998.

Rosendaal, Kara. *Real World Grocery Savings* (e-book), *PracticalSaver.com*, 2004.

Stanley, Thomas and William Danko. *The Millionaire Next Door,* Pocket, 1998.

Websites (in Alphabetical Order)

http://ers.usda.gov/publications/aib790/aib790.pdf

http://cheapskatemonthly.mvelopes.com

www.5day.com

www.about.com

www.accuquote.com

www.airlineconsolidators.com

www.aldi.com

www.alhfam.org

www.allrecipes.com

www.amazon.com

www.auctions.yahoo.com

www.autocreditfinders.com

www.autotrader.com

www.bidville.com

www.bidz.com

www.bjs.com

www.bk.com

www.blockbuster.com

www.bn.com

www.bookingbuddy.com

www.capitalone.com

www.cardtrak.com

www.carfax.com

www.carrentalexpress.com

www.carsdirect.com

www.cfbf.com

www.cheapcooking.com/pricebook.htm

www.cheapskatemonthly.com

www.cheaptickets.com

www.checksinthemail.com

www.chickfila.com

www.childrensmuseums.org

www.consumerreports.org

www.costco.com

www.couponmom.com

www.craigslist.com

www.creditunion.coop

www.crockpot.cdkitchen.com

www.crockpot.com

www.dansko.com

www.debtproofliving.com

www.dialcorp.com

www.dnb.com/us/

www.dplpress.com

www.ebay.com

www.ebay.com/university

www.edmunds.com

www.elicheesecake.com

www.eloan.com

www.elpolloloco.com

www.e-mealz.com

www.energystar.gov

www.entertainment.com

www.epinions.com

www.fabric.com

www.fabricshack.com

www.factorytoursusa.com

www.fcc.gov

www.fdic.gov

www.firstmsa.com

www.froogle.google.com

www.ftc.gov

www.gotapex.com

www.grocerybook.com

www.half.com

www.hancocks-paducah.com

www.highpointfurnituresales.com

www.hotels.com

www.hsainsider.com

www.ifi.org

www.iihs.org

www.ingdirect.com

www.insurance.com

www.insurancelaw.com

www.intelliquote.com

www.jackinthebox.com

www.kbb.com

www.kfc.com

www.libertywireless.com

www.mcdonalds.com

www.microsoft.com/money

www.mobissimo.com

www.moneyfactory.com

www.moneyspot.org

www.monstermerchantaccount.com/monsa.html

www.mrsgrossmans.com

www.msabank.com

www.myfico.com

www.myrateplan.com

www.nal.usda.gov/afsic/csa

www.netflix.com

www.nhpcalifornia.com

www.onsale.com

www.organizedhome.com

www.oshkoshbgosh.com

www.ouac.com

www.overstock.com

www.practicalsaver.com

www.priceline.com

www.quicken.com

www.QuiltShops.com

www.regalcinemas.com

www.restaurant.com

www.salescircular.com

www.samsclub.com

www.savingdinner.com

www.sears.com

www.shakerworkshops.com

www.shopping.com

www.sidestep.com

www.smartsource.com

www.soapsgonebuy.com

www.stretcher.com

www.stylemakeovers.com

www.sweetmarias.com

www.telebright.com

www.thegrocerygame.com

www.thelaundrybasket.com

www.tillamookcheese.com

www.tnfarmbureau.org

www.tracfone.com

www.travelocity.com

www.treas.gov

www.ubid.com

www.uroastem.com

www.usaa.com

www.usa.visa.com/business

www.valassis.com

www.vandykes.com

www.virginmobile.com

www.virginmobileusa.com

www.virtualcouponorganizer.com

D

G

S

T

Bold = Book titles
Italic = *Websites*

A Gift for You ...

DPL PRESS